PRAISE FOR
*HOW TO JOB SEARCH IN BOOK PUBLISHING:
THE ULTIMATE INSIDER'S GUIDE*

At last: a book I can recommend to anyone asking for advice on careers in the book industry.

Toby Faber, Faber & Faber

An invaluable guide to getting a job in this competitive industry. Take advantage of a wealth of helpful tips and advice from an expert on careers in publishing.

Angus Phillips, Author, Inside Book Publishing

A vital publication from one of the key figures in the UK publishing scene, Suzanne Collier demystifies publishing and the best ways to secure your dream job in the industry. She breaks down jargon, draws from numerous case studies and overviews the core facets of applying to – and succeeding in getting – jobs in publishing. From CVs and cover letters to interview advice and ways to bolster your experience outside of the workplace, this is an expansive guide for both in-house and freelance staff alike. *How to Job Search in Book Publishing* is full of tips, resources and wisdom learned from a lifelong career of working in the industry. Who better to help get your foot in the door than Suzanne Collier?

The Society of Young Publishers

How to Job Search in Book Publishing: The Ultimate Insider's Guide is just what's needed – a down-to-earth, practical and warmly encouraging guide to making your way into book publishing. You can feel Suzanne cheering you on as you go through the chapters, with years of lived experience behind the advice. Highly recommended for all jobseekers in our creative industry.

Marion Sinclair, Chief Executive, Publishing Scotland

A must-read for anyone aspiring to work in book publishing, this guide offers a clear and comprehensive overview of the industry's key sectors, roles and processes. Suzanne Collier expertly demystifies the nuances of trade, academic and educational publishing, providing invaluable insights for jobseekers and professionals alike.

Wayne Sime, Chief Executive Officer, Association of Learned and Professional Society Publishers

If anybody knows, Suzanne knows – and now she's put all that knowledge and wisdom between two covers for everyone to reap the benefit. Comprehensive in coverage and insight, *How to Job Search in Book Publishing* is also full of helpful tips and tricks to help anyone get in and get on... Had I had this book at the start of my career, it might not have been quite such a random walk! Could not recommend highly enough.

Chris Glennie, Chair, The Publishing Training Centre

Suzanne Collier has been working tirelessly for many years to help people find roles in the publishing industry. Her passion for book publishing and a straightforward and honest approach makes her an ideal guide to this field.

David Shelley, Chief Executive Officer, Hachette Book Group

Suzanne has huge experience in the industry, and certainly knows what she is talking about.

Amanda Ridout, Founder and Chief Executive Officer, Boldwood Books

How to Job Search in Book Publishing: The Ultimate Insider's Guide is simply marvellous. It is thorough, properly researched, comprehensive, and an essential for every aspiring (or even aspired) publisher...

Richard Charkin OBE, Founder Mensch Publishing, Former Executive Director of Bloomsbury Publishing Plc and Macmillan Publishing Ltd

I don't know of a more comprehensive guide through the world of book publishing. Suzanne Collier has covered it from every angle. This is a must-have for anyone contemplating a job in the industry. The cost of the book will be covered by your first pay cheque.

Anne Dolamore, Grub Street Publishing

Don't start your publishing job search without this book – an essential survival guide for job hunters. *How to Job Search in Book Publishing* is packed with insider tips and practical advice on navigating the industry – a must-read for anyone looking to build a career in publishing.

Jonny Geller, Chief Executive, Curtis Brown Group

Now that this book is here, it's hard to believe that it hasn't always existed: what did we DO without this comprehensive, practical guide to landing a job in publishing? It's a gift not just for jobseekers themselves but for anyone recruiting, who will from this point on receive more thoughtful, relevant applications. A great service to the publishing industry, from someone who's been working to make that industry better throughout her own career.

Alison Jones, Director, Practical Inspiration Publishing

Suzanne Collier has been writing this definitive careers bible of the publishing industry ever since I've known her (a good few years!). Now it is finally published, I can see why it took her so long. The comprehensive content, the rigorous detail and in depth knowledge offers a combined education and step-by-step process for anyone looking for a career in publishing. This will be the classic title in its field for many years to come.

Lucy McCarraher, CEO Book Magic AI, co-founder, Rethink Press, author of 14 books.

HOW TO JOB SEARCH IN BOOK PUBLISHING:
THE ULTIMATE INSIDER'S GUIDE

HOW TO JOB SEARCH IN BOOK PUBLISHING: THE ULTIMATE INSIDER'S GUIDE

Suzanne Collier

Bookcareers Publishing

Publisher's Note

Every possible effort has been made to ensure that the information contained in this book is accurate at the time of going to press, and the publishers and author cannot accept responsibility for any errors or omissions, however caused.

Neither the author nor the publisher take responsibility for any consequences of any decision made as a result of information contained in this book. When seeking career guidance always choose a registered career guidance professional from the Career Development Institute.

First published in Great Britain 2025
by Bookcareers Publishing, an imprint of bookcareers.com

10 9 8 7 6 5 4 3 2 1

© Suzanne Collier 2025
Illustrations and Diagrams © bookcareers.com
Cover image © Shutterstock

The moral rights of the author have been asserted.
No part of this book may be used or reproduced or transmitted in any form or by any means, electronic, mechanical, recording or otherwise, including for the purpose of training artificial intelligence technologies or systems, without prior written permission of the copyright owner.

ISBN (Print) 978-1-9996109-0-6
ISBN (Kindle) 978-1-9996109-5-1
ISBN (eBook) 978-1-9996109-1-3

Bookcareers Publishing always likes to give credit where it is due. These are the people who helped with the production of this book.

Editor: David Ballheimer
Research Assistant: Caitlin Palmer
Cover Design: Clare Baggaley
Illustrations: Chris Targett
Typesetter: Zara Thatcher, www.printreadyeditorial.com

Printed and bound by IngramSpark

Suzanne Collier left Beal High School, Ilford, at the age of 16 with a handful of qualifications. She loved reading and at school had always been asked to tidy the English cupboard full of books, but no one had ever told her about working in book publishing.

By sheer luck her first job was working for Andre Deutsch Ltd, in the days when Andre Deutsch and Diana Athill ran the company. At 22, she started spreading the word about book publishing careers, alongside a full-time publishing job, that took her through both trade and academic publishing, and every department, though she found her natural home in special sales and new business development. Ten years later, Suzanne founded bookcareers.com, as the ultimate side hustle.

After a rare migraine condition forced her to rethink her own career, she became fully qualified in Career Development and Guidance (RCDP). Today she sees private clients for career development, provides career support and coaching services to book publishers as well as "making mischief in publishing" by producing salary data. She is a Judge for the Business Book Awards.

Suzanne has been shortlisted for many industry awards, from both the Independent Publishers Guild and the Career Development Institute, including being shortlisted for Career Coach of the Year (Private Sector) three times.

Outside of work, Suzanne lives in Leigh on Sea, in Essex, and is a season ticket holder for Dagenham and Redbridge FC. She loves music, flowers and, having once qualified as an aerobics teacher, every form of exercise, except burpees, and, as one of her school reports said, "She is always ready to sing a song."

Suzanne describes working in book publishing as a vocation and once said: "Some people collect stamps, others enjoy painting or gardening. Me? I give careers advice."

Contents

	Introduction	1
1.	Understanding Book Publishing	5
2.	Getting Started	43
3.	Finding Jobs	75
4.	Recruitment Practices and Selection	107
5.	CVs That Get You Noticed	135
6.	Covering Letters That Work	191
7.	Ace the Interview Process	217
8.	Interview Questions and How to Answer Them	259
9.	Interview Tests and How to Pass Them	307
10.	Going Freelance	327
11.	How to Get the Career You Deserve	345
12.	Questions, Answers and Jargon Busters	363
	Appendix I	389
	Appendix II	395

Introduction

This book has taken a long time to happen, and in so many ways I'm pleased it has. If it had been published when I was first asked, back in 2001, it would have contained a fraction of the knowledge and information that appears now.

My aim in this book is not to spoon-feed you through the publishing job search and application processes, but to ensure that publishing is inclusive and open to all. Like so many people, you probably already have the practical skills required to succeed in a publishing job, but miss out because of the peculiarities of book publishing, or you may feel secret codes are used in the world of publishing recruitment.

As you'll discover, there are no longer barriers to finding a job in book publishing, and the industry is welcoming to you, whether you have formal qualifications or experience or not. The best way to show you this is by giving you the knowledge you need to ace your job search.

How to Job Search in Book Publishing would not have been complete without the assistance and feedback of the hundreds of people I have spoken to, including bookcareers.com clients, past and present, I thank you all.

Other people to thank are:

Chloe Ablett, Sydney Allen, Colin Ancliffe, Fay Angel, Suzy Astbury, Clare Baggaley, Lauren Bahorun, Louise Bainbridge, Brian Baines, David Ballheimer, Louis Barfe, Priscilla Barlow, Glenda Barnard, Jack Baverstock, Graham Bell, Kip Bertram, Catherine Bethell, Jeremy Brinton, Sally Brooking, Iain Brown, Georgina Bulga, Shakira Campion, Nick Canty, John Chappell, Richard Charkin OBE, Giles Clark, John Cleary, Sarah Conkerton, Dorothy Courtis, Isobel Cowper-Coles, Monica Craven, Elizabeth Cremona-Howard, Meghan Curtis, Angelica Curzi, Stephanie Duncan, Theresa Duncan, Lisa Edwards, Greg Evaristo, Caitlin Evans, Louise Fligman, Mindy Gibbins-Klein, Hannah Gill, Susannah Godman, Corinne Gotch, Susan Greenberg, Stephanie Hall, Anna Herve, Jas Hessey, David Hicks, Harriet Hirshman, Alastair Horne, Clare Hodder, Richard Houghton, Emma House, Penelope Ibbs, Hermione Ireland, Samira Johnson, Alison Jones, Abigail Joyce, Suzanne Kavanagh, Danuta Kean, Christian Kelly, Helen Kogan, Katerina Koulouri, Richard Lewis, Sara Lloyd, Katy Loffman, Lucy McCarraher, Julia Maciejewska, Helena Markou, Daisy Martin, Eleanor Masterman, Lisa Milton, Tony Mulliken, Lottie Murray, Norah Myers, Binita Naik, Nina, Anne Nolan, Christopher Norris, Orna O'Brien, Chris Ogle, Caitlin Palmer, Vicki Pang, Vanita Patel, Carthryn Payling, Victoria Perry, Angus Phillips, Lesley Pollinger, Jennifer Powell, David Plummer, Lizzie Quarterman, Rachel Quin, Dr Samantha Rayner, Fran Roberts, Phoebe Roubicek, Ann Sandham, Dr Paul Shanahan, Jack Shelton, Bridget Shine, Wafaa Sirokh, Freya Smith, Jane Smith, Kirsty Smith, Polly Smith, Justine Solomons, Miranda Spicer, Diana Spivey, Professor Claire Squires, Laura Summers, Chris Targett, Beverley Tarquini, Leah Tether, Zara Thatcher, Jacks Thomas, Lisa Thomas, Sheila Vaughan, Elise Watson, Jake Watson, Beth Wentworth, Beth Whalley, Esther Whitby, Annie Whyte, Debbie Williams, Brittany Willis, Kate Wilson.

And those no longer with us: Diana Athill OBE, Carole Blake, Andre Deutsch CBE, Ernest Hecht OBE, Philip Kogan, Tim Rix CBE, Tom Rosenthal, Nick Robinson, Pamela Royds, Professor Iain Stevenson.

Dedication

In memory of my Booba, Adelaide Rose, who was born at a time when women didn't have the opportunities that we have today. She was never without a book in her hand and would have loved to work in book publishing.

A note from the author

I have created an extensive number of online resources to support publication of this book, aside from the appendices at the end of the book.

If I referenced the resources on every page, it is likely that every page would say "there is a list of further resources on the bookcareers.com website", which might spoil your enjoyment and the flow of the book. So please do ensure you use the accompanying online resources that are updated regularly.

All statistics, particularly those covering employment, salaries and education level, are sourced from the bookcareers.com Salary Survey 2021/3, unless otherwise stated. Again, it would be tiresome to put a footnote at the bottom of every page.

CHAPTER ONE

Understanding Book Publishing

Publishing

"The occupation or activity of preparing and issuing books, journals and other material for sale."

Oxford English Dictionary

Before you start job hunting in book publishing, it is important to know a little bit about the industry, as it will impact the jobs you go for and what kind of books or journals you will be working on.

The Book Publishing Industry

Within publishing there are a number of different sectors and each has its own nuances and specialisations. To someone on the outside they all may look the same – in that they are all publishers and all (or most) sell worldwide. However, as you get to look inside a sector, whilst they may have a lot in common, they all have something that make them different. This might be in the way that they acquire titles, the formats they publish in (such as audio, print, eBook, online), the time of year they publish, who their customers are, and how they market or sell titles to those customers.

The main sectors are:

Adult Trade. This is consumer book publishing. The publishers produce books for the everyday general popular market and create new markets, genres and fields of interest. They are the books you predominately see in bookshops, and featured in newspapers and the mainstream media. Trade publishing responds to world trends and events. *The Sunday Times* Bestseller List is made up of trade publications and it is very rare to see an Academic book selling as many copies as a trade title. Trade publishers may publish fiction and non-fiction in a variety of formats, including audio.

As trade publications relate to the everyday world, the sales year is very much like a general retail year in that it correlates with daily lives and activities such as 'New Year, New You', 'Summer Reading' and Christmas. September to December are the biggest sales months, with the media focussing on Super Thursday, the Thursday in autumn on which most of the books predicted to be Christmas bestsellers, or by the highest profile authors, are published.

Trade books may have a short shelf life in bookshops, as the media and shops are often obsessed with new titles, so if a trade book doesn't reach its target market shortly after publication, it can quickly be forgotten and pushed aside for the next new book in a similar category. However, one of the most overlooked parts of trade publishing is the backlist. Most of the general public appear unconcerned whether a book is brand new or not, they are only interested in whether it is a good read. Editorially, trade publishers may find new titles to add to their list for publication from almost anywhere. They could receive submissions from Literary Agents, accept unsolicited proposals or commission new titles, based upon an approach, idea or format they have.

Publishers' traditional customer base includes bookshops, wholesalers, supermarkets and online retailers, but they will also sell outside of these markets, aiming to match their titles to any retailer, company or organisation that might have an interest in their publications.

Children's Trade. Children's publishers are predominantly the same as Trade publishers but often view themselves as different because they aim to publish age-appropriate titles for children, sometimes with an educational slant. For example, Picture Books (Picture Flats as they are sometimes called) are routinely 32-page full-colour illustrated titles with only one or two lines of text per page and are usually for early readers, those around 2–5 years old. It would be very unusual for a picture book to be published for the teen market. Other age groups include Middle Grade, aimed at 6–9-year-olds, often a standard format story of around 96 pages and Young Adult/YA titles, that are novels aimed at teenagers. Some children's publishers may adhere their publishing to the UK educational system of Key Stages.

Editorially, they may look at books submitted by Literary Agents or accept unsolicited submissions. Sometimes the Commissioning Editor may try to match an author with a children's illustrator on a title to make the book work.

Whilst children's publishers often participate in trade exhibitions and book fairs around the world, there is a special annual children's trade publishing exhibition in Bologna, Italy, the Bologna Book Fair, that usually takes place in April. In recent times, the Bologna Book Fair has expanded to include adult publishing, but children's books remain its prime focus.

As well as selling books to trade outlets, children's publishers will cross over into educational markets and may work to the school year, rather than the retail year, with a focus on back to school. Some of the larger children's publishers may have a special sales team whose job it is to sell new titles into schools and educational establishments.

Educational Publishers. As the name implies, educational publishers publish textbooks and educational material for the school and college markets, as well as developing resources for teachers, books for teachers about teaching and fiction and non-fiction books for the children at all levels. You might occasionally see educational books in bookshops, but that is not their main sale. As one might imagine, one aim for educational publishers is to get a book listed as the recommended textbook for a GCSE or A level course. This will result in many schools having to buy the book in high quantities in order to supply copies for the students studying that course.

In editorial terms, it is imperative that textbooks accurately adhere to the requirements of the appropriate examination board

– one mistake can cause a title to be delisted. When commissioning new titles, educational publishers are likely to either have their own bank of freelance educational authors they can call on, or find a new expert in the field who can write strictly to the examination board requirements.

As technology has moved on, educational publishers have moved to online platforms, where they put all their content (their titles) into a custom-based app. This is often referred to as Ed-Tech Publishing. The aim is to sell their platform in its entirety to a school, where the teachers can set homework and pupils can use the platform to complete the homework as well as have access to other learning resources. For the bigger publishers, this platform may include a number of titles from their children's publishing division, offering a wealth of content to the school to use at their disposal.

Academic Publishers. Academic publishing is dominated in terms of revenue by STM (Scientific, Technical and Medical – *see below*) whilst most university presses and many of the smaller academic publishers focus on HSS (Humanities and Social Sciences). Books are still important in HSS, but STM is dominated by journals and textbooks.

Peer review is a key part of academic publishing for both books and journals. Because of the specialist nature of academic work, it is difficult for a publisher to judge how good a book or journal article is, so getting a second opinion from another scholar in the field is very important to ensure that the work makes a worthwhile contribution to its subject.

TOP TIP

If you are working in Editorial for a specialist scientific publisher, to get to a higher position you might need to have a science degree in the discipline of the journal, otherwise you may find it very difficult to reach a senior Editorial role.

In the UK there is a system called the REF (Research Excellence Framework), where university departments gain funding based on how many books and journal articles have been published. There is, therefore, great pressure on individual academics to be published in order to advance their career.

Academic books and journals are routinely very highly priced, This is because their specialised nature means they will only be read by a few people and are bought almost exclusively by institutions (university libraries and the like).

For books, digital (eBooks and digital content) accounts for around 50% of sales, whilst journals are now almost exclusively digital. Digital sales via content platforms are increasingly central. Publishers may make deals with aggregators of content who sell or license bundles of content to academic institutions.

Open Access (OA) is a big issue within academic publishing. The high price of academic books and journals limits the number of people who can afford them, and many people feel that research funded by the state should be free for everyone to read. APCs and BPCs (Article Processing Charges and Book Processing Charges) paid by funders to publishers can enable books and articles to be made OA.

Commissioning and the sourcing of authors will probably come via academic conferences, where the publisher or Commissioning Editor attends a conference on the subject areas for which they are responsible and makes contacts. Alternatively, they will hunt out the leading specialist in a particular field and ask them to write for them.

Science, Technical and Medical Publishing (STM)
Legal, Professional and Society Publishers
As the name suggests, these are publishers who publish in some very specific fields and usually publish more journals than books. Their publishing model is very similar to academic publishing in the way they source authors and contributors.

Most journals are subscription based, and again conferences and peer reviews are key to publishing accurate and informed titles.

For ease in this book, I have grouped together Trade (Adult, Children's and Educational Publishing) and Academic (Academic, STM, Legal, Professional and Society Publishers).

As well as book publishers, there are many book-publishing related jobs with Literary Agents, who represent authors, or publishing service companies, who sell their services to book publishers. The skills required and the recruitment practices of both are parallel to book publishing. This is why they are included in this book.

Literary Agents act for the authors. They sign authors and then aim to license the author's works to publishers worldwide. There are differences between how a publisher and a literary agent sells. A publisher is mainly concerned with forthcoming books; what is new, and then tag on an author's backlist, if appropriate. A literary agent, however, will look at an author's whole body of work and aim to sell it everywhere all the time.

Freelancers and Publishing Service Companies may cover skills such as Editorial, Design, Sales, Marketing, Production or Publicity. They aim to fill the gaps in book publishing processes, depending on the requirements and needs. A freelancer is usually a solo person, who often has worked for book publishers, but after leaving a publishing job, now works for themselves. They will sell their services back to a variety of publishers, as and when the publisher requires. With a Publishing Service Company, the benefit to the publisher is that this is an extension of employing freelancers; they can buy in the additional services as and when they need them, to support busy times in editorial or design, without having the overheads of employing full-time staff, who may not be busy all the time.

What is the difference between a publisher, division and imprint?

If you're coming into the industry for the first time, some publishing terms can feel very confusing. The first publishing term you are likely to come across is imprint. What is the difference between a publisher and an imprint? A publisher publishes a book, but the imprint is the publishing brand name the book is published under, represented by a name and colophon on the spine of the book. Publishers usually create several imprints under their umbrella, to represent contrasting genres or collections of books and the different creative directions each list is taking, which helps both readers and buyers find books of a similar type. Larger publishers, such as Penguin Random House and Hachette, who have many different imprints, group these imprints into company divisions to make them easier to manage at top-level. For example, Hachette UK, has many divisions. One of those divisions is Hodder & Stoughton. Under the Hodder & Stoughton division, you will find imprints such as Hodder Press, Hodder & Stoughton, Coronet, Yellow Kite, and Sceptre. Likewise, a smaller publisher like Profile Books has imprints such as Profile Books, Souvenir Press, Pursuit, Wellcome Books and the Economist.

There's a list of useful jargon busters in *Chapter Twelve: Questions, Answers and Jargon Busters* of this book.

The Main Publishing Departments

Whatever sector of publishing you work in, be it Trade or Academic, these departments are common to all publishers, although the breakdown of responsibilities may alter. Some publishers are merging and blending teams as shown in Figures 1–3. There are other departments as well, but they will often reflect the demands of the individual publishing house.

Editorial

Editorial mainly commissions and compiles the content and prepares it for publication. It will source authors, find books to publish, either from a literary agent or the slush pile (the unsolicited submissions a publisher receives), or research potential authors and approach them directly. They might discover authors via conferences, finding an expert who has specialist knowledge in a particular subject area or through a collaboration. Editorial, with input from sales and/or marketing on a project's likely success, makes most of the decisions about what books are published, whilst the senior management team or editorial director will set the strategy and areas that the company wishes to publish in. There are two types of editorial role: acquisitions/commissioning (sourcing books and getting authors on board) and desk editorial/production editorial (assessing the text and getting it into shape; this is sometimes done by sending it out to an established freelancer for copyediting or proofreading).

Production

Production takes care of the whole process of producing the book or journal, whether it is print, digital or audio. This usually consists of deciding on the specifications for the book, the typography, size, style and binding, purchasing print or digital services, maintaining the quality of print or resolution of images, and the buying and managing paper stocks, if appropriate. They also might be involved in buying the print for other projects such as marketing blads, leaflets or catalogues.

Production oversees the book from manuscript all the way through to successful delivery at the publishers' distributors. If there are any issues in printing or shipping, as some printing may take place internationally, it is the Production department that will be responsible for sorting out the mess at minimal cost or disruption. If a book becomes a bestseller and additional copies need to be printed urgently, it is Production that will take the brunt of this pressure and often will already have excellent relationships with printers, binders and paper suppliers to ensure that the book is kept in stock and available.

Production is another area that can make or break the profitability of a book, so keeping a tight rein on the agreed budget is imperative. Often it is Production that will ensure that the rest of the company keeps on track with their own schedules in the publishing process. The timing of when elements of the book are prepared and delivered (such as signing the contract, editing the book, writing the cover copy) is known as the 'critical path'. Most larger publishers have consolidated a number of production processes, such as procurement, so the Production staff are focussed on the project management of the process rather than buying print or services.

Design

The amount of in-house design skill required at any publisher will vary according to the type of books being published. A publisher of highly illustrated books is likely to have a number of Book Designers or an Art Manager who work on the insides of the books – the layouts, photographs, quality of the resolution of the images, as well as the cover design and its layout. For a publisher with few illustrated titles, they might only employ one Designer and hire Freelance designers as and when they need them, usually to illustrate the cover of a book. Digital imaging has greatly reduced the number of original book covers being independently commissioned and designed.

An interior Book Designer may work to a fixed template for house style (the parameters set by each publisher as to what their books look like in layout and text). If this is the case, aside from having a good eye for graphic design, there might be limited scope within the role for any creative expression, as it has already been decided. Outside of Book Designers, there are increasing opportunities for designers who are attached to Marketing Departments, as every communication or social media post usually has a graphic attached.

Rights

This department is responsible for the exploitation of the publisher's copyright and content, in whatever formats are available (or may become available in the future). The priority within Rights is to sell. Rights deals might include reprint or audio publications or selling the (copy)right to publish an author's book to an overseas publisher, so it is published in a different language specifically for that marketplace.

They also grant permission to other publishers for small extracts or illustrations to appear in other books. More complex rights and licences might include selling the option to turn the book into a film or TV programme, to a film or TV production company (many options are sold, very few are actually taken up!), working with a games producer or app, or content aggregator, who is looking for limited content from a variety of different books, to merchandising rights and character licences.

The Rights department might sell serialisation rights to national and international press (in some publishers, this might be handled by the Publicity Department). Serial Rights are where you see what appears to be all or a major part of the book published in a newspaper. Between the 1970s and 1990s, serial rights sales were very lucrative for book publishers, often bringing in thousands. They were trailed in TV adverts ('Exclusive, read the tell-all secrets of …'), but now with the decline in sales of printed newspapers, these are no longer big money deals.

However out of all the departments, Rights can be the most profitable for a publishing company, as they can make far more money selling the right to publish, in whatever format, to other companies than they can selling copies of their own published books. Rights income can make the difference between a book being profitable or loss-making, as no cost of sale needs to be deducted from the revenue. How the division of work in a Rights department is allocated might depend on territory (a particular range of international countries) or the types of rights that can be sold (audio, international, etc.).

Contracts

Whatever size publisher you are working at, someone will have to draw up a contract relating to the copyright works being published, either between the author and publisher to write their book, or to license another publisher or organisation to publish a version of the author's book. Contracts are legal and binding agreements and even the slightest mistake, such as a decimal point in the wrong place of a royalty percentage, can be very costly.

Publishers are very likely to have their own template for every book they contract, with their ideal breakdown of royalties – how much the author gets paid for every copy of the book sold, called a boilerplate. Yet every author, author's agent or publisher is still likely to want to negotiate parts of every contract to ensure they get the best possible financial deal. Contracts and negotiations are handled by Editorial, Rights or a stand-alone Contracts department depending on the size and nature of the publisher.

There are also other contracts used across the whole business, that may or may not involve the contracts department. As well as full-time staff signing contracts of employment, part-time staff and freelancers in all departments may sign contracts for the work they do on each title or for the length of an assignment if it is a temporary, fixed-term position. Freelance sales agents will have contracts too, and there may be contracts raised with major suppliers or customers in order to outline responsibilities, payment and delivery dates.

Sales

In book publishing, Sales are very well respected as they are one of the main departments who bring in income for the publisher, and thus ensuring there is enough money in the business to pay staff salaries. It is one of the best areas to work in, as Sales staff are paid to talk about books all day, every day. A job in Sales can give you good flexibility and a substantial commission or bonus on top of your salary.

The naïve assumption with book publishing Sales is that it is a hard sell, and all about cold calling – banging on a lot of doors and getting nowhere. Yet, in book publishing, it is very much about building a customer base and generating repeat business. You might be selling to the same customer for the whole of your career, regardless of which publisher you work for. It can feel more like an account management and customer services role than a Sales role, as the onus is on you, the salesperson, to keep on good terms with the respective buyer at all times. Sales teams are usually broken down by geographic area and key (head office) accounts. Therefore, you might find a both a UK Sales team, where different team members each have a responsibility for London, South East, South West, Scotland or any part of the country, and a Key Accounts team who are responsible for the accounts with the largest turnover or have complex requirements.

Within Sales, as well as the variety of titles you will have an extreme assortment of customers, depending on the area of publishing in which you work. You could be selling to bookshops as well as organisations, associations, educational establishments, charities, mail-order websites, specialist wholesalers and general retailers. There is no end to the customers who may wish to buy books. If your role involves tapping into some non-traditional bookshop markets – any organisation that is not a bookshop but buys books – then this is called Special Sales, as opposed to Sales.

Publishing was always a business-to-business operation. Publishers sold books to bookshops (B2B) and bookshops sold to the consumer (B2C), but with changes in consumer shopping affecting the UK high street, and the dominance of the online retailer Amazon, some publishers have started to sell direct to the consumer.

International Sales

This department covers the sale of the publishers' own editions to export customers around the world (or the areas of the world the publisher has the licence to sell a particular book). International Sales often work with an international sales force of representatives and freelance agents or overseas publishers to maximise every opportunity, and the work is likely to be divided by continent and country, so that the sales team becomes an expert in their designated marketplace. It can be an advantage for International Sales staff to be bi-lingual or multi-lingual if they are selling or travelling to regions where English is not a native language.

They will work hard to get international bookshop orders and bulk and special sales, perhaps a co-edition. A co-edition is where another edition of the same book is printed alongside the publisher's original edition, but the co-edition carries the international publisher's logo and imprint. Co-editions sometimes come under the umbrella of the Rights department, and building a strong relationship with the Rights team will play a key part in International Sales. In some large publishers, where there are substantial international sales, the team may also be involved in international promotions, marketing and publicity.

Marketing

Marketing very often has two strands to it, the marketing of the books and journals to businesses, often bookshops, wholesalers, libraries and academia (B2B), and the marketing of books to the consumer (B2C/D2C). The aim of marketing is to raise awareness of the book to people who can, and hopefully will, buy the book.

This can be done in a variety of ways, including email newsletters, websites, videos, advertising, billboards, competitions, promotions, and external events. For titles with a huge marketing budget, you could be working with an external marketing or advertising agency, that manages a portfolio of marketing activities. But for most publishers, marketing is conducted on a strict low budget that might just run to a few social media adverts, if that.

Every new book is a different product, and unlike a bar of chocolate you won't get repeat purchases by the same individuals. This makes marketing books quite challenging. Marketing is about creating awareness, getting people interested, and encouraging them to buy. If you are not familiar with the concept of the marketing funnel, look it up. Marketing basics include getting the metadata optimised so that a book is discoverable, and generally getting interesting, eye-catching and relevant information in front of the potential readers.

A key part of marketing is tapping into the author's network of contacts or fans. Often, the best way to sell a book is for the author to share information with their followers on social media or other networks, so marketing often provides the author with graphics and snippets of text that they can share.

Social Media

I've put this under marketing, but where it will sit depends on the publisher you work for. Social media for book publishers is more than a few posts here and there and the occasional Facebook post or TikTok. It is a whole planned campaign strategy: for the publisher, the authors they publish and the books they produce. Having a successful social media campaign – whether a publisher uses paid social media advertising or relies on engaging posts – can turn poor sales of a book into a potential bestseller.

As social media can be very time consuming, each publisher may treat it differently, and have it fall under the department that has the best time-resource. It may be that the Editor or Publisher is in control, or the Marketing department, or Publicity. It might move around the office, with one department creating and scheduling all the regular content, and others taking it in turns to respond to posts and engage the audience throughout the week.

Publicity / PR

Publicity is responsible for all the media coverage the publisher gets. This encapsulates writing press releases, sending out review copies, arranging author interviews – online, on TV, radio or in the national press or organising author tours, that might be in person or a blog tour.

Publicity is mostly business-to-business. Publicists talk to other businesses to get as much media coverage as possible so that the resulting publicity (that one would hope is positive) encourages members of the public to buy the author's book(s). Whilst media contacts and schmoozing are key skills for publicity, what are also needed are imaginative ways of encouraging news outlets to cover books, as the amount of dedicated book pages and review coverage has plummeted over the years. Publicity may also be given the task of organising a launch party for a book, whether it's a physical launch party or a virtual event.

A launch party is sometimes given to mark publication of the book, encourage media coverage, publicity and sales of the book, but very often launches are to pander to the author's ego. A book launch can seem a very glamorous event to someone who doesn't work in publishing, but if it isn't at a hospitality venue, at the end of the event someone has to wash all the wine glasses and clear up the room; often it will be the publicity staff. Launch parties can come in all shapes and sizes, from the ones with enough champagne to sink the *Titanic*, to others that are one glass of warm white wine in the office with the author. They often take place in the evening, and you'll be required to attend as part of your job, normally with little or no recompense for working unsocial hours.

Metadata

Except in a few very large publishers, this is not a department as such, but it is critical to the success of publishing. Metadata is the bibliographic information that is a key aspect of making a book discoverable. It can be often the responsibility of the Marketing department, but it is based on information about the book supplied by the commissioning editor. In some larger publishers you might see a metadata department. If I could write 'metadata, metadata, metadata' throughout this book then I would, because regardless of which department is assigned the responsibility for ensuring it is comprehensively accurate and timely, it is part of publishing a book that needs to be learned, understood and perfected.

Finance / IT / Resources

Like every company outside of publishing, the finance, IT and Resources departments are similar. The main obvious difference is you are working for a book publisher. As a result, you are likely to be heavily involved in the future strategy of the company you work for and will often be involved in publishing activities.

Distribution / Operations

In publishing, Operations is another word for distribution. Even with online-only and digital publications, books and journals must be distributed somehow. For publishers who are producing print editions, the books will be distributed from a warehouse. Very few publishers possess their own warehouse or distribution facilities but will often share and use warehouse facilities with other publishers or specialist book publisher distribution services. You might find 100 or so publishers and imprints using the same distribution warehouse, as the customer base will be the same. It means that if a bookshop orders a number of titles from a variety of publishers, that all come from the same distribution facility, the bookshop will only receive one invoice and delivery for the whole order, covering all the publishers' books under the distributor's umbrella.

For online-only publishers, the online distribution channel is also key in ensuring that the correct online files are at the appropriate places at the right time. Distribution and operations staff are an integral part of what is called the 'Supply Chain'. The Supply Chain is critical to publishing success as without the means of getting the books to customers, none of the work from Editorial to Sales is going to have any value whatsoever.

To learn more about the different sectors in book publishing, the departments and the whole publishing process, read *Inside Book Publishing* by Angus Phillips and Giles Clark (Routledge, 7th edition 2025 ISBN 978-1032516554).

How Publishers are Changing and Evolving

Publishers are constantly changing and evolving. When I first started giving talks about book publishing in the 1980s, Figures 1 and 2 are the slides I used.

Figure 1 represents publishing in the 1970s. The different departments within the industry were straightforward and linear. All the departments within a publishing house had equal input into the making of a book.

Up until the late 1970s, Publishers in London used to have their own trade counters, where bookshops could visit during the day and collect stock of bestselling titles to ensure they had enough copies in the shops. At that time, it used to take two to three weeks for a box of books to be despatched from a publisher's distribution warehouse to a retailer, and speed was the key. It was the long delay in despatch and delivery that led to Kip Bertram setting up

```
        ┌──────────┐    ┌──────────┐    ┌──────────┐
        │ Editorial│────│Production│────│  Design  │
        └──────────┘    └──────────┘    └──────────┘
        ┌──────────┐    ┌──────────┐    ┌──────────┐
        │ Rights & │    │          │    │ Finance  │
        │ Int sales│────│   BOOK   │────│ Resources│
        │          │    │          │    │    IT    │
        └──────────┘    └──────────┘    └──────────┘
        ┌──────────┐    ┌──────────┐    ┌──────────┐
        │ Sales &  │    │          │    │          │
        │Marketing │────│ Publicity│────│Distribution│
        └──────────┘    └──────────┘    └──────────┘
```

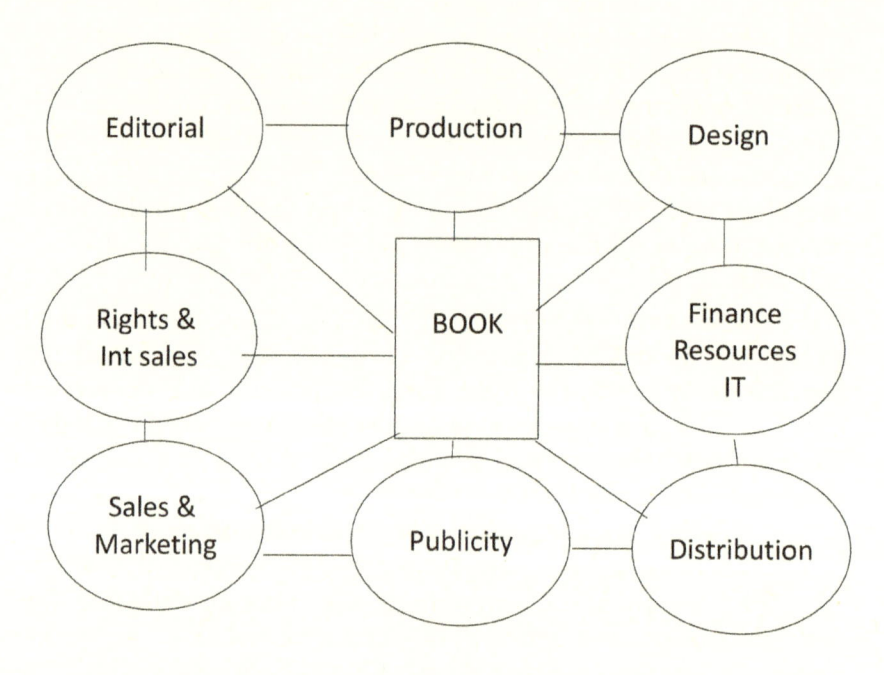

Figure 1

the first book wholesaler, Bertram Books. They would deliver next day to bookshops without an excessive delivery charge – that was unheard of. Bertrams, sadly, went into administration in 2020.

When I first joined the book publishing industry in 1983, it looked like Figure 1. Very few publishers had marketing departments. Marketing always referred to paid advertising and promotion, and very few publishers ever paid out for this! If a publisher could do or get something for free, then they would. [If, during an interview, you were asked to explain the difference between Marketing and Publicity, marketing was usually paid, publicity was usually free.] There was no real book marketing back in the 1980s, but after 1989, marketing departments started to emerge in publishers of all sizes.

As we reached the year 2000, publishing was starting to look like Figure 2.

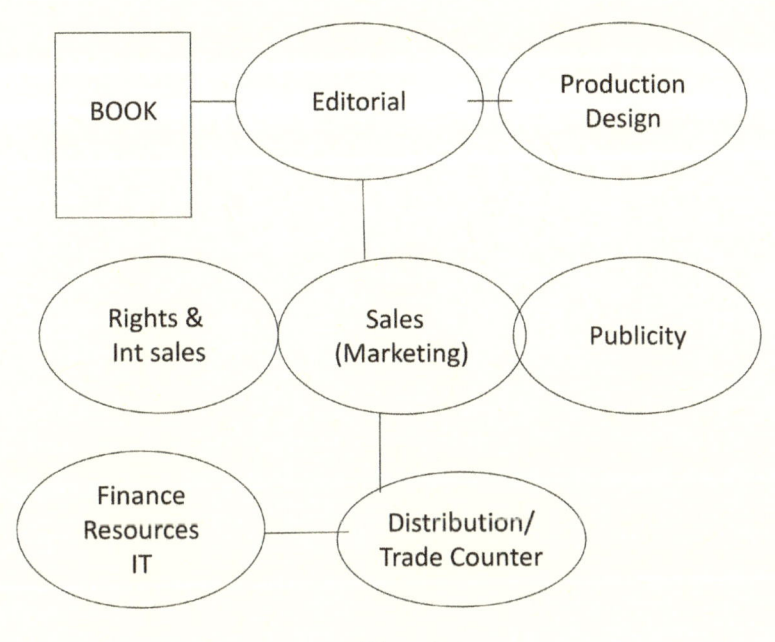

Figure 2

The departments have shifted slightly, and Editorial is working more closely with Production and Design, especially as typesetting and formatting an eBook is different to that of formatting a print edition. Sales, Marketing and Publicity are starting to blend into each other; Finance, IT and Human Resources are still out on a limb. Rights are starting to work in conjunction with International Sales, where back in the 1980s they were probably at odds with each other; Rights would always prefer to sell the copyright for a book, and International Sales would always want to sell finished copies of the publisher's own edition of the book or organise a co-edition.

Now if you look at Figure 3, this is how publishing is now.

Publishers have changed considerably. Editorial, content and production are all blended and how they differentiate depends on the company for which you work. A good example of this is the role of Production Editor. Traditionally a role unique to journal publishing, where someone controls both production and editorial, we are now seeing this role pop up in trade publishing.

Figure 3

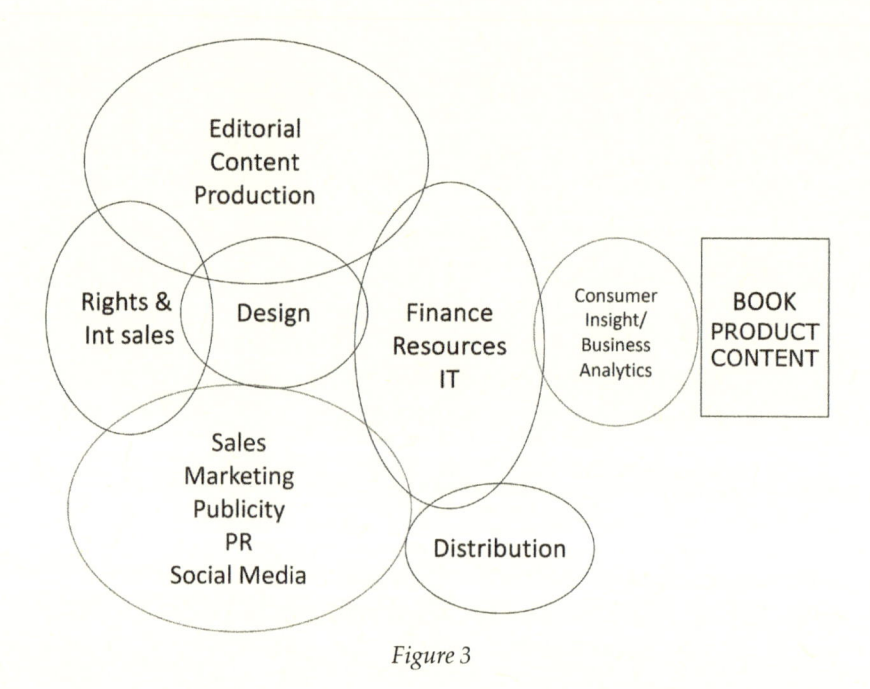

Sales, Marketing and Publicity have all but merged. As with Editorial, just how the skills, functions and work allocated within your role will depend on how your company operates.

Rights and International Sales are working in tandem to maximise all aspects of the export potential of a book.

Design, which used only to focus on book design, now plays a much bigger part. Every social media post, every blog, every aspect of book marketing and publicity now has a graphic attached. This might be a book cover or a graphic that promotes a theme or genre.

As already mentioned, the allocation of social media responsibilities varies from company to company. It will be interesting to see where it ends up long term.

Finance, IT and Resources have moved from the wilderness to be an integral part of the publishing process. As publishing has changed and become more resource-dependent, so have the responsibilities and input of these departments. There are now needs for deeper financial management and cost control and a call for administration skills that are non-department dependent, such as compiling metadata. Computer systems that support the functions and capabilities of the websites and servers need critical development and maintenance. Human resources, which used only to focus on the recruitment of new staff, now play an integral role in recruitment, staff welfare, training and helping publishers build strategic teams to support the needs of the business.

These non-specific job areas are likely to grow much more over the coming years. It doesn't mean that jobs within this area are dull and boring, they're anything but. What it does mean is that if you want to play a strategic role in the running of a publishing business you do not necessarily need to be in a traditional publishing department.

Consumer Insight

The Consumer Insight team might appear to be a relatively recent addition for many publishers, but several big brand publishers have had this department for a long time. Consumer Insight helps the Publisher and Marketing teams better understand their customers: the people who buy their books. The Consumer Insight team may have focus groups and reader panels with whom they are regularly in contact, as well as conduct surveys with both these and the wider public.

The reader and focus groups can help the Publisher learn who buys their books, their shopping and reading habits, the other interests they have, preferred price points, or anything else they wish to discover about the audience for their books. Knowing, for instance, that a mother would like a children's book that fits into a handbag and is easy to carry around could help to increase sales.

In addition to their own market research, publishers may use resources such as web analytics and social media trends. This data helps the publisher adapt their current publishing programme and find new ideas for titles, as well as sell more books. The marketing teams use this information to reach existing customers and discover new ones.

Publishers also have access to a subscription service called BookScan, provided by a company called Nielsen, who compile the bestseller lists for a fee. The information provided by BookScan allows anyone with a subscription to research and compare sales figures of all books published, not only their own but competitors' titles too. It may be possible for a Publisher to predict how well a new title could sell from the information gathered. This has taken away a lot of the 'gut instinct' feel for trade publishers, and one would assume a lot of the risk. My first employer, Andre Deutsch CBE, called publishing a legalised form of gambling, and for many publishers it still is.

The Publishers

Publishers are changing with the times, and they will continue to change and adapt, along with the marketplace.

Today's publishers are less like publishers and are moving more towards content providers instead. A lot of publishers are repurposing the content they have cultivated over a number of years and then using advances in online formats and printing technology to make titles available again in a variety of ways. Most of this was happening before Covid-19, but the worldwide pandemic has ensured that even the most reluctant of publishers are looking at different ways of operating. Publishers and Literary Agents are also looking at other services or opportunities to increase their income. It is good to be aware of this, as it could affect your future role in both a positive way, with entrepreneurial ideas, new innovation and job creation, or a negative way, by working on non-publishing projects you have little interest in.

Here are some examples of publishers and publishing organisations repurposing their content, producing items other than books, or offering different services:

- Penguin Random House often reissue classic texts packaged into value priced box sets or series. Recent examples include the Penguin Modern Classics, Little Black Classics and the Adventures in Time series.

- Hachette has acquired a number of different companies, including gift and stationery publishers, such as PaperBlanks and Laurence King who, in addition to books, publish new journals, jigsaws and puzzles.

- Bloomsbury Publishing, who issue the *Writers & Artists Yearbook*, have built a whole online community attached to the different editions of *Writers & Artists* and offer this as an online subscription, as well as other services.

- Faber & Faber launched the Faber Academy, a creative writing school that runs courses and offers mentoring and manuscript assessment for aspiring writers.
- Curtis Brown, a major literary and talent agency, also runs a creative writing school, offering courses, manuscript assessment and other editorial services
- Smaller publishers, such as Valley Press and Fly on the Wall Press, are experimenting with making money through offering subscriptions to their Substack, where they often information-share the nitty-gritty of book publishing.
- Academic Publishers allocate Digital Object Identifiers (DOIs) to books but increasingly to chapters within books, so people can buy (or rent) content at chapter level.
- Biomed Central (BMC), part of Springer Nature, has collated all their journal articles and research papers together in one website and made them available via a subscription-based service.
- Elsevier have done something similar and collated all their science journal articles and research papers together in one website, Science Direct.
- Becaris Publishing, a journal publisher, are building a whole hub, including an online magazine and community containing news and opinion, webinars and videos. Their audience respects the authority of their brand, and this expansion allows them to reach and monetarise the same audience in different ways.

Inclusivity

One major way in which publishers are changing is that they are trying very hard to be far more representative of the people who buy and read books than at any other time. Book publishing had a reputation of being full of white, middle-class graduates with private incomes, and publishing employers are working very hard to change things. Equity, diversity and inclusion (EDI) take many different forms, including employing people from lower socio-economic backgrounds, those with a wide range of disabilities and those from different cultures, backgrounds and locations. This is currently being approached in at least four ways:

- Ensuring published books are diverse and representative of a multi-cultural, multi-ability and multi-gender society.
- Participating in employment schemes, with agencies such as Creative Access, to support more diverse people joining or staying in the publishing workforce.
- Creating employment opportunities where a graduate degree is not a prerequisite for employment, such as the new Publishing Apprenticeship.
- Addressing social class and London-centric employment issues by opening offices outside of London and Oxford, and offering remote working opportunities

As inclusivity schemes change so frequently to adapt to publishers' ongoing concerns and initiatives, you will find a list of current inclusivity schemes on the web resources that accompany this book at https://www.bookcareers.com.

> **TOP TIP**
> Publishing is an industry like any other and its main aim is to make money. Once you understand and practise this, you are one part of the way to career success.

Structure of Departments

All departments are structured very similarly to Figure 4, from bottom to top. As it is a pyramid, there will always be fewer positions at the top than at the bottom. For some strange reason, publishing only recruits entry-level people at Assistant level. As a result, it is unusual to find an Editorial Assistant in the same role for four years or more.

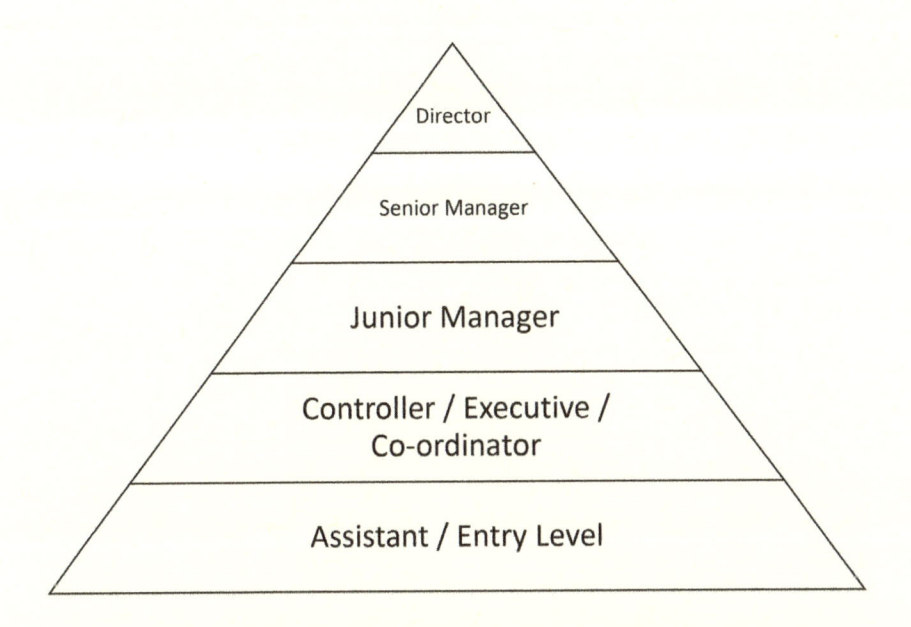

```
                    Director
                 Senior Manager
                 Junior Manager
           Controller / Executive /
                  Co-ordinator
             Assistant / Entry Level
```

Where Publishing is Now

Within each publishing sector there are opportunities and threats. To progress any job hunt, understanding the marketplace you are entering will help you immensely as it means you will be able to recognise where there might be potential job expansion or reduction, what new skills are required and see gaps within your current publishing role, if you have one. You will also be able to hold a professional discussion when you network or are at an interview.

Also, all publishers are becoming more like content providers and other media producers, such as the games industry and broadcast media, and less like traditional book publishers.

I would love to give you lots of different examples but, by the time I put it in writing, the discussions will have moved on.

Nonetheless, to give you a head-start, here are some general topics we have been discussing for a while and are still likely to be talking about in years to come.

- Amazon
- Artificial Intelligence (AI)
- Audio books

- Books as mobile phone apps
- eBook market and eBook lending
- Bricks and mortar bookshops
- Genres that are decreasing in sales
- Genres that are increasing in sales
- Libraries
- Manipulating content across different mediums and brands
- Metadata
- Open Access and DRM
- Publishing for equity, diversity and inclusion
- Social media influence on book sales
- Subscription boxes
- Where and how books are sold, B2C or D2C

Being aware of these, and other current topics, if they are relevant to the sector or publisher you are aiming to work for, could help support your job search. This type of information will enable you to ace the interview questions, 'What is trending right now?' or 'What has caught your eye recently?' You also need to know what's trending because it will give you an indication whether the publisher you wish to work for might be 'in vogue' or way behind the times and struggling.

Please don't pressure yourself to become an expert on any of the topics; you need only to have enough knowledge to understand how it may influence what and how a company is publishing or the markets it sells to.

The best way to keep up with the trends is to read widely. The UK publishing industry trade press includes titles such as *BookBrunch* and *The Bookseller*. Whilst both are paywalled, and you may find the subscriptions expensive, they do have a free daily email with the headlines, and occasionally free articles and links to external news.

> **TOP TIP**
> When you work in book publishing you need to be on top of the latest trends. So, when things like Angry Birds, Candy Crush or Pokemon Go get launched, download it, see what the fuss is all about, understand the appeal, and delete it before you get addicted! Discuss it with friends who like playing and may be addicted. Maybe let them show you and then move on. It doesn't matter whether you are working for a trade or an academic publisher because all new trends are likely to influence what your company is doing. For example, if you are working for a journal publisher there might be an article in the journal such as 'The influences of mobile phone apps on addictions and depression', so you need to know what is going on.

When you're starting out, the headlines and free news should be sufficient to give you a taster of what is going on. Trade Associations', other publishers' and competitors' websites should form an essential part of your regular reading; you need to develop a thirst for knowledge of what else is going on in the wider world. This could involve reading across all media, magazines, newspapers, watching the news and generally being aware of new potential trends and opportunities. You should be learning organically and have general awareness of what is happening in the world.

In some roles, having this knowledge could be part of your future career, such as being a Senior Commissioning Editor who is looking for the next big thing, a Marketing Manager taking advantage of a new platform or a Sales Manager approaching a new retail chain before they open.

This is probably what is noticeable about people who work in book publishing as opposed to other industries. Publishing staff usually seem far more clued up about what's new, what's forthcoming and what is going on in the world. They are great friends to take to quiz nights.

Other useful resources could be relevant, such as online forums that specialise in topics or genres and social media platforms. Apart from publishers, senior employees and the people you want to work for (more on this later), some key people to follow on social media who might help you keep on top of the trends are the Lecturers and Course Directors of the publishing Graduate and Post-Graduate courses. They often repost and share interesting articles or discuss potential new trends with their current students.

If you're interested in a specialist publisher, then it is advisable to submerge yourself in relevant magazines and media on that particular subject. For example, if you want to work for an Art History publisher, what Art publications are you reading? Other questions to consider include:

- What galleries are opening?
- What exhibitions are planned, not just for this month, but for next year and, maybe, the year after (most museums and galleries publish advance data, and their websites have lists of past exhibitions too)?
- What anniversaries are coming up that relate to major artists or art genres?
- What artworks or auctions recently featured in the national or international news?

All this subject knowledge might not seem important if you are going for an entry-level role, yet very often it is this type of knowledge and understanding that may set you apart from others when going for highly competitive roles. I have heard, too many times, a publisher say, "The candidate didn't have all the skills for the role, but their subject knowledge and understanding of our marketplace was so good that we had to give them the job."

TOP TIP

If the job you want requires you to be competent in a specific type of software that you have never used before, see if there are any free downloads and training materials available, so you can teach yourself the basics for free. Also check out YouTube for free tutorials. Paid training can be completed at a low cost via various online platforms, but often the free training could be more than sufficient for your needs.

Publishing Skills That Increase Employability

Every role in publishing has its own individual skills requirement and these will vary from role to role. However, there are skills that are key to being employable in most departments. If you currently don't have a particular skill, don't think instantly getting professionally trained will improve your employment chances, because it doesn't necessarily work that way, and not all jobs need every skill. Even so, these skills may enhance your opportunities and improve how far you get along in the recruitment process before you are rejected.

Use the following list as a guide to understand what skills are important to publishers. If you're just starting out, think about where you could get practical experience from any of these. It may be by getting involved in voluntary societies and organisations or via paid work in different industries. If you're changing your career into publishing, you may have some of these skills already.

Can you match your current experience, or non-publishing role, to any of these?

Skills are usually broken down into two sections – Hard Skills and Soft Skills.

HARD SKILLS are the technical skills that you need to perform in a job. They are traditionally skills in which you receive formal training and that you can easily sit an exam in or be tested on.

The following are the key hard skills for working in book publishing:

Proofreading and Copy-editing – the ability to edit, rewrite and rephrase text. This is often much more than spotting a few typos (typographical errors) or other errors in a text. Copy-editing requires you to rewrite and rephrase sentences or paragraphs to ensure they are grammatically correct.

Copywriting – to write fresh text from scratch, often with a marketing angle. It is about being able to write compelling copy that can draw in a reader, buyer or browser, for any manner of reasons, but often it is for the jacket copy (blurb) or promotional material for a book.

Business Analytics and Data Analysis – to understand and analyse statistics and data from a variety of sources (e.g. Internal data, Google Analytics, Business Analytic software); interpret quantitative and qualitative data and monitor return on investment (ROI).

Digital – to understand and use digital processes, apps and mobile data; be ahead of what is happening in technology and eager to try new things. You don't necessarily have to be an early adopter of gadgets, but you do need to know what is out there, and how it is being used.

IT Skills – the software that you use; the ability to learn new software quickly. In old job advertisements, the only requirement was for you to be 'computer literate', but employers now ask for knowledge of specific software packages.

The most popular software packages currently being asked about are:

- Microsoft Office (Word, Excel, PowerPoint, Outlook)
- Adobe Creative Suite (Illustrator, InDesign, Photoshop)
- Knowledge of WordPress, Drupal or blogging software
- HTML, XML and the ability to write or understand coding, and to manipulate a CSS (Cascading Style Sheet)
- Familiarity with any publishing or title software management system such Stison or Biblio or any Content Management System (CMS)
- The ability to enter any data into a Customer Relation Management (CRM) system such as Salesforce

Metadata – Metadata refers to the bibliographic information, marketing collateral and commercial information about a publication that enables the book to be easily discovered on any online system or database, and ensures the book can be traded efficiently.

> **TOP TIP**
> If you only have time to learn two software packages, a good working knowledge of Microsoft Excel and Adobe InDesign will give you a big advantage when it comes to job applications. If you learn Microsoft Excel to the level where you are experienced in Pivot Tables and VLOOKUPs, and Adobe InDesign to a level where you are experienced in creating documents or brochures, moving text and images around and resizing where necessary, you will be streets ahead of many other applicants. More importantly, these two software packages dominate job advertisement requirements. You shouldn't need to pay for expensive subscriptions or training. You'll find most software manufacturers have a free trial aspect, as well as free tutorials on their website and YouTube.

Metadata is what drives the algorithms on websites such as Amazon, Waterstones and Google and allows the book to be found in libraries. Whatever department of publishing you are in, you need to know about Metadata. If you switch off when someone mentions the word Metadata, you really might as well switch off the publishing company you work for. Good and accurate Metadata will help your employer's products sell better by allowing them to being discoverable on the internet. It will often contain the title, subtitle, a short description, a long description, price, extent (number of pages), format, number of illustrations, keywords and subject category codes. The current category codes are a in a format called Thema, BIC (though it is being phased out) and BISAC (the US system).

Customer Service – to offer an exceptional level of service to customers, whoever they may be, and no matter what constraints may be involved. This could be: taking and processing orders, answering questions and queries or serving customers in a retail environment.

Social Media – to build and engage an audience through a variety of social media and blogging platforms. The wider the variety of social media platforms you use, the better. Most publishers have their favourites, but at the very least, have an understanding of the main platforms such as Facebook, Instagram, LinkedIn, Pinterest, TikTok, X/Twitter and blogging platforms such as Substack and Medium.

SEO – this is Search Engine Optimisation. Learn how to attract more visitors to a website and make your books and webpages come up higher in searches.

Sales (1) – Business to Business (B2B) – to sell things, whatever the product, to other businesses, no matter what their different buying processes are.

Sales (2) – Business to Consumer (B2C or D2C) – to sell things, whatever the product, direct to members of the public.

Marketing – to devise marketing campaigns to specific audiences. This could involve locating audiences, writing copy, creating promotional material, understanding ROI and booking advertising space.

Publicity – to publicise an event, product or service, to deal with areas of the media, and have good media contacts.

Project Management – to manage projects, to ensure you know how to get things done in an efficient manner, within budget and to a deadline. Formal project management qualifications such as Agile and Prince2 are often not required, but some of the principles of this training may or may not be used.

SOFT SKILLS (see HARD SKILLS, P33) are the personal and people skills you have that hold the hard skills together and make them work better. They are difficult to test and can often only be demonstrated in real-life examples.

There are many soft skills, but the following tend to be key for book publishing:

Communication – how you communicate with anyone on a regular basis is a key skill that gives access to so many other skills and abilities.

Creativity – being creative, either with practical creative skills, such as writing, drawing or crafting, or in the way you approach problem solving.

Time Management – to make effective use of your time, how you spend your time at work to ensure deadlines are met.

Teamwork – how you work together with others in a team; your ability to co-operate and co-create with others.

Organisation – how to organise yourself or others efficiently. For some this might go hand in hand with time management, but time management deals with the time involved, and organisation deals with the tasks and projects. You could be very efficient at getting work done on time (time management) but not be good at deciding which tasks to do first (organisation).

Problem Solving – the ability to think for yourself, use your initiative, and come up with solutions when required. It can also be about knowing how and when to improve processes.

Negotiation – to be a top negotiator, whether it is on contract clauses, co-partnership agreements, costs, terms, discounts, with colleagues or businesses and suppliers.

Leadership or a sense of responsibility – leadership is often a senior skill, where you lead a team or organisation, devise strategy and ideas, give direction and motivate your team or colleagues. But at a junior level, you can develop your leadership skills by showing a sense of responsibility towards your work and the tasks you are given.

Management of a team or organisation – a manager takes or makes leadership ideas and organises them and the staff into actions, systems and plans. Note, if you don't know the difference between leadership and management then look them up – they are different things, and not everyone with good leadership skills has good management skills or vice versa.

If you'd like to learn more about each job within a publishing company, the Publishers Association website (www.publishers.org.uk) has information about individual jobs and the National Occupational Standards for publishing. Although they haven't been updated for many years, they will still give you a good outline (https://www.publishingtrainingcentre.co.uk/images/BookJournalPublishingNationalStandards.pdf).

TOP TIP

Do you have a friend who can support you in your job search? Why not hold a professional discussion with them about a change that you have noticed. To hold an effective professional discussion, choose a topic that might, for instance, compare the publishing programmes of Cambridge University Press and Oxford University Press, and discuss your findings and assumptions. Your friend doesn't need to have a publishing background, but if they have any knowledge about any business or workplace, they should be able to listen and contribute to the discussion and help you clarify your thoughts and points of view. It is not a test, but its aim is to give you confidence in discussing what you may have noticed about books or publishers. You might want to set a time limit on this discussion to, say, 15 or 30 minutes. This is great practice for an interview, where you might be asked to discuss, within 90 seconds, your thoughts about a particular publisher's role in the marketplace.

EXERCISE

The bookcareers.com Job Reality Scale

The bookcareers.com job reality scale will help you rate your dream job versus the reality of you being employed.

We all have dreams of the next job we want. Maybe you fantasise about working for a particular publisher, or with a select group of authors or on a genre that interests you. Unfortunately, the reality is there may be few jobs or opportunities in your preferred area.

1. What is your dream job?

First, you need to identify your dream role. What job are you looking for?

- Is it in a particular sector of publishing, such as academic, education, trade/consumer books or STM, or are you open to anything and everything?
- Is there a particular publishing department or function that you want to work in or on?
- Do you have your heart set on Editorial, or maybe you want to use your language skills in Rights, or you want to work in Sales, Marketing or Publicity, or a combination of all three? Or maybe you've set your heart on Production.
- What level of job are you looking for? Are you looking for an entry-level job or an assistant-level role? Maybe you are looking for something that is much further up the scale? Are you looking for a senior role in publishing?
- Have you imposed any specifics on your job hunt? Are you proposing to look in only one location, or are you open to working anywhere if a job arose? Are you prepared to relocate?
- Maybe you've set a specific condition that you only want to work in literary fiction or science fiction, or that you only want to work in academic books on a particular subject area.
- This involves dreaming for a moment and thinking about your ideal role.

2. How realistic is your job search?

Are you always seeing hundreds of jobs advertised every day for the job or role you are looking for? Or do you never see jobs advertised?

If you see jobs advertised every day, then that would score a full 10 marks on the bookcareers.com reality scale. If you never see any jobs advertised, then it would be 1. I'm assuming that most of you reading this will be scoring between 4 and 7. If you are Entry Level and your bookcareers.com reality scale is number 5, is there anything you can do to help move that to a 7. Maybe, you are only looking for jobs in Literary Fiction. How many Literary Fiction publishers are there? How many Editorial Assistant roles within Literary Fiction are there? Can you see that by maybe looking for non-fiction Editorial Assistant roles too, your chances of being employed will go up the scale?

If you're looking for a senior role, then a score between 3 and 5 on the bookcareers.com reality scale is okay. But, again, is there anything you can do to help widen your job search so that it becomes a 6 or a 7? If your job reality scale is stuck at 1 or 2, no matter what you do, then perhaps you need to seek professional careers guidance outside of this book with someone who can help you create opportunities for yourself.

So, after adding improvements and widening your job search, what is your bookcareers.com reality scale number now?

1. What job are you looking for?
    a. Which sector of publishing is it in?
    b. Is it in a particular publishing department or function?
    c. What level of job are you looking for?
    d. Have you imposed any specifics, such as only working on a particular genre (e.g. Literary Fiction, Fiction) or in a limited location (e.g. Cornwall)?
2. The bookcareers.com reality scale. How realistic is this job search?

    1 is hardly any jobs in that area – 10 is many jobs

    1 2 3 4 5 6 7 8 9 10

3. Is there anything you can do to improve this number?

    After adding improvements, where is your job search on the bookcareers.com reality scale?

    1 2 3 4 5 6 7 8 9 10

3. Review your skills

What skills do you already have for the job you are currently seeking?

If you are entry level, you would be expected to have between one and four skills. If you've been working for a while, you would be expected to have between four and seven skills. If you are senior, then ten or more skills are likely.

If you have difficulty completing this task, find a recent job advertisement or job description for a job you applied for, or use the *Publishing Skills That Increase Employability* list as the basis for identifying what skills you already have.

If you're entry level and you have gone through a job advertisement and thought, 'Hey, I've got seven of these skills,' it doesn't necessarily mean you should be going for a more advanced role. All it means is that you have a better chance of being employed at entry level.

What skills do you already have that match the job you are currently looking for?

1.

2.

3.

4.

ENTRY LEVEL

5.

6.

EXECUTIVE LEVEL

7.

8.

EXPERT LEVEL

9.

10.

ACTION POINTS

- What trends or big issues are there in book publishing today?
- What trends or big issues are there in the wider world that would make a good book?
- What genres or type of books are selling particularly well?
- What challenges do you think publishing faces right now?
- Can you think of two examples of content creation in publishing today?
- What major marketing campaign have you seen for a book recently that you would describe as game-changing in that it has started a new trend or fresh way of doing things?
- Where did you see the marketing?
- Why is it game-changing?
- What trend has it led or influenced?
- What book are you reading at the moment?
- What inspired you to buy it?
- Where did you buy it or how did you get it?

Pick a publisher who you most admire.
- What are they publishing?
- Who are their competitors?
- What are the differences and the similarities between the two publishers?
- Where do you sit on the bookcareers.com job reality scale?
- How many of the *Publishing Skills That Increase Employability* do you have already?
- How many do you need to work towards?

CHAPTER TWO

Getting Started

"You do not need work experience to get a publishing job, nor do you need to work unpaid for a publisher to get a job. Always choose paid work."

Suzanne Collier

The big questions any novice jobseeker faces are:

- How do you prepare for a career in publishing?
- How do you get experience if you have no experience?
- How do you stand out from the crowd?

The Magic Formula

The magic formula, regardless of your level of experience or education, is to appear employable and there are many routes to doing this.

This is not about who you worked for or where you went to university, and thankfully less about 'who you know', or having a gimmick or graphic on your CV. It is about demonstrating you have the skills and competencies to do the job. These skills and competencies don't necessarily need to be publishing connected, but relate to interests, knowledge, expertise and anything that may convince a Publisher that you can do the job.

Qualifications and Entry for a Career in Book Publishing

The majority of publishers value paid office experience higher than unpaid publishing experience. You don't necessarily need publishing qualifications or even a degree to get a publishing job, although they can help. The following pages cover a range of options for ways into the industry.

There are no definitive entry-level requirements, although, until recently, publishing was seen as a degree-level career. However, as part of their equity, diversity and inclusion policies, publishers are now more open to applicants without degrees than at any other time.

Choosing GCSE and A Level Qualifications

To get the best results, you should choose subjects you'll enjoy and do well in. However, when choosing GCSE (Level 2) qualifications and A Level (Level 3) qualifications, it is always best to seek out a qualified Careers Advisor to help you make the decision on what subjects to study. Although there are some subjects you can start fresh with at A Level, many schools and colleges request you have studied a similar subject at GCSE Level. Your A Level choices could also influence what you study at university, should you take that route.

When you reach A Level stage you have many options, the details of which are covered over the next few pages.

Continuing in Education

Going to university to study for a degree of your choice and continue your education is probably the most travelled route. Whilst at university you can pick up office and employability skills with a variety of vocational activities, such as volunteering for university societies or by doing paid part-time work in any occupation. On completion of your degree, the next step is to either look for an internship – or entry-level role – with a book publisher or to continue your education to study publishing and earn a Master's degree. Some publishing degrees and Master's courses have a requirement to undertake a placement or a minimum amount of work experience in order to gain a pass.

> **The Origins of a Degree Requirement**
>
> Publishing has always been a popular career choice, and every vacancy attracts many applicants. During the 1980s, by way of filtering and reducing the number of applicants, a number of publishers started to state their minimum qualification for an entry-level role was a graduate degree. However, these were not degree-level jobs, and it appeared the only reason for asking for a degree was to cut back on the number of candidates applying. Thankfully, the publishing industry overall has seen sense and, to be as inclusive as possible, there is no minimum education requirement for most roles.

Choosing a Graduate Degree for Publishing

When choosing a graduate degree for publishing it is not compulsory to study English, Publishing, Media or Creative Writing. Choose a degree course that you believe you will enjoy, because when we study subjects we enjoy, we often perform better. Subject specialisation for working in publishing is not important unless you have your heart set on a specialist field, such as history, art, psychology, engineering or on scientific publications. In those cases, a degree in a relevant discipline may be useful.

If you are planning to study Publishing, Media, Creative Writing or Journalism at undergraduate (first) degree level, then research the degree course. In addition to the usual questions, (location, accommodation, size of the course or campus), take advantage of any open days and ask yourself these questions:

1. Does the university specialise in a particular area of publishing or cover the precise areas of publishing in which you are interested?
2. How many former students now work in the sectors of publishing that you wish to work in, and what do people who have studied for the degree say about the course?
3. How quickly on completion of the course do graduates start work in their chosen field?
4. Who are the permanent lecturers within the faculty, and what is the staff-to-student ratio?

5. Are there any indications who will be guest lecturers?
6. How up to date is the course content? If you've read up recently on current trends within book publishing, does the course prospectus cover this?
7. What regular involvement does the university have with the publishing industry or sector?
8. Does it have an advisory board?
9. Can you work alongside study? For example, are campus days aggregated to allow part-time work or is hybrid/distance learning an option?
10. Is the university a member of the Association for Publishing Education?

The Association for Publishing Education (APE) is the organisation that nearly all universities running industry-recognised graduate and post-graduate courses belong to. Through APE, universities collaborate with each other and the publishing industry to ensure their course prospectuses reflect current trends and are of the highest standard.

You can find an up-to-date list of publishing undergraduate and post-graduate degrees and any scholarships they offer at https://www.bookcareers.com.

Studying for a Master's in Publishing

If you decide to undertake a first degree in a non-publishing or media subject, you might then wish to study for a Master's in Publishing.

A Master's in Publishing will give you great knowledge and insight into book publishing and may bring you into contact with industry connections that otherwise could take you years to meet. You'll also be studying the skills you will use every day in a future job and, depending on the Master's degree you choose, the history of publishing too. It also brings you ahead of the pack in terms of industry progression – where AI and digital are going, what's happening to the print-on-demand (POD) and eBook market, and which areas of publishing are likely to expand.

> **TOP TIP**
> The magic formula, regardless of your level of experience or education, is to appear employable and there are many routes to doing this.

However, it is a purely personal choice to study for a Master's in Publishing. Despite the fantastic education a Master's degree course will give you, there are no guarantees of a publishing job at the end of it.

Nick Canty, Senior Lecturer at the University for the Creative Arts says: *"It is purely a personal choice to study for a Master's in Publishing. Despite the fantastic education a Master's degree course will give you, there are no guarantees of a publishing job at the end of it but a Master's in Publishing will open doors for you and should get you to the interview stage."*

A Master's in Publishing is not just a box-ticking exercise. Universities continually assess industry trends and undertake a copious amount of research to ensure the content of their qualifications are of the highest standards. They liaise constantly with industry employers to remain at the forefront of developments and ensure their students are employable.

However, on the flip side, a Master's in Publishing doesn't guarantee you a job, and you still have to do an extensive amount of work for yourself. Crucially, if you're an international student, although you can work for a period on a student visa, **under current immigration restrictions, it won't help you attain permanent UK residency.**

At this point, there needs to be a few reality checks. There are probably more graduates than entry-level publishing roles. Then there are the financial aspects: will you earn back the cost of the degree in salary terms? Sadly, current statistics from the bookcareers.com Salary Survey show no difference in salary or career progression when we compare those who've studied for a Master's against those who have not. Yes, some Publishing graduates have gone on to do great things within the industry, but then so have people without a Master's.

> **TOP TIP**
> How long should you keep undertaking work experience placements and internships? For as little time as possible! All the time keep looking for a job.

If you are considering doing a Master's in Publishing, here are some questions to ask yourself:

1. Can you afford to do a Master's? Cost is a huge factor. You don't need a Master's to get a job, so don't bankrupt yourself trying to get one.
2. (a) Do you want to continue your formal education?

   (b) Are you still enjoying studying and learning in a formal environment, or are you a student who wants to move on into the world of work?
3. Can you afford to take a year out not working, or could you work and study via a distance learning degree?
4. If you're career changing or are a mature student, do you have the time and discipline to return to education? Don't underestimate the amount of work it takes to undertake a Master's degree.
5. Do you have any skills or experience to offer a publisher without a Master's? If you're straight out of university, with no extra-curricular activities, no work or office experience, or little confidence to compete in a competitive job market, then an MA may be perfect for you. A love of books alone is not enough to secure you a job.
6. If you already have some skills – maybe you've been working in an office whilst studying, curating social media for the student union or editing the student newspaper – have you now got enough to make you employable without further study?
7. Have you looked and compared the prospectus of your chosen degree with similar alternatives? Some courses are better for international publishers, and some are better for children's books or academic books over trade publishing.
8. Do you need to invest in a full Master's degree? Most universities can award postgraduate certificates (one

semester of full-time study) and postgraduate diplomas (two semesters full-time, but no dissertation) for partial completion of a Master's degree. Some will let you join individual modules as a short course. It is always worth speaking to the faculty to see what options might suit your needs.

Talk through your options with a qualified Careers Advisor. They can't make the decision for you but they will aim to guide you accordingly.

Remember, when it comes down to it, it is a personal choice. Only you can make this decision.

> **CASE STUDY**
>
> *Master's in Publishing – Manchester Metropolitan University*
>
> I realised, towards the end of my final year of an undergraduate degree, that I knew I wanted to work in book publishing but didn't have any knowledge or experience. So, I went to study a Master's at Manchester Metropolitan University. On the course we covered commissioning and editorial, children's books, digital publishing, and marketing. For the final module, I did a work experience placement, and I got a role in publishing within about a month of finishing my Master's.

Option – Studying for a PhD or Career Changing via a PhD

Universities that host publishing and communications postgraduate degrees usually also offer research degrees, aka doctorates in publishing-related topics.

These could be funded (via studentship or third party) or self-funded (student loans are available). PhDs typically take four years of full-time study, and some might include an amount of lecturing to undergraduates as part of the qualification.

If you've been in a non-publishing related career where there might be a strong overlap between your career history and a proposed topic, it is possible that you would be considered for a funded PhD; however, these are highly competitive. A word of caution: a PhD in publishing won't necessarily lead to an academic post or a greater chance of a job in publishing. Therefore, you should carefully evaluate whether a self-funded PhD is the best way to achieve your goals.

If you've completed a PhD and are looking to move from Academia into Publishing, your best bet is to look towards the publishers who are publishing the journals and publications you frequently read as part of your studies, subjects you have expert knowledge in, or towards other areas of Academic Publishing. Academics are more likely to respect the qualifications of other Academics.

CASE STUDY
Master's at City University, London

I'd graduated and was working at an Art Gallery. I always loved books and reading, so applied to do a Master's and took out a student loan to pay for it. I was accepted on to three courses but chose the one which I felt suited me.

For the first term, we learnt about the history of publishing, understanding the business and covered everything, including production, editorial and marketing. We could choose modules, and I chose the working in publishing module that exposed me to placements and getting a job in publishing.

The second term [was] more hands-on and we got to apply all the teaching from the first term into practical assignments. This involved digital product innovation and creating our own apps for what we would like to see in the world. I created a children's book using InDesign and worked on everything from the concept to marketing. Throughout the whole course we had many guest speakers who were high-profile people from across the industry. We also had international speakers too, who covered international publishing and globalisation. I'm now looking for a job in the industry and I feel far more confident about just knowing more about the industry and the individual roles and different areas. It was the most fun I have ever had. I met the most awesome people, and I felt so supported by the teachers.

Option – Entry-Level Schemes

This is where you to start looking for entry-level schemes from publishers that welcome candidates without degrees.

A few publishers, particularly the larger consumer publishing companies, periodically run internships and entry-level schemes. Formerly, these were graduate schemes aimed at those starting out but often now are open to all regardless of academic qualification or career history. The aim of these schemes is to bring in diverse talent and fresh ideas to the company.

The best-known one is called The Scheme from Penguin Random House that, in the past, has offered 12-month roles in areas such as Editorial and Marketing. The selection criteria are not judged on academic qualification but on your ability to successfully pass a number of assignments based on the skills needed, or ideas you'll be creating on the job, so if you're creative you're likely to do well. HarperCollins and Hachette have run similar opportunities. However, these entry-level schemes are not run every single year, and the criteria change, as does the recruitment process. The criteria are adapted to reflect the needs of the business or to reach those who may not have initially sought publishing as a career. As you can imagine, these are immensely popular and the publishers receive hundreds of applications for only a handful of places.

Whilst these opportunities are very appealing, don't make them the be-all and end-all of your job search. Competition is fierce and in some cases the position offered may be a fixed-term contract with no guarantee of a job at the end, although there is a good track record of successful applicants being retained as employees at the end of their contract.

Entry-level schemes will usually be advertised on the publishers' own website and promoted through their social media accounts.

Option – Publishing Apprenticeships

Publishing Apprenticeships have been running on a national scale in the UK for several years; the apprenticeship is called 'Publishing Assistant'. Publishers of all shapes and sizes, and in both trade and academic publishing, have committed to the apprenticeship scheme and have created a number of new entry-level opportunities for people who do not want to go to university.

The first intake consisted of 17 new apprentices.

Similar to apprenticeships in different industries, an apprenticeship is a fixed-term job that is aligned to the standards of an industry where you learn skills that are tied to that industry. Its intention is to leave you with skills and a recognised qualification so, at the end of the apprenticeship, you are qualified to apply for a full-time position and, hopefully, have a successful career within that industry. During the period of an apprenticeship, you will be employed in a full-time role and receive on- and off-the-job training, support and regular assessments as well as an end-of-apprenticeship assessment. These opportunities for apprenticeships cover many different departments, with the main ones specialising in editorial, marketing and production.

The Publishing Assistant apprenticeship is an A Level standard paid role and aimed at school leavers aged 18 and over. There is no maximum age limit. Publishers have embraced the introduction of apprenticeships to increase the inclusivity and diversity of their workforce. The apprenticeship will last 14–15 months, of which 12 months is training and 2–3 months is assessment. The intake of all publishing apprentices is planned for September and April every year, but you can apply at any time. You'll meet up with other apprentices and have a line manager from within the publisher that employs you. You'll also have support and mentorship from the co-ordinators of the publishing apprenticeship scheme, LDN Apprentices.

The apprenticeship is advertised – as with any other job – by the employer, but also on the Institute for Apprenticeships (IFA) website. The selection process for each candidate will vary from publisher to publisher. There is an interview process as normal, but the training provider does a final interview. If LDN Apprentices recruits on behalf of the publisher, they have a separate process of working that will be tailored to the publisher's requirements. However, some traditional recruitment practices, such as completing an online application form, attending an open day or assessment centre with part of that day being a formal interview, are in place.

Option – Work Experience and Internships

One way to get some entry-level publishing experience or find out if book publishing is the career for you is to complete a work experience placement or internship, but these are not a prerequisite for working in book publishing.

You do not have to undertake work experience to get a job, and if – from personal choice – you decide to look for a placement, you should not be working unpaid. In the UK, all work experience and internship placements fall under the National Minimum Wage or the National Living Wage.

The vocabulary over work experience and internships has become very confused in recent years, and they may now mean the same thing to many people. There was a time when work experience was just that – a two-week experience with a book publisher for prospective jobseekers to nip in and nip out of a variety of departments, see how a publishing company worked, find out whether it was a career they would like, say a few 'hellos' and make a career decision as to what to do next.

> **CASE STUDY**
> *Career Changer – Master's at UCL, London*
> I originally studied for a BA at university and had a focus on interior design. Then I worked in design sales, selling furniture to hotels and restaurants.
>
> It was a great industry, but it felt very cut-throat, and I became slightly disillusioned, even though I loved the sales aspect. I then thought, what do I love and what can I do, and I realised I wanted to work in book publishing but had no contacts.
>
> I thought undertaking a publishing MA would be a really good way of getting my foot in the door and meeting people within the industry. I joined the UCL MA programme, and I signed up for all the networking and opportunities. I got asked to volunteer at the FutureBook Conference and that is where I met my new boss, just by an informal chat. I'm now an Account Manager at a Publishing Service Company.

In the current job marketplace, some consider work experience or an internship to be a three- or six-month placement at minimum wage. Unpaid placements usually contravene UK employment laws (unless you are still a student, and even then there are caveats), so do not work for free.

If an employer takes the risk of breaking employment laws and you undertake an unpaid work experience of up to two weeks, the placement should, at the very least, pay a travel and lunch allowance. However, once these two weeks have passed, you have a value to the company. This is because you will know the names of the people in the office, how to answer the phone and how the computer system works, so if the publisher wants to retain you, you most definitely should be paid. But, as all the big UK publishers ensure everyone who completes a work experience placement is paid, there is no reason to work unpaid anywhere.

Work Experience for under 18s

If you're under the age of 18, it is very difficult to find work-experience placements in book publishing.

To combat this, one or two of the big publishers, particularly Hachette, have been running periodic remote learning work experience schemes, where you complete a number of tasks based on the skills used in the publishing process.

Be aware, however, if you are under the age of 18, it is unlikely you will find any face-to-face placements as there are usually safeguarding and health and safety responsibilities. Most publishers say that they can't let you do even a day's work experience as you 'won't be insured'.

However, there are a number of ways in which you may be able to get someone from a publisher to visit your school, via either the Publishing Ambassador scheme from the Publishers Association, or through an organisation called Speakers at Schools, via their s4nextgen scheme.

If you're under 18, you may find the following pages on Preparing for Work particularly helpful.

Choosing a Work Experience Placement or Internship

As competition for paid placements is even tougher than for entry-level roles, it is more likely that the placement chooses you, rather than you choose the placement. However, apply for the opportunities you wish to pursue. These will usually be advertised on the publisher's website. In some cases it is a lottery – Penguin Random House chooses applicants by random selection.

When reviewing the advertisement, think about why you are completing work experience. What do you hope to gain out of it? Is it in the department or sector that you have set your hopes on, or do you want to try out lots of different options before deciding on your career? If there is a list of tasks in the advertisement, do they all appear mundane office administration or do any of the tasks appear unique to book publishing?

Some publishers have well-organised work experience placements, whilst others might be more casual in their approach. Just because a publisher might approach a placement or internship differently, it should not put you off, and nor does it mean the experience will be any more or less than one that has a more formal procedure for placements.

Examples of a well-organised placement include informing you:

- What time you'll start and finish each day and an indication of the office dress code.
- Who will be looking after you.
- About others in the department, ideally by being sent an email and starter pack with photos of who is who in the department, so you can recognise them before you meet them and can look them up on LinkedIn.
- About one or two major book projects that you might be working on, so you can look up the authors and titles.
- What might be useful to read before you arrive; they may send you a book to read.
- What tasks you'll be asked to do; this might be sent as a mini job description.

However, for most placements, the only information you may be given in advance is who to report to on your first day and what time to arrive.

> **CASE STUDY**
> *Paid Internship with DK, Two-Week Remote Opportunity*
>
> This was an advertised opportunity. I was working for a kindergarten, but I really want to work in book publishing. The application process did not require a CV or Covering Letter. Instead, I applied by answering a set of questions.
>
> Every morning my day started with an online meeting with the person who was allocating me a task. Later in the day I met with them again to review the work I had completed. My first assignment was to read through an old edition of one of their books, looking for anything that might be out of date and need revising. This could be a reference to something that may no longer have existed, as well as checking for terms and phrases that were no longer appropriate.
>
> I got the opportunity to edit chapter openers and brainstorm chapter titles for a book. I experienced the marketing side too. I worked with a Brand Executive, where we would go through the calendar and look for suitable events where we could promote their books. I also undertook research for their podcast. Overall, it was a great introduction into publishing, and I really enjoyed it.

What work are you likely to be undertaking on a placement?

For the purpose of this book, I surveyed a large number of recent interns and these are the tasks that they were given:

- Writing a Press Release
- Inserting Press Releases into books
- Preparing promotional showcards – usually sticking covers of a book onto white mounted board for a bookshop to use in a display
- Sourcing a media list of contacts from a directory
- Packing review copies or other books
- Researching Bloggers for a particular title
- Running errands inside or outside the office

- Creating and posting social media posts on different platforms
- Responding to social media posts
- Reading incoming manuscripts and submissions for Editorial and writing a summary report about what you've read
- Covering the Reception desk; greeting guests
- Responding to emails, usually with a template email
- Answering the telephone
- Sorting the post
- Ordering office supplies or sandwiches for lunch
- Checking contract details and granting a licence for someone else to use copyright material from an author's work (permission agreement)
- Helping to organise events, launches and open days
- Creating a spreadsheet and a catalogue of titles
- Scanning documents
- Shredding documents
- Mailings; physically putting documents, catalogues or books into envelopes
- Researching potential customers
- Adding to and refining existing databases
- Updating the in-house system with marketing information or reviews
- Contributing to blog posts
- Writing articles for a regular newsletter
- Designing graphics for social media posts
- Drafting questions for an author interview
- Participating in the recording of author videos
- Shadowing other members of staff

- Reviewing contracts; this might involve proofreading or checking details against another document
- Checking stock levels of titles
- Copywriting
- Proofreading

Often these tasks are delegated – on a day-to-day basis – by the member of staff who is responsible for you. However, some publishers use Microsoft To Do or software such as Trello to organise regular tasks, indicating both the urgency and the deadline and who to speak to if you need help.

CASE STUDY

Temporary Role, Hospitality Assistant, Edinburgh Book Festival

I wanted to work in book publishing, so I took a temporary paid role at the Edinburgh Book Festival as an Author Hospitality Assistant. This involved a high level of author care, ensuring the authors attended their talks on time, their books were ready for signings, and they got to meet the appropriate festival teams and participate in press and publicity events. I got to meet lots of publishing staff such as agents, editors, publicists and marketers. This gave me a great insight into how everyone in publishing worked together to make the event a huge success.

If you do accept a work experience placement or internship, here are some golden rules how to make the best of it.

Some Golden Rules for Work Experience

1. Be presented well. There is no need to wear your 'Sunday best' but, if you will be office-based, before the placement ask if there is a dress code. If you are still unsure wear something 'smart casual' on your first day and gauge the rest of the dress code from there. There is no need to invest in a new wardrobe – you are on a temporary placement – but aim to look like you 'fit in'. Don't overdo jewellery, perfume or make-up; keep it subtle and professional.

> **TOP TIP**
> If you're not getting a job, it isn't necessarily a sign that you need to complete more placements and internships. It might be because there is an error on your CV or in your Covering Letter, or you're not doing enough research on the companies you are applying to or tailoring your application.

2. Before your first day remind yourself about who the company is and what they do; visit their website or google them. Have you checked their social media to see what they are talking about at the moment? Do you have a particular interest in an area of publishing that they are currently focussed on? What will you say to them if they ask you about what areas of publishing you're interested in, or what you would like to learn? Don't be upset if they don't ask these things, but it will always help you have a good experience if you know something about the company and what interests you in working for them.

3. Make sure you know the name of who you should report to when you first arrive; this is the first impression someone will get of you, so make sure it is a good one. If you want to be one step ahead, look up their profile on LinkedIn, where you may be able to see their career background and if they have a photo on their profile, and know what they look like when they approach you in the Reception area.

4. Be friendly and approachable, even if you are having a bad day. Smile and appear helpful. You are there for the experience. Even if it appears an unfriendly atmosphere, persevere, you are only there for a short while. Better that you are remembered for being the person who was always smiling rather than the person who was always grumpy.

5. Always be enthusiastic, however mundane the task, and some tasks that you might be given will seem mundane. The type of tasks you will be given are likely to include stuffing envelopes, photocopying, making up display showcards, filing and answering repetitive emails. You're likely to be invited to sit in on an internal editorial, production or marketing meeting. If you're lucky, they might ask you to look at the editorial 'slush pile' and write a report on a title.

6. There is no such thing as a stupid question. When you are being briefed for a task, if you are unsure about how to proceed or have any questions about how to process the task, then ask. However, try not to get yourself in a situation where you are asking too many questions and preventing someone else from working. If you want to be sure that you've understood what has been asked of you, then repeat back the instruction, e.g. "Just to clarify, you want me to put this leaflet in this envelope? Yes, I can do that."

7. Carry a notebook and write down essential points. Apart from helping you remember some basics, it also makes you look efficient.

The Origins of Unpaid Work Experience

It is important to understand how unpaid work experience came about. When I started in book publishing in the 1980s, unpaid internships were almost unheard of. We occasionally had one or two 15-year-olds, who were still at school, come and spend a week with us as part of a school project. Then we had a relative of an author come for a few days to work-shadow in editorial, but it was always organised with the editor concerned directly, as a favour. Everyone who worked for us got paid. We used to take on paid temporary staff during the summer to cover holidays.

Then one publisher started to say that to work for them you needed a minimum of six months' experience.

The question would come back, 'How can I get the experience if you won't give me a chance?' The publisher replied flippantly, 'I don't know, work for free or something!' As a result, people started to do just that, and work for free. But they didn't need to.

Also, the opinion that you need a minimum level of publishing knowledge might only apply to one single publisher, yet it is being bandied around like it is a universal truth, in the same way that you need to work for free. You do not need to work for free, and nor do you need publishing experience to get a publishing job.

---

8. If you get the opportunity to learn or use new software or a different computer program or method of working then USE IT. You might not get the opportunity again – and you add to your own personal skillset in the meantime. This is particularly important if it is publishing-specific software such as Biblio, Stison or Nielsen BookScan.
9. Make friends and contacts. If someone within the company is doing a particular job or role that you would like to do in the future, then why not ask them about their career path and how they got their job.
10. Don't go into work experience thinking that it will automatically lead to a job within a publisher, even if they have a vacancy. But remember, if they do have a vacancy, if you follow these rules you may be able to prove that you are their ideal candidate.
11. If they have said they will pay your travel or other expenses and you haven't yet received them, then ASK. If it was part of the arrangement, you should not feel uncomfortable about asking for something that was agreed. When arranging the work placement, if they are paying your travel expenses and the cost is more than the agreed budget, do let the publisher know. You should not be out of pocket by completing this experience.
12. No matter how long the placement is for, or what promises have been made, do not stop your job search! I've seen this happen all too frequently; you get a fabulous internship for a few weeks, it is demanding, and you're enjoying it. No one has said anything to you, but you're pretty sure they like you and think you're doing a good job, and you stop looking for a job elsewhere because you hope they will keep you on. The reality is that less than 5% of work experience applicants are offered a job at the end of their placement.

By stopping your job search you lose the momentum of how the placement can springboard you into a potential job with another publisher. You also can miss some great opportunities. This doesn't mean you need to broadcast to the company you are interning with that you're looking for a job elsewhere because they aren't offering you a job, be professional about it. Play your cards close to your chest. And if you need to take time off to go to a job interview whilst interning elsewhere, then be honest about this. You should always be allowed to go to a job interview whilst completing a placement. If the publisher stops you or makes it difficult, then please show them this and tell them I will have words with them! The whole point of you completing a placement is so that you can find a job; no one should prevent you from doing this.

Option – Anything else

You could do something else and take another route, not mentioned here. This could be working in another industry, going travelling, working for yourself or doing anything you want. There are no set career paths to working for book publishers and variety is the spice of life. Publishers are more open to people who have taken a different career path than at any other time in history. Publishers want diversity and inclusion at all levels and in all departments. This isn't only ethnic diversity but social and disability diversity too. There are no barriers to working in book publishing any more, aside from one, the lack of publishing jobs.

Career Changing

Given the lack of entry-level roles in book publishing, you might consider starting your career in a different industry first, where you are learning skills that you can bring across into publishing at a later stage. Remember that every company and organisation outside of book publishing has some sort of publishing function or department. Many of the skills that publishers want are no longer unique to book publishing.

Here are some examples:

Go and work in a bookshop and make a success of it. Bookselling used to lead to publishing roles; however, as so much of the buying has been taken out of the booksellers' hands, this is no longer the case. So, if you don't have any buying responsibilities, you need to find a role in a bookshop where you are involved in customer service, events, marketing or posting on social media for the store.

If it is a career in publishing design that you want, then any occupation where you are developing your design and layout skills could be key. It might something as basic as a company brochure or marketing flyer or a website to working for an advertising agency mocking up mood boards.

Marketing happens everywhere. Whether it is business to business (B2B) or business to the consumer (B2C/D2C), if you know how to plan and execute a marketing campaign, particularly of high value, in theory this should transfer over to publishing. If you're working within a specialist field, this could be a natural progression to publishing. For example, marketing in a law firm may give you marketing experience that is valuable for legal publishers. Marketing for an art gallery may lead to working for an art book publisher.

The same can be said for social media. Any role where you can engage and grow an audience across a variety of social platforms is welcome.

Selling anything, even cold calling and selling double glazing, or handling difficult customers, will help ground you for a career in sales, rights or customer services.

Editorial, editing, proofreading, fact-checking. All of these skills are needed by companies outside of publishing, as all produce some sort of company literature or documents. The importance for you is to use BSI Markup – the British Standard proofreading marks – and you'll be able to work anywhere. Other career choices such as teaching can lead to publishing (and to put the lack of book publishing jobs into perspective, there are approximately 500,000 teachers in the UK, and around 84,000* jobs supported by UK book publishing). You could end up working on children's books or textbooks of the Key Stage that you have been teaching. Teaching any subject or teaching English as a foreign language is always a good entry for educational publishing.

Lawyers often end up in publishing, either working on legal publications or within a contracts department, although I know of lawyers working in creative departments throughout the business. Where you start is not an indication of where you finish!

And if you're a qualified accountant, IT or HR manager, most publishers employ staff in these roles, just like every other business.

Other natural career switches are from journalism to publishing, magazines to books as well as TV and broadcast to publishing or from the games industry to publishing.

> **CASE STUDY**
> *Paid Internship at a University Press*
>
> The internship was offered as part of a scholarship for my MA in Publishing. I applied for it via the university, submitting a CV along with a 500-word rationale explaining why the MA fitted in with my career ambitions and why my financial circumstances justified receiving the scholarship. There was then a 10 minute 'informal chat' with the Editorial Director. Three days later, I was told I had been selected and would be working in the Rights department.
>
> On my first day, I reported to the International Rights Manager and Executive. It was a small office overall – about 15 staff – but International Rights consisted of just three. The task I was given was to check the contracts of upcoming titles for available rights, then research their potential for audio or translation. I also proofread the covers of foreign editions and drafted weekly 'deal round-up' emails sent out around the company. A typical day was spent training on Biblio in the morning and researching rights potential in the afternoon.
>
> Having noted my desire to gain experience in all areas of publishing, the Head of Office invited me to split my last week across Editorial and Publicity. This meant I got to attend Project Development Meetings, where new titles were pitched, and I even wrote copy for an important social media campaign. I was particularly impressed by this ability to be flexible. When the three weeks ended, the Publicity Department asked me to stay on, one day a week, alongside my MA. I believe it was having this broad and sustained experience, in addition to my MA, that allowed me to secure a job straight out of university.

Journalism allows you to bring some of your writing and editing skills across. TV and broadcasting, particularly if you've been working on any licensing, branding or audience development, sit well within publishing in roles such as editorial, rights and licensing, as does experience in the games industry. One thing that book publishers like about the TV, broadcast and games industries is that your tech skills and knowledge and understanding of the latest gadget or development could be ahead of book publishing. However, if you are thinking of making a switch from one of these industries, do check that the role you are going for will continue to keep you ahead of technology and trends and not hold you back.

There are many, many options, including different careers that are not covered here. Many people have come into publishing after experiencing a different career choice; there are no barriers and publishing really is open to all.

*Source: The Publishers Association, Vision for Publishing Report 2024.

Preparing for a Career in Publishing

If you read the list of *Publishing Skills That Increase Employability* in the previous chapter, you're probably wondering how on earth you attain some very specialist experience that might make you appear more employable. Here are some suggestions to get you started. Most of these you can do whilst you are still studying or considering your options, to help you get started. If you're about to enter the world of work for the first time, please don't wait until you've left school, college or university to acquire any skills as, by then, you'll need to earn money and find you're willing to accept any work, in any industry, as long as it pays for you to live.

What publishers are looking for at entry-level

Publishers frequently tell me this is what they are looking for at entry-level:

- An interest in their area of publishing; the books or journals they are working on.
- Enthusiasm for what they are doing and what is going on around them.
- A willingness to accept instruction and learn.
- The knowledge of office etiquette; how people in an office behave, when to interrupt someone in a meeting and when to wait.
- Excellent spelling and grammar.
- The alphabet! Filing seems to be common in most roles.

- Familiarity with major software packages (e.g. Word, Excel, PowerPoint, InDesign).
- The ability to switch on a computer, open software and start typing a document.
- Knowing how to save computer files in a logical way that enables others to easily locate the file.
- How to lay out a business letter or email, and the kind of vocabulary one expects in such documents.
- Knowing how to answer the telephone in a professional manner and take coherent messages.
- The ability to read and understand instructions.
- An understanding of how to organise yourself and your work, and prioritise the urgent and important over the fun tasks.

The good news is that nearly all of these are skills that can be taught in any environment; they are not specific to publishing. As already mentioned, the majority of publishers value paid office experience higher than unpaid publishing experience. They much prefer to see that you have a strong work ethic, the skills to do a good job, and the ability to succeed.

For publishing-related skills, as mentioned above, almost every company outside of traditional book publishing, has a small publishing or media function; they have to publish content in one form or another, or market themselves in a way that is similar to marketing any product. As a result, any company or organisation outside of traditional book publishing can probably give you some 'publishing experience'.

Thirty things you can do instead of working in an unpaid internship

1. Teach yourself a new computer skill or item of software. You don't always need an expensive training course to do this. If you see job advertisements are always saying 'must have experience of InDesign', then borrow a book from the library, download the free trial and use either the official free training or a variety of YouTube videos to learn the basics of any new software or product.

2. Read up on book publishing and industry news about publishers you want to work for. Trade magazines such as *The Bookseller, BookBrunch* and *Publishing Perspectives* are a good start. It is also useful to read internationally where you can. *Publishers Weekly* and *Publishers Lunch* (both in the USA) and *Quill and Quire* (Canada) are good for this. You can sign up for the free newsletters from the London Book Fair, Frankfurt Book Fair, Bologna Book Fair and International Publishers Association.

    In the beginning, all of this might feel like a strange world and the names of the companies or specialist terminology are meaningless but, over a few weeks, this will start to become familiar, and you'll build up your industry knowledge.

3. Learn more about the sector or genre that you want to work in. If you want to work in something specific as Crime Fiction, who are the big players – publishers and authors? What new titles are coming out? Are there any events or festivals that promote the genre? Are there any prizes specific to the genre? Do these books get published at a particular time of year? If you have set your mind on one publisher, who are their competitors? What are the similarities and differences between the publishers within the genre, such as do they market the books any differently?

4. If it is a non-fiction subject you are interested in, research what magazines or publications are available, what societies cover the topics. Are there any social media groups or experts on social media you can follow to learn more about the subject? Are there any specialist conferences or events? This doesn't mean you have to attend; often following the hashtag and surrounding conversation could give you an insight.

5. Practise putting lists of items into alphabetical order. This might seem daft and, yes, everyone knows the alphabet, but filing is a very important skill and often at entry level there is a filing test.

6. Get used to planning your day, schedule or chores as if you were working in an office. Write a list of things to do and update the list at the end of the day. First thing in the morning, review your list, and amend your priorities if

necessary. Again, this is one of the basic tasks that is key to you being organised and efficient in the office.

7. Teach yourself how to function without constantly checking your mobile phone and personal social media! When you're working for someone else, you might only get to look at your phone during lunch breaks and at the end of the day.

8. Put some logical systems and consistency into your everyday life so that others can easily find documents on your computer or takeover a computer if asked. This is about having intelligent file names. For example, instead of uninotes.doc, your file name might be Date_Lecture_GettingOrganised_V1. For future reference, most collateral in publishing, such as image files for books, nearly always start with the ISBN.

9. Practise writing work-like emails. Whilst your friends might think you've gone potty because you're no longer writing 'hiya', start being a little more formal in the way you write. And don't write in TXT MSG SPK or use Americanisms such as 'gotten' if you're in the UK.

TOP TIP

When on a placement, always be willing, happy and easy to get on with, regardless of the tasks you have been given or what is happening in your personal life. This is what job advertisements mean when they say they want someone with a 'friendly disposition'. No one wants to work with a sulky intern.

---

10. When you're reading a book, article or blogpost, notice how they have credited other sources, given a credit to a photographer or illustrator and referenced other material used. Book publishers always respect the copyright of others, so look at how this works in practice.

For the following experiences look at Voluntary Societies, Charitable Events, Student Unions, Student Newspapers and organisations around you. [The only time when you should work for free is when it is on a hobby or for a charitable cause. Companies with shareholders are not charities.]

11. Designing posters, leaflets or flyers will help you understand the principles for creating similar items for a publisher, either in a Marketing, Design or Production Department.
12. If you write press releases for any event or organisation, you'll learn how to write imaginative copy (text) that produces positive responses.
13. Using social media on behalf of a service or organisation could signal the start of your path to using social media professionally. Aim to gain as much experience as you can in creating posts, scheduling (using software like X Pro, formerly TweetDeck) and then responding to comments made on posts or Direct Messages. Make a note of the follower numbers before you start and then hopefully watch them grow!
14. Create graphics for any event, product or social media post using the online software Canva. Canva has many free elements and is used widely across publishing.

TOP TIP

Pay attention to what is going on at the company you're interning at. Are they happy or excited about a new title or project? Do they seem excessively stressed?

---

15. If you want a marketing or website role and you haven't used Google Analytics, then visit the Google website and use their free courses to teach yourself. Understanding Google Analytics is seen as a basic skill in a number of marketing roles.
16. Google Digital Garage also has a wide range of free Digital courses covering a range of skills on digital marketing and online visibility.
17. Organising or helping to co-ordinate any event (or an organisation's presence at an event) will give you experience that you may be able to transfer if organising a book launch, author signing, open day or conference. This could be anything from planning out the event, assisting where necessary or meeting and greeting on the day.

18. Publicising or advertising events such as a public meeting, after school club, fete, jumble sale or charity fundraiser.
19. Liaising with the press or media could be helpful for a career in publicity. You may be able to start building a contact list, or 'Little Black Book' of press contacts for use in a future role.
20. Writing articles and blog posts about items of interest to you or for others. You do not need to have your own blog and often it might be better to contribute to someone else's well-organised blog rather than risk your own reputation on a poor, rarely updated website.
21. Assisting with a Podcast or producing your own podcast. This could give you experience in audio production, editing digital files and marketing.
22. Creating and editing Videos either for TikTok, Reels, YouTube or for personal use. Social media is key for marketing books.
23. Selling any product. As well as understanding the principles of selling, it could also help you develop excellent communication skills.
24. Answering the phone in any busy environment. Every office has a phone. Even in the age of digital communication, an excellent telephone manner and remaining cool under duress is needed.
25. Work in retail. This can give you a wide variety of skills. The most basic one is that you turn up for work every day and work your shift. It allows you to demonstrate to a future employer that you are reliable.
26. Writing, editing or proofreading student publications might be a starting place for a career in editorial. Yes, you can also offer to proofread other students' dissertations, but what might be better is to ask a relative, or someone you know, who has been writing their life story, if you can proofread or edit it for them, to initially get a feel for what editing a book is like.
27. Any role that involves layout of text or printing might be the start of a career in production.

28. Set up, design or maintain a website, blog in WordPress (*see* the guidance in the next chapter on *Blogs/Vlogs/YouTube/TikTok*).
29. Learn how to Code or use CSS.
30. Learn how to use Excel to an advanced level where you can perform VLOOKUPs and create Pivot Tables.

These can all lead to skills that may be used in a variety of publishing departments.

TOP TIP

Everyone knows everyone else!

They say that you make lifelong friends at university, but you will find that when you work in publishing you also make life-long colleagues and acquaintances. The people you meet in your first job or internship will probably still be working in publishing throughout your career, until you – or they – retire and sometimes after retirement.

This means that you need to be nice to everyone. Try not to fall out with people. And remember that the people you meet on the way up may be the same people you also meet on the way down.

For example, on the way up, I worked as a Personal Assistant to a Sales Director. Some years later, I became a Sales Director and appointed my former Sales Director as one of our overseas agents.

ACTION POINTS

Within your studies or current workplace, think about how you can develop your soft skills as these are all likely to be skills that you need daily in most of the things you do.

- Are you communicating effectively?
- Are you using your time efficiently?
- Are you working well with others in a team?
- How organised are you?
- Do you read and understand instructions clearly?
- Do you use your initiative when someone asks something of you?
- Does anything you do require you to negotiate?
- Are there any opportunities for you to lead or manage others in your daily life?

Read through the list of 30 things you can do instead of an internship. Are there any you have already done? Are there any others you could easily do?

CHAPTER THREE

Finding Jobs

"Where are book publishing jobs advertised? Book publishing jobs are advertised everywhere."

Suzanne Collier

Let's start this chapter with a basic skill, that of reading a job advertisement. This might sound simple, but if you learn how to read and understand the detail in each and every job advertisement, rather than skim-read, you will save yourself a lot of heartache by no longer applying for the wrong jobs.

If you are looking for an entry-level role, whilst most contain the word Assistant (e.g. Editorial Assistant, Marketing Assistant, Production Assistant), it is wrong to assume that every job title with the word Assistant is an entry-level role. Some advertisements with the word Assistant may be asking for two to three years of experience; conversely, other advertisements with the word Controller or Executive may actually be entry-level roles. The answer will always be found by reading the whole job advertisement.

If you're looking for an entry-level role, it may be highly frustrating when an Assistant role asks for someone with experience. But do trust the recruiter's judgement on this; if you read the advertisement carefully and understand the tasks and work involved, you should realise why they need someone experienced in the role.

Modern publishers don't go out of their way to deprive entry-level candidates of opportunities; a business recruits staff based on the skills and competencies it needs.

In the same way, there are different layers of Managers. A Marketing Manager in one publishing house may have a very different level of skills and competencies to a Marketing Manager in another. This will only be discovered by reading and understanding the whole job advertisement.

The advice and guidance is ALWAYS read the full job advertisement. Never make a judgement on a role based on the job title, as not all job titles are equal.

> **TOP TIP**
> Always read the whole advertisement, not just the job title. Not all job titles are equal. Assistant level roles might not always be Entry Level, and likewise there are different layers of Executive and Manager roles. Always, always read the whole advertisement.

This is also why you need to be aware of ongoing developments within the book publishing industry because the traditional job titles you might be searching for no longer exist. For example, the first bookcareers.com Salary Survey started with 75 job titles and the latest one has more than 200 different contributions. Over the years, some jobs have almost disappeared (Secretary, Sales Representative) and been replaced by other jobs or titles (Personal Assistant, Key Account Executive).

It means if you are looking for an Editorial Assistant role, and searching only for advertisements with the job title Editorial Assistant, you are falling into the trap that most jobseekers make. Often a jobseeker will only search for one job title and make decisions whether to apply on reading the job title alone.

This means you could be missing out on several opportunities. Currently, it would be advisable to add job titles such as Content Assistant, Production Editorial Assistant, or Publishing Assistant to your search. However, at least one major publisher seems to invent new job titles all the time, so if you are looking for a job, ensure you look at all the jobs from a publisher; read further than the job title and understand the job function before applying, to ascertain what exactly you'd be doing in a role, as not all jobs with similar job titles are the same.

It could also help you understand the structure of the company and, if they are always advertising the same job over and over, whether it could be a good place to work or not.

How To Read a Job Advertisement

> Job Advertisement
>
> EDITORIAL ASSISTANT REQUIRED
>
> *We are a small publishing house looking for an enthusiastic Editorial Assistant with an eye for detail, who can liaise with authors, book in new manuscripts, take minutes at meetings and manage office diaries. Apply with your CV and Covering Letter to...*

If you want to work in Editorial, you would probably get very excited when you see an advert like the one above, and think that this is the job that will start your climb to the lofty heights of Commissioning Editor. You'll dream about poring over manuscripts, discussing things with authors and making editorial decisions. Yet if you re-read the job advertisement, you can see that this job has some very basic tasks. Let me walk you through them.

Liaise with authors – this means liaising with authors, it doesn't mean working on their books, editing their manuscripts or doing anything more than answering the phone or menial tasks.

Liaise is a very interesting verb in job advertisements. The dictionary definition of liaise is 'to speak to people in other organisations etc., in order to work with them or exchange information with them; to be the link between two or more people, organisations'. In effect, by liaising, you aren't really doing much aside from connecting two people, probably by phone when you put the phone call through to your boss who is doing all the hard work.

Liaise on a job advertisement is a word that may indicate basic responsibilities. If you're not looking for a junior role and the job advertisement has liaise with an essential job function, then you know you may have limited responsibility (or the person can't write job advertisements very well). In a senior role, for example, you wouldn't be liaising with authors, you'd be negotiating, nurturing or commissioning them. Do you see the difference?

Book in new manuscripts – this means just that; booking in new manuscripts and probably allocating them to an editor or reader. It doesn't mean you'll be reading the manuscripts or writing reports on them, only that you will be booking them in and probably passing them on to another member of staff.

Taking minutes at meetings – this means attending meetings for the main purpose of taking minutes. You are probably only there to record a summary of what was said, the decisions that were made and what actions need to be taken before the next meeting and by whom.

It doesn't automatically mean you will be an active participant in a meeting, only that you are there to record the discussion and outcomes.

Manage office diaries – this includes co-ordinating travel arrangements and meeting dates. It doesn't mean you are the one with the appointments or that you will ever go anywhere ever. You'll be managing the diaries of others who are having the appointments or going on their travels.

So, you can see how important it is to read beyond the job title. Unless you want a basic entry-level administration role, this might be a job to steer clear of. It is the kind of job where someone will contact me after a few weeks and say, 'Suzanne, I'm bored!' and then wonder why. If they'd read and understood the job advertisement they might not have applied for the role.

Should you apply for the job?

One question I am asked frequently is "Should I apply for the job?"

This is often because you're not sure whether you match the necessary experience or the skills required in a job vacancy. Maybe it asks for a skill that you don't have, or you are transferring from another department or different industry and are unsure whether you stand a chance.

At other times, I get comments from candidates who are frustrated because the job title doesn't match the skills or experience required and they would have applied, but they didn't feel they had the appropriate skillset.

The first question to ask yourself is, 'How much do you want the job on a scale of 1 to 10?', with 1 being not at all and 10 being can you start today?

If you answer 6 or less, then the question is whether you should be applying. It is not recommended to apply for jobs where your interest in the role is 6 or less, unless you have a valid reason for wanting the job (such as it is the only job in that location, you are unemployed or you want to make a career change). This will also help you prioritise your job applications when there are several roles to apply for at the same time, but not enough time to apply for all of them.

Don't waste your time applying for jobs you do not want to get 'just for practice'. It is much better to spend your time writing quality applications for the jobs you do want. And this is my main piece of advice: apply for the jobs you want to get. Sometimes you might feel so desperate about your job situation that you apply for roles you don't really want (true; I see it happen often). Please don't waste your time on applications that, if you were offered the job, you know you would not accept.

When we're job searching, we focus on what job we want, rather than how we can fulfil the needs of the employer. In a job

ANECDOTE
A job is what you make of it.

When I started in my first publishing job at Andre Deutsch, in the days that Andre ran the company, I had the kind of job that today's entry-level applicant would relish. I had a timetable to spend time in every single department from Accounts through to Sales, taking in Editorial, Production, Publicity and Rights on the way. At lunchtime I was required to sit on reception, and in the afternoon, it was my responsibility to despatch the daily post. This meant I probably knew more about what was going on in the company than any other employee. This was because whilst I was in a department, doing what was probably their most mundane jobs of filing or stuffing envelopes, I took an interest in who the filed letters had been sent to and what they were about. I looked at the addresses that the publicity or sales department were mailing to. As I knew what was going on in all departments, it allowed me to become an integral part of the company and complete the tasks that kept the company running smoothly. As a result, I was swiftly promoted through the ranks.

advertisement, sometimes the employer will be extremely specific about the skillset of the person they wish to employ. They need someone who can do the job and will frequently advertise the vacancy with a list of required skills, those being essential skills for the job, and desired skills, those that are not critical, but they would like you to have. Whilst you're thinking about your dream job, publishers are sometimes unrealistic with their requirements of their 'dream candidate'. This is where the bookcareers.com Tick Test comes in.

TOP TIP

What jobs should you apply for? Only apply for the jobs you want to get. Too many jobseekers apply for every single role advertised. It sounds simple, but only apply for the jobs you want to get. You'll save yourself (and the publisher) a lot of time.

The bookcareers.com Tick Test

The best way of knowing whether to apply for a job is to do the bookcareers.com Tick Test.

1. Read the job advertisement phrase by phrase. As you are reading tick, every requirement, skill or competency they are asking you to match. Often, job advertisements will have skills split into 'Essential' and 'Desirable'.

    For example:

    Break this down to:

    - *wide range of digital marketing duties*
    - *social media*
    - *website updates*
    - *email marketing*
    - *copywriting*
    - *video and audio editing*
    - *competitions and promotions*
    - *supporting the Marketing Director*
    - *interest in marketing and/or publishing*

- *excellent standard of written English*
- *eye for design*
- *Google Analytics*
- *ability to write engaging, accurate copy*
- *diary management*
- *liaising with the sales and publicity teams*
- *external stakeholders*
- *supporting events and author tours*
- *well organised*
- *busy and demanding office*

An Advertisement

We are looking for a Marketing Assistant to assist with a wide range of digital marketing duties including social media, website updates, email marketing, copywriting, video and audio editing and competitions and promotions as well as supporting the Marketing Director.

Ideally, you will have experience and an interest in marketing and/or publishing. You will have an excellent standard of written English and a good eye for design. An understanding of Google Analytics would be an advantage, as well as the ability to write engaging, accurate copy.

A large part of this role includes diary management and liaising with the sales and publicity teams, as well as external stakeholders. You'll be supporting events and author tours, so you need to be extremely well organised and familiar with working in a busy and demanding office.

---

2. Count the number of items you have ticked. Often, you'll instantly spot whether you have a good chance of progressing through the selection process, whether you are over-qualified for the post or whether it really is a job you should aspire to in the future.

3. If you have ticked six items or more, and match more than 50% of the requirements of the vacancy, apply for the job, unless you are missing an essential skill that could be described as critical.

For example, if the advertisement is for a role where you are supporting a German-speaking office and under the essential skills it asks for a German speaker, then clearly speaking German is critical for the role.

Alternatively:

This is an advertisement for a role where you are working with international territories and under the essential skills it says 'German Speaker preferred', but you have ticked and matched all other criteria. This is where it may be worth applying for the role anyway, as it could be that the publisher does not find any suitable German-speaking applicants and compromises on what is essential and desirable, especially if you have all the other skills and competencies for the role. You might have noticed the inconsistency in the advertisement quoting, "essential skills" but "German speaker preferred".

4. Now go back and re-read the advertisement. See if there are any indicators as to the cultural fit of the company or the workload you'll be given.

Check if they have any signposts in the vocabulary they have used. Phrases such as 'engaging Stakeholders' and '360-degree feedback' might, for instance, indicate that it is a corporate culture, when you could be looking for something much more informal. 'A busy and demanding workload' might not be right if you are looking for a role that is less pressurised.

Usually, a lot of time and thought has been put into the wording of a job advertisement, so see if there are any clues which indicate how you might fit into the company culture.

When you apply for a role, reply promptly but professionally. Read and understand the advertisement; read what you are being asked to send. For example, if you are asked for a CV and Covering Letter in a single document, then send just that.

Closing dates on job advertisements may be very misleading and could lull you into a false sense of security, believing you may have two weeks to apply. Often roles are taken offline before the closing date if the publisher has been inundated with applicants, or, if there is a downloadable application pack, when a certain number of downloads have taken place.

You might see in job advertisements: 'early applications will be prioritised', or 'we reserve the right to stop accepting applications before the closing date'. It is a good policy to always apply as soon as you can. However, provided the advert doesn't say, 'contact us immediately', or 'via a Recruitment Consultant', try not to apply within 15 minutes of the job going online. There is nothing worse from a recruiter's perspective than to receive an application when they know the candidate can't have read the advertisement and tailored their CV and/or Covering Letter accordingly.

TOP TIP

The clues about a working environment are often in the job advertisement. If you read the advertisement line by line, you might pick up clues as to whether you're a good cultural fit for the role, and cultural fit can be as important to you in the same way as skills and competencies are important to the recruiter. If an advertisement says the role requires a methodical approach, this might indicate that the tasks are repetitive processes. So, if you are the type of person who likes variety or gets bored very easily, such a role might not be a good cultural fit for you.

Finding Jobs

It is often said that it isn't what you know but who you know, and whilst traditionally so many publishing jobs were filled by word of mouth or speculative enquiry, this is no longer the case. Publishers are making huge commitments to equity, diversity and inclusion (EDI) and there are several ways they demonstrate this. Top of the list is advertising every job vacancy, so everyone can apply for the role, even though there might be a suitable internal candidate (never let the thought of internal candidates dissuade you from applying; internal candidates don't automatically get roles). As part of their EDI policy, publishers need to ensure candidate selection is from a wide choice of people from different backgrounds, not an elite few. As a result, the places where book publishing job vacancies are advertised has widened too.

If you asked where publishing jobs are advertised, the answer is they are advertised everywhere. Gone are the days where *The Bookseller* and *The Guardian* had a monopoly on job advertisements. Whilst those publications might still have a considerable number of jobs, there are a variety of ideas to tap into the publishing job market.

Sometimes you might feel there are no jobs available. This could be because it is a quiet time of year, or maybe a year of cutbacks, but do keep looking for jobs. People leave jobs all the time for a variety of reasons. You will also discover, even if there is a temporary recruitment freeze or an announcement about job losses, publishers may still quietly be employing staff. Yes, be aware of the marketplace, but please don't stop looking because you think there are no jobs, although do refer back to the bookcareers.com Job Reality scale in *Chapter One: Understanding Book Publishing* to check the job you want actually does exist.

What follows is a list of different ways you may be able to locate jobs or opportunities. A list of live resources is on the bookcareers.com website.

National and local newspapers – in print and online

Once the number one resource for any jobseekers, newspapers have fewer job advertisements since the rise of the internet. However, check out what is available nationally, and in your local area. *The Guardian* is still the primary resource for media roles in the national press, though occasionally the *Daily Telegraph* or *The Times* may carry director-level roles, such as PA to the Managing Director or Finance Director.

Trade Press

Every industry has specialist magazines or journals reporting the news for their individual sector, and book publishing is no different. The key players for UK book publishing are *The Bookseller* and *BookBrunch* (online only). Both regularly carry job advertisements.

Specialist Press

Other magazines and journals that have their own fields, not related to the book industry, where publishers sometimes advertise if they are looking for a broader range of skills or a diverse audience. Examples are *Design Week, Marketing Week, The Grocer, Pink News* and *The Voice*.

https://en.wikipedia.org/wiki/List_of_newspapers_in_the_United_Kingdom

Trade Associations

A Trade Association is an industry body or non-profit organisation, usually funded by membership fees and providing a wide variety of services for its members. One service they frequently offer is a job vacancy noticeboard, and it is often free for anyone to view. Some trade associations are aimed at businesses, and others are open to individuals. Book industry trade associations should be an important part of any job hunt, particularly those who welcome individual members. Whilst a full list appears in the appendices, one organisation that should be flagged up here with high importance is the Society of Young Publishers.

The Society of Young Publishers (SYP) was founded in 1948 and set up to help young people in the publishing industry learn more about the work that goes into publishing, outside their own roles. Today, the SYP has many regional branches with regular meetings, and lots of networking opportunities, including social groups and book clubs. In particular, look out for the annual conference of the London/Oxford and Scottish branches, as both bring in high-profile speakers and cover topics that would be of interest to any publishing jobseeker. If you are starting your book publishing career, there is no better organisation for you to join and network with than the SYP.

Networking Organisations

Outside trade associations, a number of member organisations have sprung up to give networking and training opportunities to those within the industry. They may, from time to time, advertise vacancies, but like other organisations, usually they give you an opportunity to network with other people within the industry.

Company Websites

As the cost of recruitment has risen, publishers use their company website to advertise their own vacancies and utilise social media to draw candidates to their vacancies.

One of the key tips for any job search is to identify the top 20 to 40 publishers you want to work for, bookmark their job vacancy noticeboard and visit it on a regular basis. If their website allows, sign up to be notified of any future vacancies. Whilst you're doing this, it is also a good idea to sign up for their newsletters, so you learn more about the books and authors they publish and how they market them. This will also give you some additional content for your Covering Letter or a future job interview.

Apprenticeships

These can be found on apprenticeship websites. Whilst the Publishing Assistant apprenticeship will give you training in publishing, a few large publishers may have other apprenticeship opportunities, such as a Customer Service apprenticeship or a Human Resources apprenticeship, so always check beyond the job title and check out the name of the employer offering the apprenticeship.

> **CASE STUDY**
> *Publishing Operations Executive, Non-Trade Publisher*
> I saw the job advertised on the publisher's website. I sent in a CV and Covering Letter through their application portal. It was two weeks before I was invited to an interview and they sent some interview tasks that I had to complete – in a week – through the company portal. One task was editing an extract of text. The second challenge was all about prioritising a number of tasks. For the third one I was given an outline and a previous example to work to, and asked to create a leaflet, taking into account the guidelines I had been given. Then the interview took place online, with two people interviewing me. They asked me a lot of competency-based questions and we had a detailed discussion about the company. Four days after the interview, they telephoned me and offered me the role.

General Job Sites

As previously mentioned, publishing has had an inclusivity and diversity issue so, from time to time, publishers will advertise in the general job market. The result of this tends to be that they get many applicants who do not have the right skills or experience. In theory, therefore, if you apply via this advertisement, you should appear higher in the publisher's list of suitable applicants than you would have if they'd advertised in the trade press.

The popularity of general job sites seems to depend on who is giving special offers and discounts to human resources departments.

Registering with them all might seem quite tedious, because they will tell you about 500 job vacancies, none of which you are looking for, but you may find the one for which you are searching. Therefore, set your search criteria high and focus on book publishing jobs.

When you register, don't upload a CV with your home address or phone number – use your email address only and – as mentioned elsewhere – never put your National Insurance number on your CV.

Set your criteria high; use the phrase 'book publishing'.

ANECDOTE

I had a client who couldn't believe I was asking them to sign up to general job sites. They were looking for a senior publishing role and were very reluctant to register outside the book trade, but realised I must be telling them to do this for a reason, so they did. Would you believe they found their dream job within about four weeks by doing this?! It seems that a new Human Resources Manager placed the role with a general recruitment consultant. What does a general recruitment consultant do to attract publishing people? They advertise on one of the five main job sites, where they usually advertise all the other jobs they are recruiting. My client appeared in the top 5% of suitable candidates and got the job.

Career Search Engines

Indeed is the main career search engine in the UK, aside from Google Jobs.

It accepts its own job adverts but also sources company websites and other job boards too. Ensure you set up an alert for any relevant jobs.

TOP TIP

Sometimes you might get overlooked in the recruitment process, however it goes. Always use your judgement as to what is best to do in each individual circumstance, but don't be afraid to check that your name is still in the process.

Specialist Recruitment Consultants

A Recruitment Consultancy is a company that helps employers (publishers) recruit new staff. They might do this by sourcing relevant applicants (this is called selection) or by headhunting suitable candidates for the role (this is called search).

They usually work on commission that is paid by the employer. You do not pay this commission, and you will play no part in the commission negotiation or even know it happened. It is the employer's place to hire a Recruitment Consultant and the employer pays the fee.

There are many myths that you may get paid less if you go via a recruiter as they take some of your salary in order to get paid. This is not true, because Recruiters agree the fee before they even advertise the position. As a candidate you will, or should, never pay to work with a recruiter or headhunter, but it is useful to be aware that this is how recruitment consultancies work.

Recruitment Consultants who work solely in the book publishing field have always been professional and maintained to a standard much higher than non-specialist consultants. One or two (such as Inspired Selection) have won awards for their professionalism in the recruitment field. This is because throughout the whole of your career you might repeatedly come into contact with the same recruiter numerous times over many years and in a variety of different roles as you move up the ladder. Also, they are aware that whilst you might be in a junior position now, in a couple of years' time you could be a manager who is recruiting, and they would hope you will choose their consultancy to do the recruiting for you.

When you're looking for a job, it is best to register with all the relevant recruitment consultants as they don't advertise all the positions they have available, and you need to open as many doors as possible. Don't be passive; do check in with them from time to time, especially if they haven't contacted you about any roles, and regularly ensure they have the latest version of your CV.

Often, when you register with a recruitment consultant, they will invite you for a formal interview, face to face, by video or telephone. This is in order to get to know you better and understand what sort of roles you are looking for or wish to be put forward for. Always be professional and treat them like a future employer. However, be transparent where you can, as hiding key bits of information or being too guarded and untrusting can also mean that they cannot represent the true you. Even if they sound like they are your best friend, and really want the best for your career, understand at all times they are only going to put forward the best possible candidates for a role. It is not in their interest to place candidates who might not make their probation, who are unreliable or who have lied about their skills and experience.

During this interview expect them to dig deeper about any gaps on your CV, and why you left certain jobs. This is especially the case if you found yourself working in a challenging situation at a publishing house they may be familiar with. Like myself, they probably have knowledge of which publishers are the best to work for and which ones could be tricky employers. Behave as you would in an interview; have your stories or answers ready. Share your aims and ambitions with them, what you are looking for in a job and what flexible working, etc., you may require. However, try not to use the conversation with the Recruitment Consultant like a confessional! You know what the suspect items are on your CV; think about what you plan to say about gaps or anything dubious, and how it may be received.

The reason you want to look like the best possible candidate when dealing with a Recruitment Consultant is because, when they are involved in selecting for a role, depending on the brief given by the publisher, they might be putting forward as few as three or as many as ten candidates. The final number will

> **CASE STUDY**
> *Editorial Assistant, Medical Communications Publisher*
> I applied for an editorial assistant role via a Recruitment Consultant, but the job had already been filled. Instead, they told me about the role of Editorial Assistant at a Medical Communications Publisher. I sent through a CV and Covering Letter to the Recruiter and then the Recruiter did all the communication; I had no direct contact with the publisher. I was invited to an online interview with two people. This was quite informal, and they told me about the company and asked about my previous editorial and publishing experience. It was very much a casual conversation. The second interview, also online, consisted of being interviewed by three people and they were asking lots of problem-solving and competency-based questions. The interview lasted an hour. Two weeks after the second interview, the Recruiter phoned and offered me the role.

depend on the brief given by the publisher and the criteria for the role. Some Recruitment Consultants will put forward only candidates who make an exact fit; or a publisher may ask for a range of candidates, including those at either extreme of the experience level. Sometimes a recruiter might put in a 'wild card'; a candidate of interest who matches the skills, but not necessarily the whole brief. Who they put forward, and the final numbers, will vary from job to job and the assignment they have been given. For some publishers, recruitment consultants are an extension of the publishers' Human Resources department and are taking candidate filtering to a higher level and conducting the first interviews themselves. For this they may ask you to write a Covering Letter or undertake a task when applying.

If you are already registered with a Recruitment Consultant don't be passive and automatically assume they will put you forward for a vacancy. If you see them advertise for a role, a friendly email to the recruiter along with a newly tailored version of your CV can make all the difference to you being selected for interview. If you're unsure of the role, then contact the Consultant anyway to see if you can have a chat about the requirements. This will also help keep you on their radar for other similar roles.

If you haven't heard from a Recruitment Consultant in a while, the best way to update them that you are still looking for a job is to send a new version of your CV.

Some publishers have preferred Recruitment Consultant suppliers – they may put their jobs exclusively with one recruitment consultant, whilst other publishers might have two or three consultants handling the same job. When you see the same role advertised with more than one recruitment consultant, your choice should be down to personal experience and the one you think will represent you the best.

The benefits of finding a job through a Recruitment Consultant are clear: they negotiate the package and the salary, they will smooth out any differences on the overall job offer, and the publisher is unlikely to withdraw the offer once made, based on this negotiation. The whole process should also be on a more professional level. This is not to say that publishers are unprofessional, but it is in the Recruitment Consultant's interest to keep both the publisher and the candidate happy, as long term, the current candidate may be recruiting for a future publisher.

However, don't rely solely on finding a job via a Recruitment Consultant: they should be part of your job search, not all of it. Recruitment Consultants are responsible for approximately 10% of the publishing job market.

CASE STUDY
A publisher advertised a role and I applied, but heard nothing. I then saw a role advertised with a Recruitment Consultant and applied, only to discover it was the same job! It appeared that my application with the publisher was either overlooked or had gone astray. Having the Recruitment Consultant advocate for my experience with the publisher made a huge difference, and I got down to the final two candidates.

Social media

There are resources for each different social media site on bookcareers.com.

If you are looking for a job, whether you are active on social media or not, there are some things you need to be aware of.

1. Even though ACAS* has set guidelines for employers checking the social media profiles of candidates, many employers ignore this and will check you out anyway. They might not be aware of the guidelines, or it could be curiosity, but remember your whole social media presence online reflects you and, in the same way, may reflect on your future employer, so even if you 'couldn't care less' about what is posted about you on the internet, you should care about how it can affect your job search and employment prospects.

   [*ACAS – Advisory, Conciliation and Arbitration Service. An impartial offshoot of the UK Government's Department for Business and Trade]

2. Ensure that your security settings on sites you use for personal relationships (e.g. Facebook) are set to the highest and that no one can tag you in photographs without your approval.

3. If there are things relating to your history on Google that are no longer relevant, but may cause a prospective employer to think twice about employing you, then you can get these pages removed by going to Google Help.

4. Remember that even if you are employed, you are not safe from the prying eyes of others and those who employ you or work for the same company. Newspapers regularly print stories about how an employee was dismissed for inappropriate Social Media or Facebook posts. It is sad to say, but if you want to remain in employment, you need to ensure your behaviour on any platform does not result in a gross misconduct dismissal.

Speculative Letters/Emails

This was the old-fashioned way of finding jobs – writing speculatively to a publisher. However, in the world of equity, diversity and inclusion, publishers have almost eradicated recruiting from speculative applications. Also, with GDPR (General Data Protection Regulation, an EU law), it is unlikely that if you wrote speculatively they would even keep your letter on file for any prolonged length of time. Publishers may be willing to accept speculative applications from time to time, but this will be mentioned on their website. Larger companies actively discourage candidates from writing speculatively; smaller ones probably don't have the resources to respond. In recent years, the percentage of candidates finding jobs via speculative enquiry has become negligible. See this as a good thing; it makes the recruitment process far more transparent. There is some guidance on how to write speculatively towards the end of *Chapter Six: Covering Letters That Work*.

Industry Trade Shows

You may get the opportunity to go to a trade show, such as the London Book Fair, that usually takes place in the spring. A trade show is often not open to the general public; it is a business-to-business (B2B) exhibition. It's usually held in a large space (in the case of the London Book Fair, London Olympia), where publishers, publishing service companies and other organisations, take stands and hold business meetings, as well as hope to find new suppliers or companies to do business with. Jobseekers are usually completely out of place here, so it is best to use these as fact-finding events, as there are usually free informative seminars going on alongside the main trade show.

Personal Contacts

Whilst, mostly due to equity, diversity and inclusion, a personal contact is unlikely to influence you being appointed in a job, what the contact can do is help you find out about roles and career opportunities that you might not see or be aware of. They can also arrange an informal chat with someone who could be recruiting in the future. Use any contacts you have and ensure they know what role you are seeking.

Informal Chat

This is where you have an informal chat or virtual coffee with a contact, knowing they do not have a job opportunity at present, but they may have one in the future. Like speculative letters, these have reduced as publishers now like to be as inclusive as possible and create wider informational events.

Publisher Open Days, Careers Events or Experiences

In order to increase diversity and inclusion, a few publishers have been hosting open days or careers evenings, both online and in person. There often aren't any jobs attached, but they give you the opportunity to find out more about the industry and how the publisher concerned works. This insightful information should help you write better job applications when a vacancy arises. Ensure you are following the publishers you want to work for on social media, as this is where events are usually advertised. Creative Access frequently organise events too.

Alumni Organisations

It is always worth keeping in touch with your university or other alumni organisation, regardless of the subject that you studied or whether your school, college or university is known for publishing. This is because people of all subject disciplines work in book publishing and might be listed as a useful contact. Alternatively, you might find someone like me, who once gave a talk at a university many years ago, listed as someone who can assist if you want a publishing job.

Blogs / Vlogs / YouTube / TikTok

If you want a job in publishing or the media, frequently people will tell you that you MUST blog, you MUST demonstrate your writing, you MUST write book reviews, you MUST have a social media channel or some such, to engage with the publishing industry. Likewise, I've been to many career talks where I've heard others on the panel recommend that you 'must have a blog' and 'you need to be visible by demonstrating your writing' to get a job.

This is not necessarily the case. Blogs are not the be-all and end-all of getting a job. Frequently, I read blogs that have been linked from candidates' CVs and I have been horrified by the end of the link – badly written blogs about personal goings on. The proofreading and errors are such that, if anything, your blog could be working against you – I always seem to click on the blogs where a graduate has misspelt their name or the name of their university. These types of errors will kill your job prospects instead of helping you land the job you so keenly want. Then there are the blogs that haven't been updated for ages, have pages missing, 404 errors or terrible design. They all work against you.

The same applies to Vlogging, TikTok and YouTube Videos. A recent candidate was publicising their new YouTube channel of book reviews, to show off their video editing skills, yet their latest video was edited so poorly, it was unwatchable. It is far better to practise these things in private, until you have them perfected, rather than going public prematurely and have them hinder your job search.

You should never be detrimental to someone who has turned you down for a job in a blog and if you publish book reviews,

---

Here are six ways to ensure your Blog/Vlog/TikTok does not kill your job search

1. Do you need a blog? The purpose of writing a blog may be to evidence your skills and experience. Is this something you need to do on your own? How often do you propose to update and maintain it? Would it be better for you to volunteer to write guest posts for someone else's blog or website?
2. If you are going to blog, make it on a subject you know about or that interests you. Perhaps you are always going to the theatre or nightclubs, watching sport, visiting lots of cafes and coffee shops or love a specialist genre of books. These types of blogs usually work well, because they are not about you, but they demonstrate your writing and editing skills and enable you to build a following.
3. Proofread your blog and check for errors. Ensure the grammar and sentence construction is correct and set your own 'house style' – and be consistent throughout. For instance, use 'proofreading' or 'proof-reading' – both are acceptable – choose one style and stick to it.

4. Check and double-check everything, including the spelling of your name. If you are going to contribute to someone else's blog, ensure they have high editorial standards. You don't want your name credited to badly rewritten or edited pieces.
5. If you are referencing your blog on your CV as a current example of your work, do ensure that your last blog post wasn't three years ago.
6. Don't expect the person interviewing you to have read your blog, but if you've linked your blog on your CV, then ensure it is a blog you are proud of.
7. Whatever course of action you decide to take, do try to see it from an employer's perspective and think the process through.

CASE STUDY
A jobseeker was blogging about their publishing job search and the people who were interviewing them. Often, they were neither kind about the publisher nor positive about their experiences. When they were rejected for a position, they wrote negatively about the publisher or said, 'I'm not going to buy their books anymore.' Needless to say, it took forever for them to find a job, because no employer wanted to be discussed in this way, nor did others want to contact them to offer advice, as they thought they'd only find themselves blogged about too.

be wary about posting extremely negative reviews. There are so many good books out there that need publicity, so spend your efforts on them instead.

If you intend to blog about your job search, remember that very often you'll be approaching this from a position of naïvety and probably make some very rookie errors. Also, most companies like things to be kept confidential, and this includes when you get a job. If you're in a job and write about your employer in a personal way or share information and occurrences without first seeking approval or permission, you might find you are not an employee of theirs for very long.

Networking for Career Success

Whilst networking events probably fall under some of the other categories, such as publishing career days, trade shows or trade associations, it is important to know how to make the most of these opportunities by networking professionally.

If you're at a networking event, it is far better to introduce yourself and latch on to something that you may have already seen or heard that day, than to use your prepared elevator pitch. Don't ever be disrespectful about the event or its speakers; even if you think the person is unconnected to organisers, positivity will always win the day.

Here are some examples of how you might introduce yourself at a networking event:

1. "Hello my name is Keerti. I don't think we've met before, what's your name? Have you been to one of these events before?"
2. "Hello my name is Keerti. I really enjoyed the last panel discussion, how about you?"

TOP TIP

Take action!

When it comes to networking, don't wait for someone else to make a move – if you do wait you may potentially lose an opportunity. You need to make the RIGHT move for you.

Here are nine top tips to get you started with networking at an event:

1. Don't pitch. When you introduce yourself, don't go straight into your full Elevator Pitch; instead, ask a question about something related to the event, such as: "What did you think of that last presentation?" "Isn't this a lovely venue? I haven't been here before, have you?" "Hello, have you been to one of these events before?" "I don't think we've met before, I'm (insert your name)."

    You don't have to shake hands if you don't feel comfortable doing so.

2. Stay focussed. Engage yourself fully in the conversation; don't keep looking over the person's shoulder for the next interesting person who comes in the room.
3. Make eye contact and smile. Everyone is nervous when first making contact but making eye contact and smiling will help to calm your nerves as well as theirs.
4. Be memorable. When asked about yourself, aim to say something they will remember about you. For example, if you are at a jobseeking event and everyone is a jobseeker, how will they remember you? What are you interested in? What career path do you hope to take?
5. Listen. Talk but don't talk too much. When you're talking, you are only hearing things you already know; when you're listening, you are hearing things you may not already know.
6. Circulate. Give yourself a target to meet and talk to at least six new people at every event. If you stand in a huddle with people you already know, you are unlikely to make any new contacts.
7. Exchange details with the person if you wish and follow up! If you've exchanged details, email the person within three working days of the end of the event and say how good it was to meet them. If appropriate, add them to your LinkedIn network and follow them on other social media.
8. Make it personal. Nothing is worse than sending 'round robin' or template emails, where it is obvious that you have sent the email to everyone but changed their name. This particularly applies to LinkedIn; if someone isn't expecting you to connect, personalise your connection requests if you can.
9. Stay in touch. Don't lose people from your network; keep in touch with maybe an occasional email when you hear they have had good or bad news (you have seen they have got a new job, changed job, been promoted or their job is at risk) or if you are going to the same event again – ask if they are going too. Make sure you are in contact aside from when you need their support, advice or connections – please don't be one of these people who only gets in touch with others when they need something.

Elevator Pitch

You may have already heard of an Elevator Pitch. It is how you introduce yourself to a stranger. An American term, Elevator Pitch is based on what you might say if you and the Managing Director get into an elevator on the ground floor, and both are going to the 15th floor. This could be your one moment in time to meet or impress the MD. What would you say to them? How would you respond if they asked you who you are or what you do?

I've read a lot of advice about Elevator Pitches, and most seem to encourage you to go on for too long. Initially, it is best to be short and punchy and then move into longer conversations, particularly when you have found out with whom you are talking. What you shouldn't do is go into a prolonged monologue of 60 seconds or more, so the other person loses interest and wants to move on. You might have several different versions of your Elevator Pitch, depending on where you are and with whom you are talking. If you're the kind of person who gets nervous at events, practise what you want to say, as this will help you not to panic much later. And remember to breathe.

The best type of Elevator Pitch lasts for 15–30 seconds and has three sections.

The first part is a brief introduction of your name and a short phrase about you, before you pause (take a breath) and read their body language to see if they immediately want to respond.

The second part is where you continue with what you want to say, and this doesn't always have to be a pitch about yourself.

The third part is to always end on a question, such as, 'Is this your first time here? What do you think of the event?' 'I learned a lot from that last speaker, how about you?' 'Would it be okay if I connected with you?'

An example of an Elevator Pitch is:

- "Hello, my name is Keerti, and I am a student with a passion for science fiction and fantasy novels."
- "I've got lots of admin experience and I am looking for a job in editorial. I came to this event to learn more about the industry and make new contacts."
- "Would it be okay if I connected with you?"

Other Ways to Find Jobs (or be Headhunted)

Write an Article

There are great opportunities for those wishing to enter publishing by writing an article about the industry. Some of the best places to do this include the *Society of Young Publishers*, *BookMachine* or *The Publishing Post* – which is a voluntary magazine designed for those wanting to break into the industry – and gain some informal publishing experience. It is also worth pitching ideas to other trade journals, but do check their websites to see if they have any submission guidelines or requirements. If you're reading *The Bookseller* or *BookBrunch* regularly, you might have a contrary opinion to one they are currently discussing, and it could be worth contacting the journalist who covered the story to ask them if they would like an alternative view.

Online Discussions

These are very common across social media. It is about offering a valid comment or point of view to an existing discussion or creating one of your own. It is why commenting on someone else's LinkedIn post or article can get you noticed. On social media, if a publisher you want to work for is posting about a cover reveal or a new title by your favourite author, then feel encouraged to respond with a positive comment. Or if they are asking for opinions, don't be afraid to offer yours, but always aim to be positive or constructive when asked for feedback.

Volunteering (not unpaid internships!)

There are lots of literary festivals of all shapes and sizes, and many require volunteers to help on the day, or days, or in the immediate run-up to the event. All are run on minuscule budgets, and the smallest ones may contribute to your travel expenses or have a lunch allowance; larger ones may pay minimum wage. However, they may bring you into contact with publishers or marketers for publishers, as well as authors. Some of the larger festivals have paid year-round roles.

If there is a big publishing conference or event, it can be worth checking if they use paid volunteers.

Both of these volunteering opportunities will help give you some industry knowledge and bring you closer to publishers, as well as increase your skills for a future publishing role. Every publishing house holds some sort of event!

How to use a Trade Show

Here are my top tips if you are job searching and going to a trade show, such as the London Book Fair. Use these tips wisely during the Fair:

1. There is usually an entrance fee, reduced if you buy a ticket in advance. Students can sometimes purchase a discounted entrance ticket.
2. Don't expect to find a job at the trade show. If you go it should be to seek information, look around and keep up with developments. Be prepared to potentially make contacts and network.
3. Exhibitors. Unless they are recruitment consultants or training providers, they are unlikely to be at the trade show for you; Exhibitors are there to buy, sell and do deals. A publishers' output for the next few years may rely on the business they do at a trade fair, so bear this in mind if someone is curt with you if you are asking questions.
4. Do not go around handing in your CV. There is probably no one on the stand who is from HR, and even if someone does accept your CV it is unlikely to make it back to the office. It is much better to check their website afterwards

and see if they accept speculative applications before emailing your CV to the office. Business cards, however, are the standard level of communication that one would expect at a trade show.

5. Go through the list of exhibitors via the online catalogue in advance and make a note of which stands you want to see. Check out the floor plan too so you don't walk endlessly for miles.
6. Wear flat comfortable shoes and if you are on a limited budget, take refreshments with you, as food and drink in trade show food outlets often come at a premium.
7. Look at the stands of the exhibitors that you want to see, and note the following:
    - How busy are they? This could be an indication of how well they are doing at the moment.
    - How many staff are on the stand?
    - Is the stand design and layout good or bad? Would you do anything differently? These are always useful discussions for future sales and marketing staff to have at job interviews.
    - What book or series are they promoting? Look at the walls and the sides of the stand. What are their lead titles? Again, these are excellent points to discuss at an interview.
    - If they give out catalogues or brochures, and you are up to carrying stuff, then take one, but be wary of picking up too much as you'll be carrying it around all day. Check the catalogues are free; and bear in mind that if it is a trade show, copies of books on the stands are not for retail sale. Although you can view publishers' catalogues online, taking a hard copy to an interview still speaks volumes.
    - Check out the competitors of the publishers that you want to work for.
    - What are they doing differently? Is it better?
    - Make some notes so you don't forget what you have seen!

8. Look around all areas of the exhibition, so that you are informed of new developments and opportunities.
9. Visit the recruitment consultants if they have stands, especially if they have had your CV for a while and you haven't been put forward for anything. Putting a face to a name is a great way to remind them that you exist.
10. Seminars – there are frequently many free seminars during a trade show. They are a great way to learn things about the industry. At the London Book Fair, you'll find the bookcareers.com Careers Clinic as well as some informative seminars run by the Society of Young Publishers.
11. Parties – towards the end of the day you will notice a number of stands setting up for drinks parties. If you are fortunate enough to be invited, don't get drunk, and use my tips on networking to see you through the event.
12. Follow up! If you've made any useful contacts at the fair, don't waste the opportunity and follow up promptly.

EXERCISE

Review some of your recent Job Applications against the bookcareers.com Tick Test:

- How many Ticks did you make against the requirements for the role?
- Were there any signs as to the cultural fit of the role?
- Can you see why you didn't make the shortlist or get called into an interview?
- Are there any instant improvements you can make to your applications, based on the skills and competencies you already have?

ACTION POINTS

- Read through a number of job advertisements at different levels to learn how the vocabulary within an advertisement changes along with the level of the role.
- For example, if you are looking for an Editorial Assistant role, also read advertisements for Editors and Commissioning Editors and you'll notice that words like 'liaising' may become 'communicating' or 'managing'.
- Practise the bookcareers.com Tick Test on any job advertisement before applying.

CHAPTER FOUR

Recruitment Practices and Selection

"Whatever the method of selection, if you know how to ace a CV, Covering Letter or Interview, you'll ace any job search, as the principles are the same."

Suzanne Collier

Now you've completed the bookcareers.com Tick Test, I thought it would be useful to show how publishers filter candidates for selection to interview. It will demonstrate to you why often you only need to meet 50% of the criteria for a position, as so much of selection is based on the ability to read and understand a job advertisement and your soft skills, not necessarily about all the skills that were asked for in the advertisement.

This is how candidates were selected for an internship. The process involved sending a CV, a Covering Letter and in the advertisement the candidate was asked to write 100 words about a book they had recently read. All the applications received were reviewed and scored as per the example below. Then only the top three, who happened to score 40 and above, made it to the shortlist. As it was an internship, only the top candidate was interviewed and if they had declined, then the second and third candidates would have then been interviewed. If this had been for a permanent role, all three candidates would have been interviewed before a final selection was made.

The main part of the advertisement read:

> We are looking for an office friendly Intern for one day a week (paid role).
>
> We are a reasonably new publisher focussing on children's and adult books. (Link to website)
>
> Ideally we'd want someone on a Monday or Wednesday and someone who is at a competent level who can help us produce commercial work and assist with Social Media. A knowledge of InDesign, Photoshop and a familiarity with Social Media an asset. Most of the work will be based around sales and marketing – but being small we all get involved in everything.
>
> To apply please send a CV and Covering Letter detailing 100 words about a book you have recently read to Lesley@

CASE STUDY

Publishing Operations Executive, Non-Trade Publisher

I saw the job advertised on the publisher's website. I sent in a CV and Covering Letter through their application portal. It was two weeks before I was invited to an interview, and they sent some interview tasks that I had a week to complete through the company portal. The first task was editing an extract of text. The next one was all about prioritising a number of tasks. For the third task I was given an outline and a previous example to work to, and asked to create a leaflet, taking into account the guidelines I had been given. Then the interview took place online, with two people interviewing me. They asked me a lot of competencies-based questions and we had a detailed discussion about the company. Four days after the interview, they telephoned me and offered the role.

This is a small selection of the candidates and how they were scored.

Can you see how the candidates who scored lower, could have made their applications better?

Read and understood	InDesign	Photoshop	Social media	Office friendly	Marketing brief	Comment	Score
10	0	0	10	10	10	Love them but no InDesign	40
10	3	3	10	10	10	They said they can work Mondays	46
8	0	0	10	10	10	Letter "to whom it may concern"	38
0	0	0	10	10	0	Looking for role for next year	20
8	0	0	5	5	10	Mentions social media but doesn't show where	28
10	0	0	10	10	10	Good candidate	40

For another role, a similar criteria were operated.

We have an opening for an Administrator to help organise our office, administration and busy workload. This is a varied role but is likely to suit someone who loves administrative processes.

Duties could involve (but this list is by no means complete):

- updating a database
- updating mailing lists
- answering incoming enquiries
- diary management
- editing information on the bookcareers.com website

- resizing an image file
- creating PowerPoint presentations
- covering social media
- telephone follow-up
- assisting with our stand at the London Book Fair
- advance preparation for meetings
- other office tasks such as filing, customer services and record keeping are all part of what we do here

If organisation is your forte and you have office experience then you'll fit in quite well. Ideally you would have already worked on any type of sales/CRM database and be active on a variety of social media. Excellent spoken and written English is essential, and you should be able to proofread your own work. Book publishing experience would be a distinct advantage. At the very least, you'll need to be good at Microsoft Word, Excel, PowerPoint and Outlook. WordPress or familiarity with any Adobe Suite programmes would be welcomed.

Please check the commute is manageable before you apply. Lesley@

This is an edited version of the notes made for a small selection of the applicants.

- *Candidate 1: Reject. Letter addressed to "To whom it may concern" and asking about any positions in your organisation.*
- *Candidate 2: Reject. Got my name wrong! They are studying for an MA in Publishing so have some useful industry knowledge.*
- *Candidate 3: Maybe. Excellent, but commute looks way too long for this role. Send them an email asking about the journey time.*
- *Candidate 4: Reject. Not enough PowerPoint experience.*
- *Candidate 5: Interview. No publishing experience but local to the office. Lots of office experience though which could be useful.*
- *Candidate 6: Reject. Teaching experience, no publishing experience. Initially sent a CV with a mistake then sent another CV without a mistake. Hmmm.*

- Candidate 7: Reject. Publishing experience but no mention of PowerPoint. Covering Letter was a template and not tailored to the role.
- Candidate 8: Reject. No mention of PowerPoint. Standard email not applying for this particular role.
- Candidate 9: Reject. No mention of computer skills at all! Standard letter template with words clearly inserted in a different font.

TOP TIP
If you are rejected quickly, don't assume that the publisher hasn't read your application. Even if you're rejected within 15 minutes of applying, understand that it takes only a brief amount of time for a recruiter to gauge whether you have the skills and competencies for the role.

How publishers select a shortlist and sift through applications.

"We know every candidate takes time to put an application together, and we owe it to each and every candidate to read their application."

The ways publishers select a shortlist and work through a vast number of applications will vary from role to role and from publisher to publisher. Overall, I have personally spoken to hundreds of managers, directors and recruiters across the industry about how they select candidates, but here is a summary that is indicative of the whole process.

Each publisher took actions to ensure they had a mix of candidates (e.g. by advertising on Creative Access or other inclusive job boards), as well as taking other actions to reduce unconscious bias, and ensure roles were recruited from candidates with differing backgrounds. A couple of publishers are starting to pilot AI to help them filter down initial applications, but up to this point, I hope you find it comforting that every publisher I spoke to has said that every single application was read by a human.

The way AI is being used in recruitment is an ever-changing situation, but even those trialling AI are wary of it ruling out candidates who may be suitable. The primary AI filters are being used to check whether someone has the right to work in the UK, attached a Covering Letter (if requested) or answered any application questions fully. By this I mean, not filling a box with the minimum number of characters requested or using AI to generate a summary of their experience. Being selected through AI isn't about dumping meaningless keywords into an application but writing clearly about your skills and experience and how they relate to the role for which you are applying.

One of the publishers involved in an AI pilot study said of the candidate selection, "The candidates who stood out were the ones who wrote authentic and tethered applications," meaning the candidates who tailored their application and their skills and competencies to the role were the ones who got through to being read by a human. So, always write your application assuming it will be read by a human and, please, don't get too caught up in what any applicant tracking system might be looking for.

Here are some real-life examples of candidate selection in action.

Publisher A

Editorial Assistant

They received 200 applications, read every one and sifted this down to 60 by ring-fencing the people who had aligned themselves to the company in their Covering Letter and who had answered the question in the advertisement. Those who failed to answer the question were instantly rejected, as well as those who had sent a generic CV. They were looking for transferable skills, such as those who had immersed themselves in books in other ways, not necessarily working for a publishing house, and who had an authentic story about why they wanted to work for this publisher (like reading to their siblings or other children). They interviewed 50 candidates, asking them all the same questions, and those who passed the first interview were sent a test. Sometimes this was a prioritisation scenario or a basic proofreading test. Two out of this 50 were given a second interview and one was offered the role.

Publisher B
Editorial Assistant

The vacancy was open for 10 days and they received 100 applications, so they closed it early. The recruiting team read all the applications, looking for the essential requirements in the job advertisement. Candidates who did not meet the essential requirements did not get through the first sift. The recruiting team noticed that the first batch of applications they received were weaker; the stronger candidates applied closer to the deadline (probably because they spent more time on their applications). They passed 20 candidates on to the manager of the department with the vacancy for them to decide who they would like to interview. They interviewed six candidates, all with two members of staff. At the end of the first interview candidates were given a test using InDesign (it had been an essential requirement) and a scenario where they had to pass on information to an author. Usually, they make a decision after first interview, and only invite one person back before offering them the role.

Publisher C
Rights Assistant

They received approximately 100 applications and went through all of them, skim-reading (but everything was opened and looked at) and searching for the criteria they asked for. The Director was ruthless – any with a mistake was rejected. The comment was, "Nobody in the business will take you seriously if you make the slightest mistake in an email or letter." Ten candidates were selected for interview and, at the interview, they were given a timed test to review a contract and point out what was wrong. Two candidates were called back for a second interview, and one was offered the job.

Publisher D
Publishing Assistant

A total of 670 applications were received, but a lot were instantly unsuitable as they had no right to work in the UK or had made mistakes in their application. Of the 670, 20% had not sent a Covering Letter. All of these were rejected, along with those who had not read the job description or thought about the job.

The rest were divided into three piles. Pile one were those who had mentioned wanting to work for the publisher; they felt particularly drawn to these candidates. Pile two were those who had prior publishing experience. Pile three were those who had no publishing experience but had thought about how they matched the job description and the skills required.

They were humbled by the number of over-qualified people who had applied, including those from industries such as financial services, who wanted to career change into publishing. They ended up with 100 CVs and these were read quite carefully. Twenty of these made it to a longlist where their skills were examined closely. Six were invited to interview with two members of staff, and three of these made it to second interview, where they were given a test.

As they are a small company, and everyone gets involved, one of the tests involved outlining a marketing campaign. The Publisher commented that there is no game-playing at interview; there is no good cop or bad cop. It is about finding the right candidate as, from the employer's perspective, this is a lengthy and time-consuming process.

Publisher E
Journals Publishing Assistant
They received 120 applications and rejected those who were not based in the UK. They reduced this further by eliminating those who had not sent both a CV and Covering Letter, those with mistakes or those who hadn't written a tailored letter. The first shortlist comprised 25 applicants, and from this they identified those who had understood the role or mentioned the name of the publisher. This gave them a shortlist of seven who they called for an interview, but only six were interviewed as one had already got a job elsewhere. From those six, two candidates were called back for a second interview.

Publisher F

They recruited for a wide variety of entry-level roles – **Editorial, Marketing, Publicity, Sales, Rights, Audio**

The process is highly dependent on the vacancy and the hiring manager's needs. They would either ask for a cover letter or application questions. The application questions can range from asking why they think their skills would suit the role, their motivation for applying or demonstration of problem-solving skills. They may also ask candidates specific questions such as a book that they enjoyed reading or a book they would market differently to understand their business acumen.

Some of the roles went on *The Bookseller*, LinkedIn, Creative Access, Twitter and select diversity and inclusion jobs boards. For each role they received around 250–450 applicants. Every application was read by a human.

They looked for any previous office-based experience, passion for the role that they had applied for, and passion for the division/imprint/genre. Anyone who was a bookseller or had a BookTok or Bookstagram is a plus for certain roles as well. If they saw that it was a copy-and-paste job, for example, or another publisher was mentioned in the cover letter, then they didn't put the candidate forward in the application process as that may have indicated a lack of eye for detail. Any obvious spelling mistakes for roles where attention to detail is needed would be noted as well.

If someone had relevant experience and had a good application but did not ever mention the publisher they were approaching in their application, they usually were not put forward to the next stage.

They rejected candidates who they detected were using AI. In some circumstances the applicant had copy and pasted the entire prompt and conversation from an AI platform (that was, without a doubt, generated by AI).

Usually, they would invite five to ten candidates to be interviewed for entry-level roles. This often started with an initial phone screening, confirming interest, salary expectations and notice period. Then they would be invited to a first-round interview (usually online) with two interviewers (most likely the hiring manager and their colleague/HR). Typically, there would be a task (prioritisation, proofreading, arithmetic, scenarios, copywriting, etc.) either before or during the interview. Then the final two to four candidates would be invited to in-person interviews with other members of the hiring manager's team. There may also be a task at this stage. Sometimes the process took as long as two months to complete.

Publisher G
Editorial Assistant

They used application questions, as they wanted detailed relevant answers to the questions asked on the application form. Vacancies are usually advertised on their company website, the IPG, BookMachine, Creative Access and the Publishers Association.

For this role they received 748 applications, and all were read by a human, who first reviewed if candidates had the right to work in the UK, rejecting those who did not. They also rejected candidates who did not put much effort into their application answers and rejected candidates who asked for a salary higher than was stated in the advertisement as it showed they had not read the job advertisement.

All the applications that were received seemed like genuine human answers to the questions, so they didn't have to reject any candidates for use of AI. Nine candidates made it through to the first interview for a Teams call with two team members, and from that nine they invited three for a second interview. They sent the three candidates a proofreading task a couple of days before their interviews and made sure that all candidates had the same amount of time to complete the task. The task had to be returned a day before their second interview.

The three candidates who made it through to the face-to-face interview all did very well on the proofreading task. It was a hard decision to decide what candidate to offer the position to as all three were really good. But one candidate just edged the other two with their answers and the confidence they exuded in the face-to-face interview.

Publisher H
Editorial Assistant

Part of the initial application process included an assignment to write a synopsis and review of a novel candidates enjoyed that was published in the last year.

They received 592 applications, and every single one was read by a human. They filtered them by looking for candidates who were able to show evidence in their CV that they had an active interest in getting into the publishing industry by taking part in publishing events or working as a bookseller, etc. They read all the cover letters and made sure they were tailored to the individual vacancy. Then they reviewed application question to ensure candidates had the right taste in books based on the imprint that was hiring, whilst keeping an eye on spelling and grammar.

Mostly they were keen to see that a clear effort had been made when answering the question. Three candidates made it through to an in-person interview where they were asked a mixture of questions that related to the responsibilities and capabilities required for the role. They then had a second in-person interview, with more competency-based questions and tasks testing their spelling, prioritisation and visual accuracy. The process took approximately six weeks.

Publisher I
Digital Marketing Assistant
Four hundred applications were received, and every one was read. All unsuccessful applications received a rejection letter. The Covering Letter and CV were equally important. Candidates were scored on the key skills they mentioned that matched the advertisement, as well as anything that stood out as showing an interest in the company or the industry. At the same time as being aware of unconscious bias, the publisher wanted to reflect their inclusion and diversity policies. The publisher was easily able to recognise when someone had used a template letter and hadn't tailored it to the role, and those candidates were in the first batch of rejections.

As they were keen to fill the role, they started interviewing candidates before the closing date. This was by an initial telephone chat and then a face-to-face interview. They probably spoke to 10 candidates initially, but they wanted to speak to a few more. However, the publisher was surprised how hard they had to chase candidates to fix interview times, so dropped candidates who were impossible to contact. Six were called for online interviews, where they were given interview tasks, such as writing a social media post for a book. Two were shortlisted from this. The publisher commented that any interview tasks they gave related directly to the skills needed for the job, so candidates should have felt confident that if they had the skills for the job, they shouldn't have had a problem with the tasks.

Publisher J

Publishing Assistant

Forty applications were received and all were read. Among the ones that instantly went in the 'No' pile were those that said they were looking to work in fiction (it was a non-fiction role for lifestyle books), had misspelt the publisher's name, or left the name off when it was in the advertisement.

The publisher doesn't do tests as they usually advertise in places where those already interested in the industry will look (e.g. bookcareers.com, Society of Young Publishers). Often, it was a gut instinct about how the candidates would fit in and, as a small publisher, fitting into the ethos of the company was given priority over existing publishing skills or experience. From this they would make a long list of six to eight candidates and then go through them again. There were a few candidate no-shows for the interviews, that they felt was quite poor. The decision on who to employ was made after just one round of interviews.

Publisher K

Graduate Scheme (multiple places) leading to a permanent role

They received 900 applications, and every single one was read. The Recruitment Team split the task between three members of staff, and each spent at least an hour a day, over three days, going through every application. The Recruitment Manager wanted to point out, "We know every candidate takes time to put an application together, and we owe it to each and every candidate to read their application."

During the sifting, they went through the answers to the three screening questions, looking for well-constructed responses and sensible answers as well as an adherence to the word count. This brought down the number to 100 and from this they selected 25 to take an assessment and video interview, relating to the skills they would need in the job; it was not their aim to trip up candidates. The tests involved verbal and numerical reasoning. From this they selected three candidates for the roles.

Today's publishers are frequently modifying their recruitment practices to ensure they are open to all. Gone are the days of only advertising vacancies to a specific section of the publishing workforce. Publishers want people with different backgrounds that represent the multi-cultural, multi-faceted, diverse society that we live in today.

This means that whilst some publishers may feel they are making the recruitment processes fairer, from a candidate's perspective, you might get the impression that you are being made to jump through hoop after hoop. In some instances, it can seem like the publisher is asking you to stand on your head and sing a Beatles song backwards to prove that you have the skills and competencies for the job advertised.

> **TOP TIP**
> Don't get caught in the numbers trap. If you've seen some of the numbers of people who have applied for roles and it has put you off, or you are thinking, 'No wonder I never get anywhere,' remember that at least half of the applicants will be instantly rejected. Instant rejections are usually because of one or more of the following: they don't have the right to work in the UK, didn't read the job advertisement, sent a generic application, sent a Covering Letter with another publisher's name on it, or made numerous spelling mistakes.

The following pages discuss some of the recruitment practices that do not rely solely on CVs, Covering Letters and interviews, and also show you how a publisher may make their selection criteria and score you. But whatever the method of selection, if you know how to ace a CV, Covering Letter or interview, you'll ace any job search, as the principles are the same.

Here are a variety of different recruitment practices:

A Job Advertisement that is an Editorial Test

This is where a job advertisement deliberately contains a number of spelling or grammatical errors. This might be mentioned in the advert itself, asking you – within your Covering Letter – to point out the errors you spotted. If the advertisement does this and gives the number of mistakes you need to find, remember one of the mistakes may be the number itself! This type of advertisement is specifically designed to reduce the number of applicants for popular roles such as Editorial Assistant (as applying will take time; you can't swiftly send a CV and Covering Letter). It is a fair way of filtering out applicants who may not have the skills and competencies required.

Whether an advertisement mentions errors or not, and you spot an error, it is always advisable to mention this somewhere in your Covering Letter, usually at the end or as a PS. The same goes for any spelling or grammatical errors you may spot in any online system. Treat the whole application process as a test in publishing skills.

Sample job advertisement that is an editorial test:

We are looking for an new Editorial Assisant to help support the editorial team with proofreading and copyediting.

You need to be expert at spotting other peoples' mistakes as well as have meticulous punctuation skills.

Duties include:

- *Proof reading*
- *Copyediting*
- *Research and fact checking*
- *Liason with authors*
- *Reading unsolicited manuscripts and righting reader reports*
- *Helping outwhere necessary.*

To apply pls send your CV and Covering Letter to lesley@

In this job advertisement there are three deliberate spelling mistakes or grammatical errors. When applying for this role, please point them out to us.

500 words (or more or less)

Instead of applying with a CV or Covering Letter, a publisher might ask you to write 500 words about why you are the right person for the job, what skills you can bring and, depending on the level of the role, what you'd like to learn or what changes you intend to make in the role.

Five hundred words is frequently used when recruiting candidates for roles where they may expect a lot of applicants. The fact that you can't instantly send off a CV and/or a Covering Letter will reduce the number of applications. It is also used for roles that may involve copywriting and should be seen as an initial copywriting test.

These 500-word count questions are marked on content, tone, spelling, grammar, punctuation and sentence construction.

- Content – ensure you have answered the points they have raised in the advertisement. This is a clear example of being able to read and understand instructions.

- Tone – they want to see if you have the right company tone for working with them. For example, if the advertisement is written in a friendly and non-formal way, then writing in a formal way could possibly count against you. You should aim to match their writing tone or the tone that the advertisement is asking for. If you find this extremely difficult, it could be a sign that this might not be the publisher or publishing job for you.

- Spelling, grammar, punctuation, sentence construction – obviously, the publisher wants to check your written English, and if you use words correctly. This is never about using big or complicated words or flowery language; it is about whether you can get your message across clearly to the reader. It should go without saying, but never go over the word count specified.

A Video CV or Showreel

One or two roles have asked for a video or showreel. The first was for a previous HarperCollins Graduate Scheme, and it was very similar to a pre-recorded video interview (*see Chapter Seven: Ace the Interview Process*), where the job advertisement asked you to answer in the video a number of questions and your video was how you answered them. This was the publisher's way of saying 'no CVs'.

As with any interview or application, read and understand the questions, stick to the criteria set, and you'll be well on your way to being shortlisted, as most people won't take the time to do this.

Another advertisement was for a marketing role, where you'd be producing author video interviews. Obviously, the publisher wanted to see what you produced about yourself to gauge whether to invite you to an interview. In the future you might be required to use a different type of medium, but the principles of preparing any of these are always the same:

- Read and understand the instructions
- Answer any questions or provide any information required along the guidelines given
- Stick to any time frame or set criteria
- Keep to a similar tone and vocabulary

Overall, so far, video CVs have not taken off in publishing. However, if you learn how to answer the "Tell me about yourself" question (see *Chapter Eight: Interview Questions and How to Answer Them*) and follow the points above, you'll go a long way to making an excellent video CV.

TOP TIP

Every communication you send is an editorial test. Whether you are emailing a recruitment consultant, commenting online to a potential employer about a book you love, or replying to anyone you correspond with. I still can tell you exactly who sent me an email that said, 'I was wandering if you could...' rather than, 'I was wondering if you could...'

Your correspondence at all levels must be faultless.

Blind/Anonymous Recruitment

Blind/anonymous recruitment is where all personal and identifying details about yourself are removed before your application reaches the publisher. It is becoming increasingly popular across most industries, as it allows any candidate who has the skills and competencies for the role to be measured on these, rather than your name, who you know, where you went to university, your ethnic origin or background. The applications go through a third-party system that will automatically recognise different sections of your CV, remove the personal information and focus only on the critical parts of your career history in relation to the role. It also randomises the order that applications are served to the publisher, so if you normally find yourself missing out on roles because you're at the wrong end alphabetically, blind recruitment will assist you. (Don't always assume that if you've applied and your name begins with A or Z, you'll be first or last in the queue; publishers have lots of random ways in which they approach applications in an inbox!)

This is why, if the application involves uploading a CV, it is important to ensure that you've incorporated as many relevant skills and as much of your experience as possible.

Application Questions (usually three)

Instead of a Covering Letter, you're asked to answer a number of questions, usually three, that will focus on the skills for the role. For junior and entry-level roles, they may focus on your soft skills; if you're applying for a senior role, it is likely to focus on the hard practical skills required. The questions are likely to have a word limit (do not go over this!) and one is likely to be a longer, practical question, such as a mini copyrighting or editorial test.

Examples of a three-question application are:

1. What are your career highlights to date?
2. What are your strengths/personal qualities
3. What interests you about a career with us?

OR

1. What attracted you to this role?
2. Why do you want to work in this area of publishing?
3. What do you think are the major challenges for this genre?

OR

1. Please give an example of how you have been creative either in the workplace or outside of work?
2. What things do you keep in mind when approaching an author for the first time?
3. Please read this excerpt and make suggestions to the author as to how you would rephrase the paragraph so it covers inclusion and diversity.

Guidelines for answering these questions are incorporated into *Chapter Eight: Interview Questions and How to Answer Them*.

Application Forms

A number of publishers have application forms as part of their applicant-tracking system, and you'll also find other publishers from time to time may use forms. If the system allows you, fill in the basics, make a note of the questions, go away and work on your answers, and then copy and paste your answers into the boxes. This gives you time to think about your answers and to proofread your work too. Any typing, spelling or grammatical mistakes on any application form are likely to count against you.

If the application form is a replacement for a CV and Covering Letter, think clearly about what you want to say in relation to your skills and the job vacancy; don't automatically copy and paste parts of your CV – if the publisher wanted your CV, they would have asked for it. Think very carefully about how you match the job, what skills you can bring, and what you can do.

When it comes to filling in the sections of an application form, I'd steer you towards well-laid out narrative rather than using bullet points, mainly because if they wanted a bullet-pointed answer, it is likely they would have requested your CV. It also gives you time to think closely about what skills and competencies you already have for the role.

Add some extra detail so the publisher can gauge your writing skills; it is better than copying and pasting lines from your CV. It demonstrates that you have put time and thought into your application. However, the choice to use bullet points or narrative remains a personal one.

One of the drawbacks of completing a full application form that replaces a CV is that if you aren't currently employed in a similar role elsewhere, or feel you are over-qualified or on a much higher salary, you might feel you are not really given a chance to prove yourself, or show you are happy to work at a lower level or at the salary band advertised. This is why it is really important not to copy and paste your career history into the question boxes. Use words tailored to the skills required in the advertisement, so you can demonstrate you are the right person for the role.

Usually, application forms ask for salary expectations rather than current salary. So, if you're changing careers or downsizing your career, and are on a much higher salary but prepared to work for less, this should help. If the publisher isn't using #BookJobTransparency and including an approximate salary in the advertisement, you can check approximate salaries for publishing roles on the bookcareers.com website.

Assignments

Sometimes, after you've applied for a post and before you are selected for interview, you may be sent an assignment, such as a prioritisation, editorial or copywriting test to complete.

This is to check you have the skills and competencies for the role before the publisher spends time interviewing you. Detailed assignments might include drafting a marketing or sales plan for a particular title.

These types of requests are all perfectly normal and as these assignments often overlap with interview tests, I'll discuss them in greater detail in *Chapter Nine: Interview Tests and How to Pass Them*.

If you are at a senior level, the assignments may be more complex and you could be asked for long-term strategies, ideas for developing the sales or lists, or produce a list of authors you would aim to attract. Sometimes it can feel like you're being used for free consultancy advice, though it is very rare a reputable publisher would do it.

Whilst you want to share your ideas and prove you're the right candidate for the job, you shouldn't be asked to complete a detailed strategy for the publisher, give away all your ideas, or feel obliged to share company confidential information from your current employer.

If you are asked to put together a presentation, the request should be fair and appropriate, and you should only share as much information as you are comfortable with, for example, one top-level idea, but not the detail. The main aim of these senior tasks should be for you to demonstrate to the publisher how you think and what you can do.

Always trust your gut instinct on this. Add a © copyright line to any materials you produce and, if appropriate, don't be afraid to question the process or in extreme circumstances, suggest a consultancy fee. If a Recruitment Consultant is involved in the process, always ask them for guidance; they know the publisher concerned and will advise the publisher as to what is a reasonable request.

CASE STUDY
Editorial Assistant, Medical Communications Publisher

I applied for an Editorial Assistant role via a Recruitment Consultant, but the job had already been filled. Instead, they told me about the role of Editorial Assistant at a Medical Communications Publisher. I sent through CV and Covering Letter to the Recruiter and then the Recruiter did all the communication; I had no direct contact with the publisher. I was invited to an online interview with two people. This was quite informal, and they told me about the company and asked about my previous editorial and publishing experience. It was very much a casual conversation. The second interview, also online, consisted of being interviewed by three people and they were asking lots of problem-solving and competencies-based questions. The interview lasted an hour. Two weeks after the second interview, the Recruiter phoned and offered me the role.

Assessment Centres and Open Days

When a publisher has a number of similar roles to recruit, such as Oxford University Press wanting to recruit four new Marketing Assistants, it is not uncommon for them to recruit via an Assessment Centre or hold an Open Day.

This is where, after initial selection, 50 or more candidates are brought together, divided into teams to listen to presentations or undertake a group assignment and then interviewed one by one.

If you are given a group assignment you need to think about:

- How you work with the other team members, even people you don't like.
- Whether you are helpful to someone in the team who might be struggling or being left behind.
- How well you read and understand the instructions.
- What direction the team leader is giving and if you are supportive of them.
- If you are questioning things that don't feel right or you think have been missed.
- If you are relating well to people from different backgrounds to yourself.
- How you will meet any task deadlines, specifics or creative input.

It almost goes without saying, group assignments are tough; they don't suit everyone and you're not alone if you find them intimidating. Often the most competitive candidates think they outshine others but, in book publishing, teamwork and collaboration are key, and the loudest, most competitive or visible candidate might not be the one who gets the job.

Open Days are similar, except often they are friendlier and less pressured. Even if the Open Day is advertised as a fact-finding event for the candidate, and the publisher is not actively recruiting, always remember that informally the publishers might be assessing you for future roles and opportunities, so be on your best behaviour.

Further guidance on Assessment Centres is in *Chapter Seven: Ace the Interview Process*.

> **TOP TIP**
> If you're asked to complete an online form that has application questions, start the application by reading the questions, then copying and pasting the questions and working on them offline on your computer. This gives you the opportunity to construct your answers properly, check your spelling and grammar, and ensure you stick to the word count. Then paste your answers into their form. It also means you will have saved your answers on to your computer, so if you get called to interview you know what your answers were.

Reading and Understanding Instructions

By now, you've probably seen that I've mentioned the ability to read and understand instructions several times.

The truth is that if I could give you only one piece of advice to take away from this whole book, one piece of knowledge that would underpin your whole career – every job you ever go for, every application you write, every task you ever complete, the one thing that will help you stand out and get noticed, get promoted, and make everyone think you are a complete and utter genius, it is this:

READ AND UNDERSTAND INSTRUCTIONS

Ah! But that is easy you say. That's simple, that's nothing special.

If it is nothing special, and it's a simple thing to do, why do so many people fail to do it?

We seem to be living in a world of skim-reading. From reading a salacious headline on a celebrity news website and jumping straight to the comments; from when you read the job title on a job advertisement and jump straight in to apply without reading the detail; from when you complete an online application, repost or comment on a social media post without clicking the link and reading and understanding the content.

People fail at reading and understanding every single minute of every single day.

This is why if you learn how to read and understand instructions, you will have the best possible career and be the best possible version of yourself.

For example, when you are applying for the job and the advertisement says 'Apply to Suzanne Collier at bookcareers.com,' why would you address your Covering Letter 'Dear Sir or Madam'?

If someone shares a link 'apply now' and attaches a link, click the link and read through the whole page before replying to the post by asking the question, 'Where do I apply?'

Recruiters often comment, 'Why didn't they read my email?' And as you may have read in the comments from publishers who sifted through applications, they were looking for candidates who had read and understood the job advertisement.

When I'm working with clients, I have to put a heading to my emails:

Important – Action Required – Please Read Carefully.

Why do I have to do that? I shouldn't have to do that, but I do, because people do not automatically read and understand instructions.

When applying for jobs, you'll be amazed at how many people do not read the small print on job advertisements. I hear this all the time from recruiters. "This vacancy was an office-based role in our Scottish division, and I've got applications from people in London, yet when I invite them for an interview they respond, 'Oh, I didn't realise'". But if they had read and understood the job advertisement they would have known.

Once you have a job, if you continue to read and understand instructions, you will perform so much better in that job than your peers – all because you read and understood an email before actioning it – and you can be absolutely certain that your colleagues will not. Your colleagues will skim-read, probably missing some very important points.

It is reading and understanding instructions that will help you get promoted and might help you get a salary increase because you will be outstanding in everything that you do. All because you read and understand instructions.

So please, if you are looking for a job in book publishing, make sure you read and understand the job advertisement and the instructions before applying.

The Lost Art of the Rejection Letter

If you apply for a job do not automatically expect to be told if you are unsuccessful. A number of publishers and Recruitment Consultants currently advertise with the line, "Due to the volume of applicants if you have not heard from us within six weeks, please take it that you have been unsuccessful," or something similar. It really is down to sheer volume. For an Editorial Assistant role, a publisher may receive 300–600 applications, and they may not have the staff resources to personally reject everyone. This is one benefit of many online recruitment systems; it is usually quite easy to let the candidates know en masse that they didn't make the shortlist.

Sadly, there are a few publishers who neglect to tell someone after an interview that they have not been successful, or you are kept hanging on for what seems like an eternity before they tell you. Part of this could be down to the candidate who has been invited to an interview, and they sent some interview tasks that I had a week to complete through the company portal. The first task was editing an extract of text. The next one was all about prioritising a number of tasks. For the third task I was given an outline and a previous example to work to, and asked to create a leaflet, taking into account the guidelines I had been given. Then the interview took place online, with two people interviewing me. They asked me a lot of competencies-based questions and we had a detailed discussion about the company. Four days after the interview, they telephoned me and offered the role.

EXERCISE

Here are three standard application questions that are often used instead of Covering Letters.

Before moving on to the next chapters, that will show you how to answer them fully, why not see how well you can answer them now. Each answer should contain no more than 200 words.

1. Please can you give an example of when you worked with others as a team to complete a project. What components did you enjoy?
2. How do you prioritise your workload? Can you give an example of good prioritisation in action.
3. Please give an example of when you've been creative.

ACTION POINTS

Read through the pages on how publishers sift through candidates.

Answer the following questions:

- How many publishers said they read every application?
- What are the key points that publishers said they were looking for from the candidates?
- Are there any new actions you will now take when putting together your next job application? If so, what are they?

CHAPTER FIVE

CVs That Get You Noticed

"Even though most of us are relatively intelligent people, that intelligence goes out of the window when it comes to writing our own CV."

Suzanne Collier

Over the next few chapters, I am going to discuss CVs and Covering Letters, as well as job interviews.

Some of this information might conflict with what you've already been told or what you've read on a publisher's website or blog. However, I have rigorously tested all the information I give out. I've studied the psychology of what happens when a Recruiter receives an application for a role and how their brain works when reading an application. This doesn't relate to unconscious bias, unless, of course, that unconscious bias is geared towards someone who cannot spell, uses incorrect grammar, misuses words or punctuation, or writes poorly.

The brains of those in publishing are wired slightly differently from other industries. What is different about those who recruit for book publishing roles? They usually read all day, every day. Their whole job, regardless of the function, revolves around words. This means that everyone who reads your application is likely to be an avid and accomplished reader. Whether they realise it or not, their brain is automatically proofreading or copyediting your application, and subconsciously thinking 'this reads well' or 'what on earth?!'

The other point I feel I must make is that when a publisher writes, "This is what I like to see in an application", suddenly every applicant will include the information mentioned. By the very nature of how someone's brain works, the publisher is likely to become bored by such formulaic applications. This is why you need to tailor every application to every job you apply for and work with each individual advertisement as the starting base.

Also, I've seen very misleading advice given. Candidates are told they've got a great CV or Covering Letter, that they then use for every job, but the reality is that their documents won't get through the most basic of applicant-tracking systems or they are using too much "CV speak" or hyperbole.

Many people will insist you write your application their way. In the following chapters, you'll learn how to write your application the right way – so that you stand out in a competitive jobs market and hopefully get a job swiftly.

Everyone has an opinion about what makes a great CV. Ask 37 different people about your CV and you'd get 37 different responses. If there was an exact template for a perfect CV, there wouldn't be at least 45 books on the subject. A perfect CV is one that gets you an interview and ultimately gets you the job. Your CV is your marketing tool and you should use it as such. That doesn't mean you need to add gimmicks, as a gimmick only works once. Here is an example of a gimmick that hasn't even worked once – the candidate entitled their CV: "The Graduate, a brave story of a student getting a job in book publishing". I've seen SO many of these over the past 30 years; we've called none of them in for interview.

In a situation where you are always applying for jobs and not getting anywhere, analyse which part of your job search is letting you down. If you are not getting interviews, it is down to your CV and covering letter; if you are getting interviews but not getting the job, it is a mixture of your CV, covering letter and interview performance.

Most people think that your CV will open the door, and the rest is all about how you perform at interview. This is not the case; your CV has to be brilliant enough to stand up through the whole process.

What happens when you leave the interview? The interviewer is left with your CV, covering letter and their notes. Very often at this stage, the recruiter is directly comparing your career history with someone else's, so you want to ensure that the skills and competencies you have for the job are clear from the vocabulary you use on your CV. Please don't get hung up on the 'your CV versus someone else's' part of the job hunt, as no two candidates are identical, and if you focus on this, it will distract you from being the best candidate you can be.

Also, you should not get hung up about how AI may or may not be used in candidate selection. When you have the skills and competencies for the role, you're more than likely to be selected, regardless of whether it is a human or AI doing the initial sifting.

This is why it is so important to tailor your CV to every job for which you apply. Do not send a generic CV with only a few top bullet points changed. The CV that got you your current job or part-time temping roles may not be the CV that will get you your next job. What worked in another role or industry might not automatically work for the job you want now. In the same way, what worked for a friend won't necessarily work for you.

By tailoring your CV and covering letter for every role, you are likely to be in the top 20% of applicants for any job you go for.

Always remember your CV is a statement of fact, showing where you have been and what you have done. Your covering letter says where you are going, why you want to work for the publisher and what skills you can bring with you.

At all times, you must retain ownership of your CV. You need to know every single word written on it; after all, you will be quizzed about everything on your CV at interview. All my clients are responsible for their own CVs; I never write a client's CV word for word. Instead, I guide clients towards expressing their skills and competencies in the best possible way. Your CV must be written in your own words, because at the end of the day, it will be you getting a job based on your CV, not the person who has written your CV for you. People who don't successfully pass their probation period in a new job frequently had their entire CV and covering letter written for them by someone else. Please do not use Artificial Intelligence (AI) to either write your CV or amend it, unless the job advertisement has specifically requested that you do. You are coming into a words business. Always use your own words.

Publishers are currently asking candidates to tick a box that confirms they have not used AI and that their application is all their own work.

Remember, too, that your CV is a living document; it will need changing and adapting every time you gain new skills or experiences. Trends in CVs change frequently. What I aim to do in this chapter is to help you build a CV that will please all of the people most of the time. The rest is up to you.

TOP TIP

Don't let anyone else write your CV for you. I don't write CVs for any of my clients; I guide them as to what should be included and train them how to write their own CV. This might sound surprising, but no client has the same background, so why should they have the same CV?

CV Basics

You might be inclined to skim-read this section, but please don't, even if you are the most experienced Editor. It contains valuable insights into what are very common mistakes from people who think they know it all already!

No matter what job you are going for, you'll need to incorporate the following factual information:

- Contact Details
- Employment History
- Education

Aside from this, there is information you may wish to add, including interests, training or vocational qualifications, references or anything else you'd like to mention. We discuss these sections later in this chapter.

In the next section – on CV Tools – you'll learn how to present your CV and make it stand out. Most errors seen on CVs are all basic ones, so go through the basics first.

Contact details

When laying out your CV, it should have your name and contact details clearly at the top.

You don't need to type the words 'Curriculum Vitae', as it is assumed it is your CV as your name is at the top. Also, the words 'curriculum vitae' are often misspelt.

Your contact details are:

- *Name*
- *Email address*
- *Telephone number*

You don't have to include your date of birth or age, and it is optional whether you add your home address. You might leave on your home address if the advertisement makes it clear they are looking for someone local or who lives within a certain distance of the office. Never include your National Insurance number on your CV.

When uploading your CV to various job-hunting websites, it is advisable to include only your email address and phone number unless specifically asked for your street address or other information. If you are a student putting your address on your CV and you have both home and term-time addresses, make sure it is clear which address you are at, or only use one address.

ADELAIDE ROSE
Adelaide@emailaddress.co.uk, Tel +44 000 000 0000

You might be tempted to put your contact details elsewhere on your CV, like the bottom of the page – don't do this! Most recruiters expect to see your contact details at the top; it is the natural place for your contact details to be, so do keep them there.

One essential thing to check is that your contact details are correct. Every now and then, I contact a candidate and their mobile number or email address is wrong – digits or letters have been reversed. Always make it easy for a recruiter to get in touch with you. So many recruiters tell me that they couldn't get in touch with candidates as the contact details weren't clear. It isn't unusual to make a typo in a phone number; do ensure this doesn't happen on your CV.

And remember, if you are giving your phone number ensure it is easy for the recruiter to reach you. If your mobile phone still has a daft message on your voicemail, think if it represents the best possible version of you. Also check that your voicemail is switched on to receive messages. I have lost count of the number of times I've phoned a mobile only to get a message, "Sorry, your call cannot be taken at present; please try again later."

I have recently come across candidates who automatically block unknown or withheld numbers. This is a risky game to play when you are job hunting; a number of recruiters block their outgoing numbers. Even if a recruiter has been in touch with you before on a visible number, if they are working from home their number may be withheld. In a competitive job market, you want to ensure you don't miss any calls.

Always duplicate the exact same contact details, in typeface, font size and layout on your covering letter. By doing this you instantly demonstrate you have some publishing skills as the documents match. It is useful, too, in case your CV and covering letter get separated, but if emailing, don't be tempted to merge your covering letter and CV into one document unless specifically asked; for instance, Creative Access often ask for one document. In other situations, the recruiter may instantly assume you haven't sent a covering letter.

There is no need to number the pages of your CV or repeat your contact details on every page. It takes up space that you probably need elsewhere, and the chances of both of the two pages of your CV becoming separated are extremely rare. It is not advisable to set your CV up for double-sided printing; have it as two separate pages.

If you are currently in a job, never use your work email address to look for another job. Firstly, it shows you are looking for a job on your current employer's time and resources (why would a recruiter want to employ someone who does that?) and secondly, emails sent from a company email address are likely to be monitored.

Always use a personal email address, and ensure it isn't a funny name or prone to typos. For example, *llladelaide@*. Are they three of number one or three of letter l, or a combination of both? And an email address *iamanidiot@* might not be the best first impression to give.

Another important thing to check, especially if you are using a Gmail account, is how your name appears on sent emails. You can check this by looking at your email settings or emailing yourself. Very often I see candidates' names appearing as AR (initials only) instead of their full name, or even being a symbol only. When a recruiter is going through hundreds of applications, they might think that the application is spam, whereas you want to be the best professional person that you can be.

Spelling, punctuation, grammar, tense and vocabulary

Book publishing is an industry like no other. Spelling, punctuation, grammar, tense, vocabulary and editing are paramount; I cannot express this enough. The major difference with book publishing compared to other industries is that book publishers are the purveyors of the English language. We need to be better than anyone else in getting the nuances of the English language right; the rest of the universe relies on publishers to set standards that others follow. You should demonstrate that you have these skills by getting these things right.

Spelling and Punctuation

Always check and double-check your spelling. Running your CV through spellcheck might be good some of the time, but it doesn't pick up everything – misused words, for instance. Spellcheck won't pick up words that are the wrong expression for the phrase. For example, I see documents that say *affective* instead of *effective*; spellcheck often won't pick up things like this! Nothing beats a manual proofread. Read the words out loud to yourself and check they make sense.

Check the names and spelling of places where you have worked and lived, especially if they are likely to come up on spellcheck. If you are sending your CV as a Microsoft Word document, don't protect it or set it to 'do not spellcheck'. I know of someone who copies protected documents into new documents and spellchecks from there.

Here are some examples:

- *I am an affective coordinator who can manage dairies* would pass through Microsoft's spellcheck program.

- Words, such as license, have different spellings in UK and US English. In the UK, the verb is license and the noun is licence; in the USA, the noun is license and the verb is licence.

- Many people have worked at *McDonald's* whilst at university, but on their CV they have the name incorrectly as *MacDonald's*, not *McDonald's* (and don't forget the apostrophe).

- Be very careful to check place names and street names for apostrophes. For example, three towns are *Bishop's Stortford* (possessive), *Bishop Auckland* (singular) and *Kings Norton* (plural),

- When you need to double-check any of these individual points, Google is often your friend.

Vocabulary

You need to ensure you are using the correct nouns, verbs and adjectives in the right context. If you are unsure use a dictionary.

For example, I worked with a client who said: *"I have worked on books from contraction to publication."* They believed that contraction was the correct extension of the word contract without realising that contraction has an entirely different meaning.

Tense

Your current role should be written in the present tense and previous roles in the past tense. Always write in the first person but ensure you write in coherent sentences, varying the language so the statements flow. Never write in the third person; after all, it is your CV – a document written by you – so why would you write about yourself in someone else's voice?

It is not a good idea to copy and paste words and phrases from other documents, such as a previous job description. The vocabulary from job descriptions often miss details that, in respect of tasks, bring them to life. You then need to ensure that the tense and vocabulary is consistent with the rest of your CV. As a result, it can be easy to see when someone has done a cut and paste job.

For example:

Sandra is an experienced Editorial Assistant

should be

An experienced Editorial Assistant

or

I am an experienced Editorial Assistant

Current job
Editing manuscripts, preparing them for publication

Previous jobs
Edited manuscripts and prepared them for publication

Inconsistencies – both of these appeared in the same CV:
I learnt how to proofread
They studied modules on proofreading

If you struggle with this, then get a friend with excellent spelling and grammar skills to check your CV. Remember, this should be a learning exercise – you need them to point out grammar and spelling errors so you can learn from the experience and make your own corrections in future.

Consistency

Consistency is extremely important. Imagine what this book would be like to read if we hadn't been consistent in our editing. You should use the same quality of consistency with your CV.

Look at the margins, headers, indents and layouts you are using. If you were editing a marketing document or a book, would you let inconsistencies through? No? Then ensure everything is consistent all the way through. Check that all the paragraphs line up, and all the headers are the same typeface and font size.

- If you use a date format such as 'May 2025', don't then use 'May 25' elsewhere.

- If you have put the full name of the company for one previous employer then do that for every previous employer.

E.g.
Bloomsbury
HarperCollins Publishers
should be
Bloomsbury Books
HarperCollins Publishers

Set yourself a 'house style' and follow it.

A house style is the standard layout and formatting you use across your whole CV. Choose how you are going to lay out and present your CV and stick to it. If you decide you want three-line spaces between each previous role in your career, then ensure there are three-line spaces across your whole CV. If then (for reasons of space) you go back to reduce this to two lines in one section, then reduce it to two lines across your whole CV. In the same way, if you decide headings are **BOLD BLOCK CAPITALS** then ensure all headings for the same purposes are the same and don't have headings at the same level that are **Bold Lower-case Underline**, unless it is a subheading or used for a different purpose.

Likewise, if at the end of a bullet pointed phrase you put a full stop (full point), ensure it is there for all the phrases laid out in the same way. I always recommend leaving out the full stops at the end of CV phrases as it is too easy to miss one, and to a trained editor, missing a full stop may then look like an error.

Another issue with consistency can be company names. Some publishing organisations always have their name in lower-case, like we do at bookcareers.com.

However, on a CV, adhering to this can look like an error.

For example:

Hachette UK
bookcareers.com
HarperCollins Publishers

At first glance, the company bookcareers.com, without an upper-case character at the start, may look like an error. However, the format for bookcareers.com always has been lower-case throughout, so that it matches the website and all the graphics. (There is a simple reason why I chose lower-case throughout all usage as our company identity. When I chose the format for the website, the usual style was to have the whole website name in lower-case.) Whilst your past employer might have always nagged you to ensure their name was always lower-case, don't follow this on your CV; a lower-case initial letter will look like an error to everyone except those in the know.

Errant characters and page endings

Every time you update your CV, before you send it off via email, if you can, print out a hard copy. This is critical because, as well as giving it a final check, you want to see how it prints out. By doing so, you may find an errant character at the top or bottom of the page, or things haven't printed out as you wish. Even though you intend to email your CV, you never know if it may be printed out at the other end, especially if you are invited to an interview.

If you are using bullet points, always use the standard bullet point symbol or *. On someone else's computer other characters may not print as you think, and the symbol may appear as something else. This can happen in a PDF as well as Microsoft Word if the appropriate character set is not installed on the recipient's printer. On one client's CV, their non-standard bullet points printed out as love hearts not the bullet points they intended.

If you press print and get the message, "the margins of the page are outside the printable area", then change the margins. You have no idea what the person at the other end will do when they see the message, so you need to ensure that the message doesn't occur and that your CV text is all within normal margins.

Ensure you print only pages with text and not blank ones.

> **TOP TIP**
> When you grasp that job hunting is a marketing process, and you are the product, then you are part of the way to winning.

Dates

I am seeing a recent trend on CVs where candidates remove all dates from their CV thinking this will help them. Don't do this. A recruiter needs to know when and how long you were at a place of employment or in training. They are not going to discriminate against you for giving this information.

Date Formats

Although you might set your own house style for dates, it is highly recommended to write the name of the month, rather than the number, and use a four-digit number for the year. This makes the dates you use automatically global in their interpretation and far easier for someone to read.

For past jobs, always put the month and the year, not the year alone. That way, a recruiter can instantly see how long you were at a job.

When describing short-term placements, it is critical that you explain how many weeks or days this was for. I often see misleading time periods on CVs and these can instantly kill your trustworthiness as an employee.

For example: *Internship, Bookcareers Publishing, November to December.*

When you word your CV like this, a recruiter might take this as face value and believe you have two months of experience. You go to the interview and they say, "Tell me about your two months at Bookcareers Publishing," and you say, "Actually, it was only… a day a week for two months, or six weeks, or two weeks over a two-month period."

As a result, you instantly lose all credibility as a candidate and the recruiter thinks perhaps you have tried to mislead them, albeit unintentionally, into thinking you have experience that you clearly don't have. The result is they then question every item on your CV and start to believe you may not be entirely honest and can't be trusted. It has happened with several clients (before they saw me) and I have interviewed candidates for roles where they attempted to mislead. It isn't big and it isn't clever. Go for honesty all the way. No one will think any less of you for being honest.

If you are not honest and make out you have greater experience, it might lead to the unfortunate situation of getting the job but not making your probation period as you are not capable of fulfilling your role. It is much better to get a job that meets your skills and competencies and hold on to it than to be employed in a role where you are out of your depth.

So always go for

November–December 2024 (2 weeks)

as a format when describing short-term placements.

Track Changes

If you've been editing in Microsoft Word and been using 'Track Changes', ensure that you have definitively removed all evidence of this. (Email your CV to a friend to be completely sure.) This is because I frequently see CVs uploaded online with all the comments still visible and very often containing notes that you would not want a future employer to see.

CV Templates

Do not use a CV Template unless you are asked to do so.

CV Templates do you no favours at all. If you are using a standard résumé template supplied by a well-known software producer, the chances are that in a batch of 300 CVs, there are probably at least six other people using the same thing. This means that when someone is skimming over your CV, they may feel like they've already read it and put you in the rejection pile.

Most CV templates are also poorly designed, and you cannot include all the coherent information you need. They also don't always work well with any Applicant Tracking Systems that recruiters may use.

I also advise against using Canva or InDesign to write your CV. You want to be able to update or tailor your CV in a matter of minutes. Having your CV with a fancy layout in design software can delay your application or make it awkward when all you want to do is add an extra line of text. Please also don't believe the myth that you need to use InDesign to produce your CV to demonstrate you can use InDesign; this is not the case.

Spacing

Very often I see page wastage on CVs. Indents that start a third of the page's width in is a typical example of page wastage. Always align the text to the left. This is common from people who tell me they have no space on their CV and don't want to go over two pages. Yet, by removing the indent and aligning all the text left, suddenly they find their CV fits on two pages and they have room to spare.

Alignment

As I said above, always align text to the left, and I recommend not using justified text on a CV or covering letter because of the way it sometimes spaces out the words. Centred text or headings are also not recommended because of the way people's eyes read (in English, this is left to right).

> **ANECDOTE**
>
> When I first started giving advice about CVs, Christian Kelly (a former Human Resources & Training Manager at HarperCollins) told me that when you are writing your CV, do not centre text or indent it, as your eye naturally starts at the left-hand side of the page, and sentences that start a third of the way in or centred are not read.
>
> I didn't believe this was true, but when you spend your day reading or skimming through CV after CV, you realise that Christian was quite correct. I've seen it too with the clients I work with; a client might not be selected for an interview, because somehow vital information was missed when skim-reading. On reviewing the client's CVs, the text has always been indented.

Columns

Newspaper columns might sit well on a Journalist's CV, but they don't sit well in book publishing, so if you are planning a career transition from journalism to book publishing, then do not have columns in your CV. This is because people who read books in English expect the text to run from left to right. When you have a CV in columns it makes it very difficult to skim-read; your eye doesn't know what to focus on first. You also lose a lot of space when using columns, and this is not good when you have so much you want to say!

Although at the time of writing, Applicant Tracking Systems (ATS) are not heavily used to filter candidates in publishing recruitment, some ATS have difficulty in reading columns.

Avoid using headers, footers and text boxes

If you are using Microsoft Word, and not saving to PDF, then avoid using headers, footers and text boxes.

This is because traditionally in Microsoft Word, different views (Normal, Print, Outline) gave different viewing experiences and, in some views, text in headers, footers and text boxes disappear. For example, if you have all your contact details in the header, in certain views they are faded out or invisible. Not great if you want to be contacted.

Text boxes are also a hindrance as they can disappear completely or can be easily dragged and dropped over other text. If you need a format to organise your layout, use a table and hide the table borders. As with columns, headers, footers and text boxes don't work well with ATS.

Location

If you are applying for a job in a completely different location to one where you currently live, then you have two options.

1. Don't mention your current address at all, although it might be obvious that you are based 150 miles away from the publisher, as that is where your current job is based.
2. Mention your location and under your address insert the words "(can relocate swiftly)" if you intend to relocate or "(1 hour commute)" if you intend to commute. But ensure you have done your homework about relocating first.

Length of your CV

Don't make your CV longer than two pages for jobs in the UK. Even if you have been working for 30 years, your CV should not be more than two pages. If you are applying for a role with an academic publisher and you want to include a list of your published articles, then a third page is acceptable, but only use it for this purpose. Keep all your articles and publications on the third page.

Aim to keep the length of each of your descriptions for each role relevant to the time you spent in each role and level of responsibility you had, along with how long ago the role was. This will help you edit and revise your CV as your career progresses. When it comes to condensing your CV, spend less time giving full descriptions of earlier roles, where the experience and descriptions have been superseded by current roles. For example, if you were a Rights Assistant and are now a Rights Manager, you can reduce your descriptions for the Rights Assistant role and keep only essential elements, maybe a particular market or skill, that are the keys for the role for which you are applying.

If you are a recent student and have held on to holiday jobs, some of the bad CV advice says remove these, as they are not relevant to publishing. However, any holiday, part-time or student job demonstrates that you have a good work ethic. Each opportunity may also have given you a wide variety of skills, such as customer service, prioritisation, dealing with difficult people, etc. Never underestimate how much these experiences can help your future employability. If a lot of your short-term roles were similar experiences (e.g. you worked in three different coffee shops as a barista), you could list them with the dates and merge the experience rather than detail every experience individually.

For example:

Barista, Costa Coffee. May to June 2023
I did all the cashing up

Barista, Starbucks. July to September 2023
I was front of house and often dealt with difficult customers

Barista, Independent. September to October 2023
I cleared the tables as well as made coffee

Could become

Barista May to October 2023
At the end of my time at university, I worked for Costa Coffee for six weeks before returning home. I then spent more than a month with

Starbucks before the branch closed and I joined an independent coffee outlet. At all three stores, I helped with everything from making coffee, to clearing tables and cashing up, as well as – I believe – being friendly and approachable, even when there was a difficult customer.

Photographs

Do not put a photograph of yourself on your CV or send in a photograph unless you are asked. In some countries it is compulsory to add a photograph, but not in the UK. In fact, what you might find is that if your photo is included on your CV, you could be instantly rejected as part of their unconscious bias selection process. The recruiter does not need to know what you look like in advance.

Graphics

If you are not a designer, then steer clear of any graphics.

If you are a designer looking for a design job, then a graphic border, small illustration or your logo on a CV is a good thing alongside your portfolio. In this case, colour may be acceptable but ensure the colours you use are easily readable on screen. Too many times I see text in yellow, a colour that does not read well on a white background or on screen.

Many designers think they need to over-design their CV in order to win a job. This is not the case. Let your CV be the business document, the statement of fact, and your portfolio, showing many different styles, be the advertisement for your design skills. If you demonstrate one of your design styles on your CV, and it isn't to the recruiter's taste, then you could miss out on the job. But when you force them to look at your portfolio, so they see all of your design styles and your versatility, you have far more chance of success.

Coloured Text

Always use black text on a white background. When you reverse text (white text on a black background), and the interviewer goes to print out your CV, you will waste an awful lot of their black ink; it also is sometimes harder to read. In my research for this book, 75% of recruiters surveyed said they sometimes printed out CVs, often when getting ready to interview a candidate, so whilst you might be uploading to an online platform, or emailing your CV, always take the print option into account.

Unless you are a designer, avoid colour completely. You do not know how the colour will print at the other end, and more importantly, you do not know if the interviewer is colour blind and there are now more recognised varying degrees of colour blindness. Also, if you are colour blind, then ask a friend to check your CV isn't in colour. I was working with a client who, before they came to me, had been unemployed for eight months. When I checked their CV it was in brown type. They were colour blind and hadn't realised they'd been sending their CV out like this. Call it a coincidence, but within three weeks of changing their CV to black text, they got a job.

Fonts

Use fonts that are current TrueType fonts or standard ones: Arial, Times New Roman, Verdana and Tahoma are all good fonts to use. Avoid Comic Sans or any handwriting fonts. Don't use more than one font style and three font sizes (e.g. Arial, 14, 12, 10). Avoid going below 10 pt anywhere on your CV. You want your CV to be read, and if you make it 9pt or even 8pt, firstly, it makes your CV very difficult to read; secondly, it indicates that maybe you have got too much information on your CV (as you have condensed the typeface to fit two pages) and your CV needs a good edit.

- Using **BOLD** or underline to emphasise words in sentences about your skills.

  It is fine to use **BOLD** and underline in your headings, but these should be avoided in descriptions on your CV, especially where you express your skills. The words or skills you highlight might not be the ones the publisher is concerned about. The recruiter might actually be looking for other things, and not only the skills mentioned in the job advertisement. Using the example below, you will see the words 'digital' and 'email marketing' highlighted, but the publisher could be more interested in your social media skills. Or they might see the word 'digital' highlighted and completely miss that you have print experience too.

Example

*I have 2 years print and **digital** experience, focusing on **email marketing** and social media*

If you are going to make a bullet point about your skills, then it should stand up on its own; there is no need to add any further emphasis. If the skill is a critical one for the job you are applying for, then the recruiter knows what they are skim-reading for; you don't need to emphasise it further.

- Italics

    I don't know if you've noticed, but when you are skimming lines of text, italics are sometimes difficult to read.

    This is why the only time you should use italics on your CV is when mentioning the title of a book, newspaper or journal you want to name that you have worked on, such as *Pride and Prejudice*, or if you have been working for a music publisher, music albums should also be italicised. Other titles are also italicised, such as television programmes, plays, films and music albums. Singles (songs) and individual poems in a poetry book would be set inside double quotes.

    As with other sections of your CV, when you are formatting the dates of past employment or education on your CV, it is always best to use the month and the year as four digits. (e.g. June 2024). Think of it as good practice. Remember that publishers like words, so they will react best to letters rather than numerals.

- How to lay out the name of the company and your job title:

    Depending on what you want the recruiter to pick up on first, choose to lead off with the name of your employer or job title.

    For example, if you are already an Editorial Assistant, it would be best to lay out your job title and employer as:

Editorial Assistant
Bookcareers Publishing, either below or to the side.

The reason is, when skim-reading, the employer's eye is likely to absorb the words EDITORIAL ASSISTANT, before skimming over the name of the publisher and then read through your experience.

Alternatively, if you've been working for a book publisher, but not in the department you are applying for, it might be better if you lay out the heading as:

Bookcareers publishing,
Assistant, Sales & Marketing

Again, the employer's eye will fix on the name of the publisher, might see the word assistant and then read about your skills and competencies.

Gaps on your CV

If you talk to any Human Resource or recruitment professional, they will tell you that you need to explain every single gap on your CV, as well as point out any gap with your university experience or education and add an explanation. Therefore, on a CV you might see things like:

- *Career Break – caring for relative*
- *Career Break – family bereavement*
- *University – It took me 4 years to complete a 3-year course as I had a period of ill health in the middle.*

This advice is WRONG. Don't do it. It is fine to have gaps on your CV, or just explain them with the words 'Career Break' with no detail.

As for you taking four years instead of three to complete your degree, no one is going to realise it was a three-year course instead of a four-year one, so don't volunteer this information unless you are asked.

Gaps due to Covid-19

It is fine to have a gap on your CV from February 2020 to June 2020 or longer. You shouldn't need to explain at all why this gap has occurred.

If your job was furloughed, you may want to mention this on your CV, but it shouldn't influence whether you get a job or not. It was a company decision to furlough you, not a personal one.

If you were undertaking training courses or learning new skills during the lockdown, it is good to add these to your CV. However, don't feel pressured to add anything in this gap. A pandemic isn't a war; this is no badge of honour. Your job was to stay safe and stay at home.

Any recruiter should not probe what you did during lockdown as they do not know your personal circumstances. However, if they do ask, it is fine to say you caught up on some reading, DVDs, home chores or helped neighbours. It is perfectly normal to say that you stayed at home during Covid-19 as that is what you were asked to do.

Naming your CV (and your Covering Letter) file names

Before you send your CV to a publisher, name the document or file correctly.

Best practice is to name it one of:

- *FirstnameLastnameCV*
- *LastnameFirstnameCV*

And do the same with your Covering Letter:

- *FirstnameLastnameLetter*
- *LastnameFirstnameLetter*

On every document you will work on in your future publishing role – all the books, publications, catalogues and leaflets – consistency is key, and it should be no different in your job applications. Ensure consistency on both the file names of your CV and Covering Letter, and what you use as capitals and lower-case. Be the professional publisher you are.

It is not recommended to put the name of the publisher or imprint in the file you send, e.g. HarperCollins, because sometimes you will forget and send the same CV to Penguin Random House. Also, never call your CV 'publishingCV', or have the words 'publishing, editorial or another department' as the title. This is because it instantly indicates to the employer that you are looking for a job in another industry or department.

I've seen discussions online about these points, in that having the name of the publisher or department indicates you have tailored your CV, and you really want to work for them. No, this isn't going to make the slightest bit of difference, but sending with the file name of Hachette to a different publisher or sending a 'MarketingCV' for an Editorial role could see you instantly in the first batch of rejections.

The risks are always too high, so stick to best practice. After all, you want the recruiter to learn and remember your name, and what better way than by ensuring all your file names use it!

Always keep a copy of your CV and Covering Letter

I recommend you first save your letter as the name of the company and role on your computer, then save again, as the files with your name, for emailing. This way, you always know exactly what version of your CV is the most recent, so when you do your next application, you're using the latest versions as the starting point.

It also means that if you are on a prolonged job hunt, and you find yourself applying to the same publisher again, but for a different role (or maybe the same role again – these things happen), then you can instantly refer to what you sent to them previously and avoid repeating phrases and terms.

Using Tools on Your CV

You can use a number of tools on your CV to make your application and skills stand out.

Some of these come in and go out of fashion, but you should pick the tool that is relevant for the job you are applying for. This will vary per job application, depending on what parts of your career history or skillset you want to emphasise. This is why it is so important to tailor your CV for each role you are applying for. You might use one, two or even three tools on the same CV, but it is not recommended to use four.

Which tool should you use?

For every single job application, read through the job advertisement and assess what skills and competencies you want to highlight on your CV to show the recruiter you are right for the job.

In conversations with Human Resources Managers and Recruitment Consultants, each has their own personal preference for which tool they like to see on a CV. Even two people from the same publishing house will disagree about what makes a CV stand out. The truth is, no matter what someone says they like to see, the reality is often very different, because each person reacts in a positive way to the skills on a CV that match the job they are currently recruiting for.

As the components for a job change, so will what a recruiter is looking for on a CV. This is why there is so much conflicting information about what makes a great CV. However, in the many successful and unsuccessful job applications I have analysed, both for clients and as research for this book, the successful CVs are always the ones that match the skills and competencies for the role.

There are five main tools:
1. Jumping straight in with your employment history
2. A heading or strapline
3. A personal profile or personal statement
4. Key skills / Skills profile
5. Separating your experiences

1. Jumping straight in with your employment history

This only works if you are currently in a job that matches the role you for which you are applying, and you don't wish anything else on your CV to detract from that. It applies to those who already have an employment history and are working for a big-name publisher, a competitor or supplier to the publisher you are applying to. For example, say you were working at Bloomsbury, and were applying for a similar role at Hachette, or you were working for the BBC and the role you are applying for has one of its key tasks as liaising with the BBC, then sometimes it is best to minimise the waffle and go straight in with your employment history.

2. Heading or strapline

This is a single sentence emphasising your skills and experience. It is concise and to the point.

This was a very big trend on CVs in the 1990s, and it is starting to come back in fashion.

Examples

- *A MA in Publishing graduate with a strong interest in marketing*
- *A recent Psychology graduate with basic editorial experience*
- *A bookshop assistant with excellent customer service skills*
- *A Primary School teacher with experience of children's publishing*
- *A Rights Assistant with experience in co-editions and the Bologna, London, Sharjah, Beijing and Frankfurt Book Fairs*

3. A Personal profile or personal statement

A personal profile is an introduction to you and your CV; it is a summary of who you are and what you can offer. This is slightly different to the personal profile you may have written when applying to university or applying for training or funding, as it is focussed on what you can bring to the job rather than what you want to do.

A good personal profile consists of three to five narrative lines emphasising your skills, experience and key information.

An example of a good personal profile:

A Marketing Assistant with experience of email, social media and print leaflets. I have been responsible for initiating campaigns that regularly delivered a 75% open rate and generated an increased income of over £250,000 and added 50,000 followers. I'm adept at measuring analytics on a variety of platforms.

A lot of clients I see have difficulty in writing a good personal profile. My advice is, if you can't write a good personal profile, then use another tool to express yourself.

An example of a bad personal profile:

A recent graduate of English Literature who is enthusiastic, organised, methodical and has an eye for detail. I want to work for a book publisher so I can continue my love of literary fiction. I am an excellent communicator and team player. During my degree I learnt how to work under pressure and keep to strict deadlines and was a volunteer editor for the University Newspaper. I would be an asset to bookcareers.com Publishing.

Or a profile that starts:

A highly motivated and versatile English Graduate.

Or

An ambitious graduate

This is a bad personal profile because how many English Literature graduates do you think are applying for the same job as you? Lots! The rest of the profile is about your soft or unquantifiable skills. It is also subjective and full of hyperbole, cliches and stock phrases. What is an 'excellent communicator'? How can this be gauged? Who are you excellent at communicating to (or with)? There is little within the profile that is worth retaining. I also suggest you don't waste words by saying, '*I would be an asset to .... Publishing*' on your CV as it is using up a line of text where you could add different information that will directly encourage the employer to employ you. Of course you think you'd be an asset to the publisher; that is why you are applying for the job!

As well as all of this, a personal profile can expose how poor your copywriting skills are. It is why writing a personal profile is often a bad idea for many people. Also, the less experience you have, the harder it is to write a personal profile that is based on skills and competencies.

If you are going to write one, aim keep to these three points:

1. Who are you? (This doesn't mean write your name!)
2. What skills can you bring?
3. What things are you good at? What can you do?

Aim to keep these relevant to the job you are applying for, using coherent sentences.

When you write your personal profile, think of your USP, your unique selling point. What skills have you got that are unique to you, and relevant to the skills and competencies of the job? Is there anything extra you can add? How can you give your personal profile a distinct element, so your own writing voice can be heard?

Therefore, the above profile might be reworded as:

An entry-level assistant with experience of proofreading via a University Newspaper. This has given me a love of editing, in particular literary fiction. It taught me how to communicate with writers and contributors, as well as work under pressure and keep to strict deadlines. I'm also adept at social media and a regular user of Instagram and TikTok.

Can you see how, within the second profile, some of the hyperbole, cliches and stock phrases have been grounded and given validation? That is what you need to do if you intend to use a personal profile as your tool. You should also notice that it feels relatable, and you can hear the candidate's voice, rather than CV speak.

BEFORE

To pursue a career in publishing, preferably through either an editorial or publicity assistant-based role at a major trade publishing company. A broadly skilled postgraduate with successful work experience in several sectors looking for a fast-paced, rewarding environment to specialise in. Proven capabilities in research, support and communication. Attention to detail prominent. Flexible and capable of working independently and as part of a team. Postgraduate and undergraduate degrees in literature and history.

AFTER

This is good, but it still needs work; whilst factual it is missing the candidate's voice.

An Editorial Assistant with a qualification in Proofreading and Editing and experience as an Editorial Intern. Proven capabilities in research, data collection, preparing presentations and administrative support whilst showing a strong attention to detail. Flexible and capable of maintaining favourable working relationships in any situation. Postgraduate and undergraduate degrees in literature and history.

AFTER AGAIN

An Editorial Assistant with a passion for Science Fiction and Fantasy. I have a qualification in Proofreading and Editing and experience as an Editorial Intern within Trade Publishing. I've proven capabilities in research, data collection, preparing presentations and administrative support whilst showing a strong attention to detail. I'm flexible and always enjoy good working relationships with colleagues. I also have postgraduate and undergraduate degrees in literature and history.

> Please do not copy the examples in this book word for word. Publishing is a small industry. The chances are high that others have been daft enough to do this.

This is another example of a personal profile that doesn't work for jobhunting and is full of CV-speak:

A dedicated self-motivated person who possesses outstanding communication and organisation skills, enjoys working alone and as part of a team. Works well under pressure, strives for excellence and ensures deadlines are consistently met. Motivated to learn from new experiences and always ready to face a challenge with an open mind.

Yet when I looked at this candidate's CV, they had studied Publishing as a first degree, and whilst at university they had worked in an office as an administrative assistant and worked in a busy mobile phone shop as a sales assistant.

I have a BSc in Publishing, covering all aspects of book publishing in print and digital formats, and I am trained in CSS, HTML and Web Analytics. Whilst studying I held down two jobs, one in a mobile phone shop, the other a coffee shop. Both of these have given me administrative and customer service skills. I'm the best person to have around in challenging situations.

This could be rewritten as:

I'm a recent publishing graduate with a variety of administrative and customer service experience gained while holding down two part-time roles in order to fund my studies. I'm extremely self-motivated, love working in challenging situations, and have grasped the basics of editorial, marketing and social media as a volunteer for a university society. I'm experienced in a wide range of software including Microsoft Excel and Adobe InDesign.

Other examples:

Recent Graduate

BEFORE

As a recent MA graduate and former bookseller, I am a dedicated and hardworking individual who is driven to improve my literary skills and build on my previous experience in the field. After spending my postgraduate studies focusing on my passion for editorial work, I am now seeking an entry-level role with a publisher who matches my drive to promote strong individual voices and powerful commentary on social issues.

AFTER

I'm passionate about editorial work and have gained proofreading and copyediting experience through publishing two anthologies whilst studying for a MA at university. I love the teamwork aspect of publishing, and got involved with every task, so have an understanding of the whole process, including bookselling, as I've been working in a bookshop. Most of all, I enjoyed collaborating with authors to ensure their voices were heard.

Marketing

BEFORE

I am an industrious and reliable individual with over five years in communication-based roles.

I have completed my degree in Sociology, and I am currently looking for full-time positions in an admin facing role.

AFTER

I'm a Marketing Assistant who has been creating weekly newsletters, meeting with potential clients, writing copy for social media posts and covering general office administration. I enjoy collaborating with others and supporting a busy office.

Rights

BEFORE

A highly motivated and dynamic University of Oxford graduate with a BA in German. My academic background has equipped me with strong analytical thinking, creative writing, and a deep understanding of literature. I have proven organisational and project management skills, the ability to manage multiple tasks efficiently, and a passion for collaboration. Adaptable and quick to learn, I am eager to bring fresh perspectives and innovative solutions to diverse professional environments.

AFTER

I have a keen interest in rights and translation rights. Being an Oxford graduate of German, I have a love of languages and all things international as well as experience in Creative Writing. Having spent a month work shadowing in a publishing house, I learned how the business runs, the basics of project management and the importance of teamwork and collaboration.

Career Changer

BEFORE

I'm currently teaching in a primary school and always loved books. My day involves lesson planning and teaching lessons, finding interesting projects for the children that align with the curriculum and deputising for the headmistress. I'd like to bring these skills and a qualification in proofreading to publishing.

AFTER

I'm a primary school teacher with a qualification in editing and proofreading, whilst having full knowledge of the key-stage curriculum and excellent administrative skills. I've also been immersing myself in the world of Educational Publishing and have gained an understanding

> **TOP TIP**
> Analyse which part of your job search is letting you down. If you are not getting interviews, it is down to your CV and Covering Letter; if you are getting interviews but not getting the job, it is a mixture of your CV, covering letter and your interview performance.

of the demands and challenges, as well as how to appeal to readers of all ages and develop a child's imaginative skills.

4. Key skills / Skills profile

This is where you list your skills as bullet points, so that the immediate focus is on your skills matching the job you are applying for. On the surface it appears to be a relatively simple tool to use, and that is why it is probably the most popular of all the tools and it has been around a long time. Yet, when you delve into people's key skills profiles, you realise that they can actually be as poorly written as a personal profile.

The aim of a skills profile is to highlight and emphasise your skills across ALL your career history, not necessarily the latest role. Key skills can help immensely if you are transferring from a different industry (e.g. in an editorial or marketing role in a bank or restaurant chain) or sector (e.g. from academic to trade, or from sales to editorial) as the recruiter instantly sees you have the skills for the job rather than focusing on the fact they aren't necessarily gained in the exact publishing environment.

How many bulleted points should you go for? This depends on your experience. I estimate a minimum of four if you're starting out and up to nine for senior staff, but it really depends on the message you want to get across instantly to the recruiter.

This is an example of a poor skills profiles:

- *Editing Skills*
- *Communication Skills*
- *Administration Skills*
- *Social Media Skills*
- *Managing Skills*

At senior level I have seen these written as:

- *Writing*
- *Commissioning*
- *Editing/Copy editing*
- *Page Layout*
- *Proofreading*
- *Events Management*

You might rewrite the skills like the following:

- *Editing catalogues, newsletters and business documents*
- *Communicating with internal and external suppliers*
- *Dealing with daily administration*
- *Responsible for the company's social media profile*
- *Experienced at managing a team*

You may think you have done a good job with the rewrite, but still it has limited context.

However, the best kind of skills profile is one that has foundation and gives quantities and achievements – if you have them – so it reads less like a job description and more like what you CAN do. All the time, think what you CAN do and what you CAN bring and make the job your own.

For this I created a CAN acronym to use with clients:

- Context – What you did, the skill; how did you use it?
- Achievement – How well you did it; were there any notable successes?
- Numbers (or people) – Add numbers and quantities where possible. Think about the size or frequency of what you did and who you were interacting with. This is where, if parts of your job have been measurable – sales, followers, return on investment (ROI), increased turnover, engagement – then mention the measure without necessarily disclosing what could be seen as confidential company information.

- *Editing bi-annual catalogues, weekly newsletters and proofreading regular company mailshots for other departments*
- *Communicating on deadlines and printing costs with internal colleagues in production, marketing and editorial*
- *Liaising with external suppliers, freelance contributors, printers and distributors throughout the production process*
- *Responsible for daily administration including answering incoming calls, providing customer service, managing the diaries for three directors and filing for the department*
- *Experience in developing TikTok, Facebook and Instagram Accounts from scratch to over 10,000 followers*

If you are writing these when replying to a job advertisement and you have the experience they require, look for the keywords they used in the advert (e.g. printers and distributors), and ensure they are your keywords too. However, do not replicate every single word on the advertisement – it is lazy and way too obvious.

It is personal preference here whether to use active or past tense for your key skills as a tool on your CV. The format usually is past job, past tense; current job, present tense, and always watch word repetition. You should not have the word "experience" in every single line!

Other examples of well-written skills profiles could be:

Recent Graduate

BEFORE
- Self-Motivated
- Excellent Communication and Organisation Skills
- Works well as a team and alone

AFTER (using information from their CV)
- Administrative experience, including diary management and answering enquiries
- Familiar with being the first point of contact in a customer service environment
- An understanding of editorial, marketing and social media (Instagram, TikTok)

- Organised and can prioritise a busy workload
- Experienced with Microsoft Excel and Adobe InDesign

Marketing Assistant

BEFORE

- Creating social media content for personal book blog, book review account
- Creating accessible synopsis of a broad variety of literature, offering recommendations and explanations as to why
- Creating social media content
- Liaising with authors and proofreading the work they send to ensure it is understandable and gives suitable insight to their work

AFTER

- Creating social media content for a personal book review Instagram account
- Writing a synopsis of each book so that it is accessible to readers, offering recommendations
- Developing a new social media network in order to promote the work of unpublished writers I have met through local book clubs and reading groups
- Proofreading authors' works to ensure they are fit for publication

Editorial Co-ordinator

BEFORE

- Writing & Communication: Expertise in creating engaging and articulate content, adhering to diverse style guides, and ensuring clarity and coherence in written materials.
- Organization & Project Management: Skilled at prioritizing and balancing varied workloads, ensuring the timely achievement of personal and team goals.

- Collaboration: Experience in team environments, collaborating with colleagues to achieve seamless communication and task completion.
- IT Proficiency: Advanced user of Microsoft Office Suite, with basic skills in Canva and Adobe InDesign. Eager to upskill and quick to learn new programmes.

AFTER

- Expertise in creating engaging and articulate content, adhering to diverse style guides, and ensuring clarity and coherence in written materials
- Excellent in team environments, collaborating with colleagues to achieve seamless communication and task completion
- Skilled at prioritising and balancing varied workloads, ensuring the timely achievement of personal and team goals
- Advanced user of Microsoft Office Suite (Word, Excel, PowerPoint, Outlook), with basic skills in Canva and Adobe InDesign

AFTER EXAMPLES

Generalist

- Comprehensive knowledge of trade and academic book publishing across all departments, roles and tasks
- Understanding of current and future developments in publishing and the skills that are required to deliver these, such as Digital, POD, eBooks, Audio, AI and new markets

Sales Executive

- Consistently produces higher sales over budget, achieving 65% increase last year
- Selling, marketing and negotiating to wholesalers, supermarkets, chains/multiples, key and specialist accounts at a management level

Commissioning Editor
- Commissioning 20–25 books a year, via agents, ideas sent into the publisher and sourcing authors through relevant organisations and other contacts
- Experience in quality illustrated non-fiction in print and eBooks
- Structural editing and re-writing: helping authors to present their material in the clearest, most readable and most accessible form and clarifying their ideas

5. Separating your experiences

Separating your experiences is a great tool for those who are career-changing or are mature students, or if you are working in a different industry whilst looking for your first publishing role. It involves separating your publishing and book industry experience and all your non-publishing experience, and if you've completed a Master's in Publishing, worked in a bookshop or volunteered at a Literary Festival, including them under your publishing experience. See the example below:

Example:
BEFORE (with your full information for each role)
- *NHS Healthcare Administrative Assistant (current role)*
- *Work Experience Joe Blogs Publisher (2 weeks)*
- *Carphone Warehouse (past role)*
- *Publishing Internship (6 months)*
- *Volunteer Literary Festival*
- *Publishing Degree*

AFTER (with your full information for each role)
- *Publishing Experience*
- *Work Experience Joe Blogs Publisher (2 weeks)*
- *Publishing Internship (6 months)*
- *Volunteer Literary Festival*
- *Publishing Degree*

Other Experience
- *NHS Healthcare Administrative Assistant (current role)*
- *Carphone Warehouse (past role)*

Writing your job and career history

When it comes to describing your career history you should follow the same principle as if you are writing your key skills, except use more narrative if necessary. Your brief should not only show the responsibilities you have or had, but also your achievements within them too. If possible, the style should reflect the job advertisement you are responding to, as well as the skills and competencies required.

If you are already in work and have a current official job description to work from, you might use this as a guide, but do not copy and paste it into your CV, as the vocabulary is likely to be very wordy and too formal. Instead, write your skills and competencies clearly so it is easy for someone else (who might not understand your current role) to see what you were actually doing, what you achieved, and how you made the job your own, as well as any skills and competencies you can bring to a new role.

It is no good saying:

Production Assistant – I assisted the production department.

What did that involve? How did you do this?

Instead, by writing the following, you could give some clarity:

Production Assistant – I helped co-ordinate the production schedules, liaising with the editorial, marketing and sales departments.

If you are repeatedly not getting selected for interview but have the skills and competencies for the role for which you are applying, the reason may be a poorly written CV. Read through your CV word for word and understand the points you want to get across so that a recruiter employs you.

For example:

I spent six months here as an intern and have since been promoted to Production Editor.

This would read much better on a CV as:

I am currently employed as a Production Editor (list the tasks). Prior to this I was an intern for six months and they were so happy with my work they decided to keep me on and have since promoted me.

However, you need to avoid buzzwords – topical words and phrases that come in and go out of fashion, as well as stock CV phrases and hyperbole. Buzzwords to avoid, unless they are mentioned in a positive way in the job advertisement, are phrases such as 'Blue Sky Thinking', '360-degree feedback' and 'engaging stakeholders'.

Industry buzzwords or trends relating to publishing are fine.

For example:

- *Digital*
- *eBooks*
- *Online*
- *Open Access*
- *Web*
- *Social Media*

So, when you are making the job your own, think about:

- What have you done to make a difference?
- What impact have you made?
- What have you achieved?
- Have you introduced any systems?
- Did you reorganise anything (even something like reorganising the filing system to improve efficiency counts)?
- Did you create any new strategies or make any suggestions that resulted in increased turnover?
- Did you develop social media platforms to increase follower count and engagement?
- Did you attend any festivals or conferences to learn or help increase brand awareness?

All these points add weight to your role and demonstrate how you could make a difference in a new role. If you are struggling with this, think about something that you did that you know your predecessor didn't do, and if you haven't done anything differently to your predecessor, maybe you have already been asked to leave the company or your job is being made redundant.

There is a tendency when writing bullet points to strip them down completely, skip words (as in CV speak) and make them all single sentences. Remember, this is book publishing; we are a words business. The person reading your CV is likely to be an avid reader. Clear, coherent explanations of tasks that a recruiter can relate to are more likely to gain an affirmative response than short soundbites with words missing.

For example:

Responsible for booking in manuscripts

could become

Responsible for booking in manuscripts and allocating them to the appropriate editor

However, if you are following the CAN guidelines, your bullet point should read more like this:

Responsible for booking in more than 300 manuscripts a year, and allocating them to the appropriate editor, chasing up readers' reports where necessary

Example – Marketing Assistant
BEFORE
Within this role, I am mainly responsible for finding new independent advertising partnerships from across London. I assist the Magazine's Head of Partnerships in maintaining our roster of clients. My daily tasks include invoicing, creating our weekly newsletter, meeting with potential sales leads, and attending important events across the city as company representative.

AFTER

- *Creating a weekly newsletter using MailChimp that was sent to over 10,000 subscribers*
- *Raising monthly invoices and tracking payments, chasing where necessary*
- *Writing copy for social posts (Instagram, Facebook, LinkedIn) and checking on engagement. I increased our following by 50%*
- *Using Google Analytics to check on our website and social media performance*
- *Attending launches and local events as a PR representative, deputising for the Department Head*
- *Administrative support for the whole team, including booking meetings, typing up minutes and following up sales leads*

Example of Journal Publishing to Trade Publishing

BEFORE

Journals Editorial Assistant

- *Editorial Office management of multiple STM and SSH titles, including the migration of journals from external to internal editorial management; the implementation of procedures to improve and enhance client service; and updating systems and revising websites to improve efficiency and ethical practice.*
- *Managing the submission systems for multiple journals, checking papers against specific journal style and returning to authors when necessary.*
- *Promptly answering correspondence. Providing system support, managing authorship concerns and reconciling author, reviewer and editor disputes.*
- *Training and overseeing external (vendor) editorial assistants. Creating procedures manuals, giving training and acting as a point of contact.*
- *Writing copy and author guidelines for journal websites. Updating relevant media platforms using HTML and Rich Text.*

AFTER

Editorial Assistant

- *Managing the submission systems for multiple publications, checking against specific house style and returning to authors where necessary*
- *Promptly answering correspondence. Providing system support, managing authorship concerns and reconciling author, reviewer and editor queries*
- *Training and overseeing editorial assistants. Creating procedure manuals and acting as a point of contact and team leader*
- *Writing copy and author guidelines for websites. Updating relevant media platforms using HTML and Rich Text*

Adding a preamble

Very often, when writing about your current or previous role, particularly if you want to explain something unique about it, a good idea could be to add a preamble or introduction to your role or employer. That way, the person assessing your CV can understand precisely your relevance to the role you are applying for.

This is particularly useful for career-changers, as well as those working in different sectors of publishing, or whose job title might not instantly seem an immediate fit, such as working as an Editorial Assistant at an organisation that was not a book publisher or for a book publisher in a different sector. If you are going to use a preamble, then do a good editorial job and be consistent by writing a preamble for similar past roles.

Example

Photographer's Assistant, Bookcareers Photography Ltd

I work for the agency used by major publishers such as Bloggs, Joe and David for all the interior photographs of their books. I communicate on a daily basis with the publishers' editorial and art departments

- *Taking bookings for meeting rooms, liaising with the editorial departments and assisting with layouts*
- *Editing photographs using Photoshop to ensure they are of a file format and quality suitable for publication*

Describing Placements and Internships

Many people decide to do a placement of two weeks or more at a publishing house before they look for a job. Most of these placements are now paid the living wage, although if you are still in education, under the 1998 National Minimum Wage Act, you may be able to find an unpaid placement (but you should still receive expenses). However, these are increasingly rare, and hopefully will soon be phased out altogether. As I said earlier, always choose paid work.

Very often on a CV, I see students exaggerating what they did within a placement or trying to make it look as if it was for a longer period of time than it was. There is no need to do this; no one expects you to be running the company during a brief placement.

Example:

During a two-week placement I edited a manuscript, wrote a book report and participated in an Editorial Meeting.

And whilst the placement was for two weeks, it crossed over into different months, so on a CV, it might look like:

November–December Bookcareers Publishing Work Placement

During a two-week placement I edited a manuscript, wrote a book report and participated in an Editorial Meeting.

The reality is that everyone who works in book publishing knows what happens in a two-week placement. You might have been given some tasks, but it is highly unlikely that you were given a level of responsibility that you have described. Even if you think you were, you can guarantee that someone in the company has checked or, in some cases, not used your work. As a result, it is far better to explain it as a two-week placement where you got to learn about publishing and the different departments, rather than dress it up as something it was not.

To avoid any misleading information about the dates of the placement (see above section on dates under *CV Basics*), it is always best to be clear how long it was on your CV.

Therefore, a well-worded placement might look like:

Bookcareers Publishing Work Placement

During a two-week placement I shadowed the Editor, wrote a book report and sat in on Editorial and Marketing Meetings. It was a great opportunity to find out how a publishing house operated and confirmed my commitment to a career in Editorial.

BEFORE

J. Doe Publishing London – October 2024 (1 week)
- Work experience as part of the sales team
- Completed a variety of office-based tasks and took part in team meetings
- Gained valuable experience working with Microsoft Office (Excel, PowerPoint, Teams) and software Biblio and Nielsen
- Received an expansive overview of different roles within a publishing company

AFTER

J. Doe Publishing London – October 2024 (1 week)

I spent a week in the Sales Department where I got to understand the whole publishing process and work with the wider Sales Team.

I undertook the following tasks:
- *Created a PowerPoint of the titles that were being published next year*
- *Updated an Excel Spreadsheet with current sales figures*
- *Helped the Team Assistant create book dummies*
- *Attended a team cover meeting, where rough designs were previewed and discussions held*
- *Other meetings I participated in were a Special Sales Meeting and a Design meeting*
- *I learned how to use Biblio and Nielsen BookScan*

CVs for those leaving education / When you have no work history

One of the hardest things to do is write a CV when you feel you have little or nothing to say as you are just starting out after having left education. During your time in education, especially if you are at university, make the most of the University Careers

Department. They are usually very helpful in preparing students for the world of work. Whilst you're at university, and even for a limited time when you become an alumnus, this guidance is free. It is also very important for the university to know if you are not yet in work after graduating, because they rely on student success stories when recruiting new students, so may give you extra assistance.

However, I often see recent graduates advised to fill their CV with a faux skills profile, as aside from your education and maybe part-time jobs, you have limited experience. Whilst it might work in other industries, in book publishing, it instantly says that you have nothing to offer:

Example of a bad/faux skills profile:

Communication Skills *I was an effective communicator at university. I communicated with all of my fellow students and my lecturer*

Writing Skills *I wrote a thesis of 20,000 words*

Research Skills *I researched my thesis and did a huge amount of research for my lectures*

Teamwork *I shared my research with my fellow students*

Proofreading *I proofread my thesis and those of my fellow students. They always said I was grate at spotting mistakes*

This uses lots of words that say nothing, and an experienced recruiter is likely to instantly dismiss it as waffle, especially if it takes up most of a whole page. So please do not create a faux skills profile like this. Even if you have only a little to say there are much better ways of expressing it.

For example:

- Any holiday work – see if you can expand on this.

Costa Coffee, Barista, [add dates]
Serving coffee, keeping the kitchen clean, welcoming customers, having a friendly disposition and learnt how to deal with difficult people

SEC Lawyers, [add dates]
Filing Assistant

If you really have nothing but your school, college or university experience:

- What did you do away from your education?
- Were you a member of any special societies or organisations?
- Have you volunteered anywhere?
- What social media do you use, how do you use it?

University Rowing Club
Used Instagram to promote social events for the Rowing Club

Even if you have absolutely no experience, focus on adding a little more detail to your education or any of the computer software you can use.

If you're a graduate, write two to three lines about your degree. Did you choose modules, and what were they? Did you complete a dissertation or major project, and what was the subject?

If you can't find anything else to add to your limited career history, this is where you might add things such as, "This involved researching more than 5,000 different photographs and choosing a cover photograph."

Alternatively, you created a survey, designing the questionnaire, garnering more than 200 responses and analysing the responses before writing a report.

By spending time to break down your limited experience in this way, as opposed to taking the faux skills path, someone can instantly see what you can do, rather than being made visibly aware of what you can't do or haven't done.

On every CV, either as the last line of your skills profile, or on the second page, under 'Other Information', you should list your software skills. There are a few reasons for this:

1. We are still living in an age where some people don't have a wide variety of software skills, and this affects both young and old. When you don't mention an aspect of software, the instant assumption is that you do not know how to use it.

2. When you upload your CV to any generic job site, the software they use is doing a keyword check looking for keywords relating to computer software.

Many people are caught out when mentioning software packages on their CV. Some people have just basic words:

Microsoft 365 and Adobe Creative Suite

This is not enough information. Do you think the keyword checker will be looking for the word 365 (as in Microsoft 365)? Or do you think it might be looking for a unique word like PowerPoint?

Even then, you need to expand further and demonstrate some of those brilliant editing skills.

Often I see:

Microsoft 365 (Word, Excel, PowerPoint), Adobe InDesign and Photoshop

However, if you do a good editorial job on your CV, the correct format should be:

Microsoft Office (Word, Excel, PowerPoint), Adobe Creative Suite (InDesign, Photoshop)

Consistency is vitally important if you are to edit a book with any lists, so follow this style on your CV and make sure the names of the software manufacturers, their packages and components of the packages are consistent.

When you are grading your software experience, be honest. If you are a beginner at InDesign, mention that you are a beginner; if you are advanced, then say it.

How much of a beginner are you? When can you mention a software package on your CV? These are the guidelines I recommend you to use when describing your levels of software skills:

Beginner
If are confident enough to sit at a computer, open a document and start working on the basics.

Intermediate

If are confident enough to sit at a computer, open a document, start working on formulas and funky stuff, and know the protocols of the software.

Advanced

You should have every confidence that you know the software like the back of your hand, can create amazing things with it and can teach others.

One word to avoid using when describing your experience on your CV is the word proficient. Sadly, proficient has become frequently misused on CVs, and some people think that the word actually means basic and adequate rather than the dictionary definition (competent, skilled, accomplished, practised, seasoned). Because of this abuse, I advise clients to avoid using the word altogether and use more descriptive and quantifiable words, such as 'beginner', 'intermediate' and 'advanced' or any adjectives that are in a dictionary as definitions of proficient.

Education

An important section of your CV will be your past education. This should be on your CV after your work history, not before it. The only time this advice might differ is if you've studied publishing at degree or master's level and you are separating your publishing and non-publishing experience. Otherwise, have your work history first.

It is important to list all your qualifications and places of education, although you might condense the words and information. If you are a recent graduate or you have studied publishing, it can be handy to list a dissertation or major project as part of the description for your education, as well as any special modules and your pass mark, if known.

For secondary level experience, a list of qualifications attained is usually sufficient.

Example

BA English Literature 2.1, UCL

Modules: 18th century crime fiction, female authors

Dissertation: Diverse voices in 20th century literature

A Levels: English Literature (A), French (B), Music (B), Clare School, London

GCSEs: Maths (B), English Language (A), English Literature (A), French (B), Music (A), Geography (B), History (A), Clare School, London

Training

If you've undertaken any training that could be relevant to your job search, either informal self-study or via a formal training course, you might want to add a section on your CV to cover this or include it in an additional section.

Languages

Mention on your CV if you are able to speak or write in more than one language. The importance of languages within the role you are applying for, such as Rights or International Sales, will depend where on your CV you place this information. If it is essential, critical or desirable for the role, it could be best to mention them in your Profile, Strapline or Key Skills and then duplicate the languages elsewhere on your CV. This can be either as part of a job description, education, training or in an additional section. Be clear about the languages you can speak and the ones you can write, and how fluent or basic you are.

Interests

The section on your CV relating to personal interests was created at a time when most people left school at 15 or 16 and had nothing but a handful of qualifications when applying for a job. Try to imagine you are an interviewer during those times. In front of you is a 16-year-old. You are thinking about giving them an entry-level job and they are extremely nervous and very shy, What do you think you would ask them to help them relax and maybe talk about themselves? Maybe, you'd ask them, "What do you like doing outside of school?" The 16-year-old would then go on to talk about their interests, and this could lead into some of the tasks and skills that might be involved in the job.

Your situation is very different from this. I've seen one or two large corporations, outside of publishing, say that if you don't put your interests on your CV that you are not a well-rounded person, or you are one-dimensional but, in all honesty, I have yet to see such a negative attitude in book publishing. Aside from which, even if you don't mention interests on your CV, you could still be asked about them at an interview, and one of those questions is likely to be about the books you like to read.

Surveys outside of the publishing industry give mixed views on the importance of interests on CVs; some said that interests on a CV were irrelevant. However, interests can be important if they are relevant to the job you are going for, or on a subject that could be beneficial to understanding the genres of your future employer. They can also be a useful discussion point or icebreaker at the start of an interview; in the same way they can also be prejudicial and allow stereotypes to be formed.

I leave it up to you whether you keep your interests on or off your CV, but I would recommend keeping them on if the interests you have relate to skills, experiences or interests that are relevant to the job you are applying for.

Examples:
1. Travel publisher, a love of travel (maybe with a list of places you have visited)
2. An Art History publisher (visiting museums, galleries, exhibitions)

There also might be voluntary experiences or other achievements you have attained that you might want to mention or feel are relevant.

For example, it may surprise you to learn that I am a qualified aerobics teacher. For many years I left this qualification off my CV, until I realised that this demonstrated, aside from having some basic teaching skills, I could motivate others enough that they wanted to join the classes I ran. It also meant that I could plan a lesson and keep people interested enough that they would come back the following week.

TOP TIP
Always remember that your CV is a statement of fact showing where you've been. Your Covering Letter says where you are going, why you want to work for the publisher and what skills you can bring with you.

Additional or Other Information

Sometimes on your CV you might want to add additional information that doesn't fit into any other subheading of work history, education or voluntary work. In this case, a heading of 'Additional Information' or 'Other Information' could come in handy. Items that could go in this section include if you have a current Driving Licence, for instance. This is also a good section to include information about languages or training, if you haven't been able to find a suitable place for them elsewhere on your CV. It is up to you what you put under this heading.

References

Unless you have a key Referee, who might be good to name drop on the bottom of your CV (although this carries less weight than it previously did), the expected format and phrase is "References available on request". This will also release some space on your CV if you have referees listed.

General Office CV

Whatever level you are, from time to time you might be in between contracts and need to find some temporary office work, either in publishing or any industry. For this a generalist office CV is usually best. It lets the recruiter see instantly what you CAN do, and you may find you get more interviews and temporary assignments as a result.

This type of CV is less about your career history and more about your skills.

An example is:

- *Office Skills*
    - *Excellent at communicating with clients, customers and internal colleagues and external suppliers*
    - *Typing 60 wpm; familiar with both Windows and Mac computers*
    - *Organising events, meetings and conferences from 10 to 300 people*
    - *Good telephone manner*

- *Familiar with all office equipment (list any special equipment you can use)*

- *Computer packages:*
  - *(Advanced): Microsoft 365 (Word, Excel, Outlook)*
  - *(Intermediate): Adobe Creative Suite (InDesign)*
  - *(Basic): Microsoft 365 (Access, PowerPoint), Adobe Creative Suite (Photoshop), HTML*

And then list your work history.

Final checks

There are three final checks to do before emailing your CV.

1. File size

    It is always a good idea to check the file size of your CV to ensure there are no bugs in it. A CV is usually less than 1MB in size. Whilst computer speeds are faster and it will still download quickly, imagine that the HR Manager might view CVs on their mobile or iPad.

2. Page count

    The second check is to print out your CV and make sure there are neither errant characters nor extra pages (that the page endings are working and you're not printing three pages, two with text and one blank) and give it a final proofread.

3. Date and time

    The last check before you email your CV is to ensure the date-stamp on your CV is the same day as you are emailing it (and ideally the time isn't at 3.00 am). If the date or time is older, it is quite easy to change – it won't matter if the time is a few minutes out. If it is an old CV (and I hope it isn't!), resave the document. If you haven't edited it, you'll probably need to 'Save As' and overwrite the file.

This is particularly important if you are asked to quickly send a CV and you want to send a version that you used for a very similar job and don't have time to update it. This may happen at a networking event, a chance conversation on social media or an informal approach on LinkedIn.

Always ensure the date and time stamp is the same date and time you are emailing your CV, because recruiters do check.

For example, when I advertised a part-time job on social media, I had about 10 CVs through within the first 24 hours. At least seven CVs were dated three months earlier. This indicated to me as a recruiter that the candidate hadn't even bothered to look at or update their CV before applying.

You want to give the best possible impression of yourself to a recruiter; you want them to believe that you crafted your CV especially for them, for that job, because your skills are perfect for the role, and that is how much you want to work there.

Be the best possible professional version of yourself that you can.

> **TOP TIP**
> Tailor your CV and Covering Letter for every job you apply for. By doing this you are automatically likely to be in the top 20% of candidates for the role, because 80% of applicants won't bother to do this.

Is your CV too good?

I was working with a client who always seemed to end up in the wrong job. They'd end up in a job where they would be working on something they weren't interested in or would take on a role that was too complex, too demanding or not appropriate for their favoured skills. When we started to analyse why this was happening, I came to the conclusion their CV was a generalist CV and they'd made it too good, too perfect, and they were getting every job they applied for, whether it was appropriate for them or not, and whether they had any interest in it or not, as they always interviewed well.

They had emphasised skills on their CV that they may have had and been competent in, but in discussions, they admitted they hated using. Nonetheless, they were applying for jobs that had these skills at the forefront. In the job interviews they were saying, 'yes, I can do that', and getting the job on the back of this, and then wondering why they were always unhappy.

EXERCISE

If you're always updating and adding to your CV, instead of giving it a complete rework, or you think now is the time for it to have a complete rework, then do the following exercise.

Print out a copy of your CV. Take a pair of scissors to it and cut it into sections, different jobs, skills, interests, education and switch it all around.

You might think you would be better served doing this on a computer and cutting and pasting. However, if you've been in employment for a while, it can be a good idea to examine every part of your CV and start again.

Be sure of every word and phrase that is written. It might be there is something on your CV you haven't updated in many years as it is part of your past history, and it now needs to be rewritten or removed. You also need to review your whole CV now you are rewriting your skills to give them some context. This is part of what I described earlier as Context, Achievements and Numbers (CAN).

ACTION POINTS

Without looking at your CV, think about three skills that you HAVE NOW that you believe you will need or utilise in the job you want.

Write down these three skills. Now, look at your CV and count to 5. How many of the three skills you identified can you find in 5 seconds? Sadly, when an employer looks at your CV, they may glance at it for as few as 5 or as many as 10 seconds. That very sorry state of affairs is why you need to identify the skills you need for the job you are applying for and that you already have. Make them clear on your CV; you can do this with the use of the tools detailed in this chapter. It also explains why narrative CVs, ones that are complete paragraphs of text, rarely help you get a job.

Look through the last CV you sent in response to a job advertisement. On reflection, how well do you think it matched the skills and competencies required?

Which tools do you think you could have used to express your skills clearly?

What tools are you thinking of using in the future?

CHAPTER SIX

Covering Letters That Work

"Nothing excites me more than reading a well-written Covering Letter."
Charlotte Hussein, former Director, Human Resources at Wiley

"Whatever you write, when you write your Covering Letter, make sure you APPLY FOR THE JOB in the first line of text. So many people fail to do this and then wonder why they don't get called back for an interview."

Suzanne Collier

Writing a winning Covering Letter is a challenge but the good news is, once you get into the habit of writing a Covering Letter that gets the right response, it is easy to emulate it, without you copying words and phrases that you have used before. One client kept a folder of words and phrases that they liked to use again and again and wondered why they were always being rejected. The problem with reusing old words and phrases is that they are unlikely to be directly related to the job you are applying for, and therefore the letter would read like a page of soundbites, rather than a well-crafted and well-written Covering Letter. Plus, if you didn't get a job or interview when you first used those words and phrases, what guarantee do you have they would work another time?

The quote at start of the chapter, by Charlotte Hussein, formerly Director of Human Resources at Wiley, "Nothing excites me more than reading a well-written Covering Letter," came when we were discussing video applications. This is particularly true in book publishing because our lives revolve around words.

Always write a Covering Letter from a fresh page; it is much easier to do this and add words than to edit a previous letter. The skills you will learn in this chapter will show you how easy writing a Covering Letter can be.

Before we go into how to do this, let's get some basics right:

Length of the letter

Your Covering Letter should be no more than one side of A4 paper, excluding any additional information they have asked you to include (such as "Tell me about a book ..."). If you are looking at word count, you should aim for a total of 450–850 words, including your name, contact details and their name. Less than 400 words, you have not written enough, and if it is 900 words or more, you may need to give your Covering Letter a good edit!

Contact details

Always ensure your contact details are clear at the top of the letter and include your telephone number (or numbers) and email address. For consistency, I recommend that you copy and paste the contact details from your CV, so the documents match.

As with your CV, don't use headers, footers or text boxes as they may not be read in certain views or be picked up by applicant tracking systems.

Consistency in font size

For the best impression, it is recommended to use the same font size as you do on your CV. This is another reason why you should not go below 10pt, and aim to use the same readable, current TrueType font as your CV. It's a publishing thing; you want your documents to match.

Do not top and tail your Covering Letter

Topping and tailing a letter means changing the first paragraph and the last paragraph and changing all instances of where you have used the company name. It is SO obvious when a candidate does this. It is lazy, unprofessional and because it is so easy to spot, the recruiter might assume you haven't read the advertisement properly.

Do not use AI to write any part of your Covering Letter

Unless you are specifically asked to use AI in your Covering Letter or application, do not use AI. The way some grammar-checkers work can introduce AI speak into your letter. It is very important that the letter is in your words, phrases and grammar; it is a test of your writing skill – after all, you want to work in a business that values writing as a skill. Whatever role you get, you are likely to be writing emails and correspondence, as well as marketing or editorial collateral too. In addition, the way AI currently machine learns could mean that someone else will have precisely the same words and phrases as your letter, even though these words originated from you.

Remember to lay it out like a letter

Align the text to the left, put the date on your letter and the name of the publisher or imprint. You don't need to put the full address of the publisher; you'll need the space as you need to stick to one side of A4 paper. When you have a job, you may have to communicate via written letter instead of an email, so this is your opportunity to demonstrate that you know how to lay out a business letter.

> Dear Whoever,
>
> When starting your letter "Dear ...," if you do not have the name of the person to whom your application is being sent, but only a Recruitment@ email or know it is for a particular imprint, then address it to them.
>
> E.g. *Dear Recruitment at Hachette*
> Or *Dear Sales Team at Vintage*

If you know the name of the person who is recruiting but applications are still being sent to a generic recruitment @ email address, then it is fine to start with "Dear Name".

If the email address is the name of the person, e.g. "janesmith@" and it gives two names and you don't know them, then address it as "Dear Jane Smith,". If it is one name "jane@" then it is fine to address it as "Dear Jane," but do double-check the rest of the advertisement hasn't mentioned her name in full.

> E.g. *please apply to Jane Smith, Jane@*

If you do not know the name of the person who will receive the application, always aim to personalise it with the company name rather than using the staid term, "Dear Sir or Madam," and never use "Dear Sir," on its own. This is because if you know anything about book publishing, 80% of people who work in the industry are female; also, there are other gender options aside from Sir or Madam.

If you are going to use the word "Madam," please ensure you use "Madam," and not "Madame," as one client did.

You no longer need to search for hours for the name of someone to whom to address a letter if you don't already know it – unless it is a sole person business and then it should be easy to find (e.g. Suzanne at bookcareers.com). This is because EDI policies mean you are unlikely to be marked up for finding out the name; someone who is from a lower socio-economic background and busy working in other jobs might not have the time to go searching. However, if you have the name of a person and you misspell it, then you are likely to be marked down.

Yours faithfully or Yours sincerely

The correct usage of the words 'faithfully' and 'sincerely' are as follows:

> Opening *"Dear Sir or Madam"* (or any version of this); closing *"Yours faithfully"*.
>
> Opening A company name, an individual name, a friendly address, or anything else *"Dear"*; closing *"Yours sincerely"*.

If the letter is addressed to someone you know already, then it is fine to sign off with "Best wishes" or "Kind regards", or a similar term, but remember, professionalism is key when it comes to Covering Letters.

TOP TIP

Always write a Covering Letter from a fresh page and write it around the job advertisement. The publisher has told you what they want. How in the letter can you demonstrate you are the person they are looking for?

Your opening sentence

This is really important, as you need to apply for the job! I undertook considerable research on this after working with a client who sent out six letters and only got called to an interview for two jobs, but they were the perfect candidate for all six. The four they missed out on all started the opening paragraph with waffle about the company and not saying: *"I would like to apply for the role"*.

When you write your opening sentence make a firm statement:

- "I am applying for the position"
- "I would like to apply for the role of"
- "Please accept this as my application for the role of"

Or something similar.

What you don't want to say is:

"I hope you will consider me for the role of …"

'Hope' indicates that you have little confidence in your skills and expertise.

Or

"I am writing to apply for the role of …"

Of course you are writing, it is your letter!

Or

"Hello, my name is …"

It is your letter, your name should be at the top of the page, not in the content of the letter. In addition, starting your letter like this detracts from the matter in hand.

File Size

As with your CV, check the file size isn't too large.

Page Layout

If you asked me if there was a template for writing a Covering Letter, I would say "YES, there is!" Although I wouldn't call it a template; they are more like a set of guidelines.

We live in a world where, whilst we are all readers, our attention span has dropped, and this means that the best Covering Letters have no paragraph with more than eight lines of text. If you tend to write overlong paragraphs yourself, you can test this by splitting the paragraph halfway and seeing how much more readable the text on the page appears.

The page should look like:

Dear

2-4 lines

4-8 lines

4-8 lines

4-8 lines

4-8 lines if you need them

2-4 lines

Yours sincerely / faithfully

Traditionally you might have been told to break down your Covering Letter as per the example below. This order is not set in stone, apart from the first and last paragraphs, and you should reorder the paragraphs so that it reads like a letter. Yes, I cannot reiterate this enough, a Covering Letter should read like a letter, not a stilted statement of puffed-up facts about yourself.

Dear

2-4 lines – Apply for the job in the first sentence, where you saw the job advertised and the date of the advert if it was in a print publication.

4-8 lines – Why you want to work for them and how your critical skills match the role without saying, "I want to work for you because …"

4-8 lines – The hard skills you can bring – the skills you can be tested on, such as editorial, sales, marketing, rights, production.

4-8 lines – The soft skills you can bring – the skills you need to put the job together, and demonstrate you work well with others such as communication, organisation, time management.

4-8 lines – Any Other Business (AOB). Anything else they have asked for, such as salary expectations or availability for interview, or other relevant information you would like to mention that you haven't yet.

2 lines – Look forward to hearing from you shortly and am available for interview at your convenience.

Yours sincerely/faithfully

The reason why this traditional guidance no longer works as well as it did previously is because, when you follow the rough outline, it isn't indicating what exactly to say. You need more flexibility than this to write the best Covering Letter, one that will win you an interview and ultimately the job.

You need to make the letter feel less formulaic and about you, when really you need to be writing about them! Writing about them? Yes, the best Covering Letters focus on the company, the job and what skills you can bring. Remember from *Chapter Five: CVs That Get You Noticed*, your CV is a statement of fact showing where you have been. Your Covering Letter says where you are going, why you want to work for the publisher and what skills you can bring with you.

Initially, this might seem a time-consuming way to write a Covering Letter but with practice you will speed up. However, without realising it, when you really want the job, you're probably already spending hours or days stressing and mulling over what you want to write.

The following process will help you organise your thoughts, take the worry out of the situation and should find your application-to-interview ratio (your hit rate) go up. In addition, when you write your Covering Letter in this way, you will automatically include the key points, and this will help you sail through any human selection or AI system that might be used for the initial sift.

How to plan your letter

Find the job advertisement, or the full job description if they have made one available, grab yourself a notebook and pen and go through the job advertisement line by line, highlighting key words but also noting how you match each skill or requirement, remembering to include your transferrable skills.

To make it easier, look at each statement as a set of questions:

- Can you do this?
- Do you have experience of this?

Then write down your answers:

- I have done this.
- I have the skills for this.
- This is like something I've already done.

Think, too, about any connection you have with the publisher, its books, any other skill you think is important, anything else you want to say about the role and any relevant achievements you can mention.

This is very much like the preparation you will do for an interview but is not necessarily so detailed as you don't need to evidence every single point.

By doing this, you should have a good list of points now.

TOP TIP

Just as with your CV, your Covering Letter should have a date and time stamp from that day or the one before, and with a reasonable hour. By this, if the time stamp shows you saved the document at 3.00 am, you would hardly be at your freshest or most alert for work later that day. Also, you should ensure the Covering Letter and CV have either the same or consecutive working days on the date stamp. This may seem irrelevant, but a discrepancy or inconsistency might be picked up by someone.

Now compile all these points so they make sense.

As you bring everything together aim to construct real sentences. One of the best ways to do this is to dream that you have been successful, got the job and it is your first day. Think about how excited you are to see this opportunity come up and that you can't wait to get going on your first assignment. Use this enthusiasm and excitement to help you write a proper letter, as though you were writing to a friend. Think about the skills you would be using, the projects you would be working on, the experience you can bring.

Academic, Children's Publishing or different publishing sectors

There are subtle differences in how you write a Covering Letter for different types of publishing sectors, such as Academic or Children's Publishing. However, when you use the method of writing a Covering Letter based around the job advertisement, your observations about the role and tone of writing should naturally adapt to the sector.

For example, with a Journal Publisher, you may be talking about how you are either familiar with the area of journals they publish or the subject area. It is not unusual for you to have no knowledge of the publisher, journals or subject area, in which case, focus on why you want to work for the publisher, and add some information about your academic achievements, if you do not have any work history to discuss. With Children's Publishing, particularly at entry level, they may be looking for signs that you engage with children or still interact with children's books at some level. Again, this should be drawn out when matching your experience to the job advertisement in question.

A practical example of how to write a covering letter

Here is an example of the full process. Whilst the example has been written for this book, and of course, I am used to writing Covering Letters, responding to the job advertisement in this way took approximately 15 minutes from writing out how the candidate matched the job and crafting the initial draft of the

Covering Letter, excluding the time taken to write the example of a book. For someone doing this for the first time, I would expect this to take no more than 60 minutes.

1. Read the Job Advertisement. Here is a job advertisement. (A real job advertisement has been used, with permission, but some specifics anonymised.)

    Bookcareers Publishing has an opening for an Editorial Assistant for our non-fiction list, covering business, leadership and entrepreneurship. This is an entry-level role where enthusiasm and a passion for our books are valued over prior publishing experience (although if you have prior experience, you're welcome to apply too).

    You will be the sole Editorial Assistant and the first port of call for the department.

    Your responsibilities will include:

    - Managing the department inbox that includes all editorial queries
    - Reading and responding to the submissions inbox, looking out for anything suitable to pass to the editorial team
    - Supporting a busy editorial team of three Commissioning Editors and two Desk Editors and liaising with the sales, design, marketing and publicity teams
    - Liaising with authors where necessary
    - Once trained, proofreading, copywriting, proof-checking and clearing permissions
    - Administrative tasks including minute-taking, phone and email queries, post
    - Reading and reporting on manuscripts

    Essential skills include:

    - A voracious reader with demonstrable interest in bookcareers publishing

- An energetic and flexible approach to work, self-motivated with excellent organisational, time management and planning skills
- Excellent verbal and written communication skills and meticulous attention to detail
- **Strong IT skills**

Please apply with a CV and Covering Letter, including no more than 150 words about a book you've read recently.

2. Understand the job advertisement and match your skills; identify any transferable skills. Key words or phrases are underscored here.

Imagine the person wanting to apply for the role is a recent English graduate, who has been working in customer services for a supermarket. They'd previously worked in an office for a month, during summer break, so have good office skills, and, of course, they love reading. They also have a personal interest in the genre. For the purpose of this example, any titles mentioned have all been published by Rethink Press and are used with kind permission of the publisher.

"Bookcareers Publishing has an opening for an Editorial Assistant for our non-fiction list, covering business, leadership and entrepreneurship."

I have a keen interest in business books, as well as leadership and entrepreneurship.

"This is an entry-level role where enthusiasm and a passion for our books are valued over prior publishing experience (although if you have prior experience, you're welcome to apply too)."

I first read **Making College Happen** *as I was trying to find ways to go to university on a budget. I thought it was so well thought out, I looked out other titles and discovered a passion for instructive non-fiction.* **The Uni-Tasking Revolution** *helped me learn to prioritise and organise a heavy workload and* *whilst it is a long way off in the future,* **Become a Successful First Time CEO** *piqued my interest to read further than books directly relevant to me.*

"You will be the <u>sole Editorial Assistant</u> and the <u>first port of call for the department</u>."

As I have office experience as well as working on the customer service desk, I am used to being the first port of call in a very busy environment.

"Your responsibilities will include:

- <u>managing the department inbox</u> that includes all editorial queries"

    I have office experience where I was required to manage the enquiry inbox that received over 200 emails a day, sometimes from very angry people.

- "<u>reading and responding to the submissions inbox</u>, looking out for <u>anything suitable to pass to the editorial team</u>"

    Whilst at university I joined the book and creative writing club and we would often read each other's manuscripts and offer feedback in the form of a reader report. It helped me learn what could have publishing potential, against what writing needed improvement.

- "<u>supporting a busy editorial team</u> of three Commissioning Editors and two Desk Editors"

    During time spent in an office, I reported to three senior members of the team.

- "and <u>liaising with the sales, design, marketing and publicity teams</u>"

    I worked across the business, liaising with other departments.

- "<u>liaising with authors</u> where necessary"

- "Once trained, <u>proofreading, copywriting, proof checking and clearing permissions</u>"

    reading and proofreading other students' manuscripts.

- **"Administrative tasks including <u>minute taking, phone and email queries, post</u>"**

    In the office job I was answering phone and email enquiries.

- **"<u>Reading and reporting on manuscripts</u>"**

    "Essential skills include:

    "<u>A voracious reader</u> with demonstrable <u>interest in bookcareers</u> publishing"

    I am a voracious reader across all genres but really enjoy personal development and business.

- **"An <u>energetic and flexible approach</u> to work, self-motivated with excellent <u>organisational, time management and planning skills</u>"**

    Self-motivated, at times I juggled two jobs around my university work. This required me to be highly organised and practise excellent time management. I like to be productive.

    In my office job I learned how to use Microsoft outlook and to organise tasks.

- **"<u>Excellent verbal and written communication</u> skills and <u>meticulous attention to detail</u>"**

    "Strong <u>IT skills</u>"

    Attention to detail re reading the manuscripts.

    In my office job I learned how to use all aspects of Microsoft,

- **"Please apply with a CV and Covering Letter, including no more than 150 words about a book you've read recently."**

    There is not much direction about what type of book you may have read, but I am lucky enough to have read some of this publisher's books in this genre so I will choose one of theirs.

3. Bringing all your points together. In this example we have ended up with the following:

    I have a keen interest in business books, as well as leadership and entrepreneurship.

"I first read Making College Happen *as I was trying to find ways to go to university on a budget. I thought it was so well thought out, I searched for other titles and discovered a passion for instructive non-fiction.* The Uni-Tasking Revolution *helped me learn to prioritise and organise a heavy workload and whilst it is a long way off in the future,* Become a Successful First Time CEO *piqued my interest to read further than books directly relevant to me."*

As I have office experience as well as working on the customer service desk, I am used to being the first port of call in a very busy environment.

"I have office experience where I was required to manage the enquiry inbox which received over 200 emails a day, sometimes from very angry people."

Whilst at university I joined the book and creative writing club and we would often read each other's manuscripts and offer feedback in the form of a reader report. It helped me learn what could have publishing potential, against what writing needed improvement.

"During time spent in an office, I reported to three senior members of the team."

"I worked across the business, liaising with other departments. reading and proofreading other students' manuscripts,"

"In the office job I was answering phone and email enquiries."

"I am a voracious reader across all genres but really enjoy the personal development and business sectors. Self-motivated, at times I juggled two jobs around my university work. This required me to be highly organised and practise excellent time management. I like to be productive."

In my office job I learned how to use all aspects of Microsoft,

"In my office job I learned how to use Microsoft outlook and to organise tasks."

"A book I have read recently was Jonathan Hemus's Crisis Proof *about overcoming any crisis in business. The book takes you on a journey of how to prepare for any crisis as well as why crisis planning is important, and why it needs to be done before*

the crisis happens. Author's credentials as a crisis planner are important, and it is supplemented with real-life examples. From taking control of a social media storm to dealing with a plane crash for a major airline, you'll learn key skills which can be used in any situation."

4. Turning it into a letter: It is really important that the letter flows like a letter and reads well. You should never include the phrase, "as you will see from my CV". They've asked for your letter AND your CV; the two documents should work in tandem and stand alone.

   In addition to the notes you've made, can you think of anything else you might want to mention, such as:

   - What can you do?
   - What other skills can you bring?
   - How will the company benefit?
   - Do you have any specialist knowledge of software packages?

Do you remember how, on your CV, you wanted to write some 'chatty things' about where you wanted to go, and what you wanted to do? If appropriate, your Covering Letter could be the place to add it.

TOP TIP
If time allows, don't be too hasty sending off your Covering Letter. Take your time over it. A good letter should be written and edited over a 24-hour period (one sleep) or slightly longer to allow your thoughts to mature, particularly if it is a job that you are desperate to get. One way I know I've written a good Covering Letter is when, after sending it, I want to keep reading it over and over.

Dear Bookcareers Publishing

I would like to apply for the role of Editorial Assistant that I saw advertised on *The Bookseller* website.

I am a voracious reader who has a keen interest in business books, as well as books on leadership, entrepreneurship and personal development. I first read *Making College Happen* as I was trying to find ways to survive at university on a budget. As well as containing valuable advice, I particularly liked Howard R. Freedman's no-nonsense writing style. This book led me to looking at other similar titles, and that is how I discovered a passion for instructive non-fiction. *The Uni-Tasking Revolution* taught me how to prioritise and organise a heavy workload and, whilst it might be some way off for me, David Roche's *Become a Successful First Time CEO*, piqued my interest to read further across the genres.

I have some experience in reading and recommending manuscripts and basic proofreading skills, learned whilst I was part of the university book and creative writing club. We would often read each other's manuscripts and offer feedback in the form of a reader report or suggested corrections. It helped me to understand what books could have publishing potential, against what writing needed improvement. I also learned how to be diplomatic when giving any feedback, appreciating that the author might not want to hear the observations made.

I'm currently working on a busy customer service desk, so I am used to being the first port of call in a demanding environment, where I am helping people over the phone as well as face to face. This requires me to be highly organised and adhere to established processes and schedules. Previously, I spent a month working in an office for a housing association, where I reported to three Directors. I managed their email inbox that received more than 200 emails a day, sometimes from people in difficult situations. I was responsible for liaising with other departments and external suppliers in order to resolve the queries, and I had to use my initiative to try and smooth things over as best I could in arduous circumstances.

I juggled two jobs around studying at university and as a result I'm self-motivated and have gained good IT skills. I have used all aspects of Microsoft 365 including Excel, PowerPoint, Outlook and To-Do as well as a bespoke CRM. I like to be productive, manage time effectively, and am always willing to take on new responsibilities and challenges.

A book I read recently was Jonathan Hemus's *Crisis Proof: How to prepare for the worst day of your business life*. It enables a business and its employees to react calmly and objectively in a time of panic and crisis, whilst resolving a stressful situation and averting any further incidents. The book was well-structured by being divided into sections, as well as chapters. It took the reader on a clear journey where they learn all aspects of crisis planning and its importance, before moving on to a practical exercise and implementation. The author's expertise shone through by the use of real-life examples and responses and his concise writing style. The advice about the decisions to make in advance was especially helpful. Whether taking control of a social media storm or dealing with a major disaster, this book will teach anyone how to prepare for any business eventuality.

I would love to talk to you more about the role and how I could benefit bookcareers publishing. I'm available for interview at your convenience and look forward to hearing from you shortly.

Yours sincerely

Adelaide Rose

[NB if this letter was on A4 size paper, no paragraph would be over 8 lines of text]

Checking your content

Even though you think you've written a fantastic Covering Letter, it is time to check your content, as well as giving it a meticulous proofread and grammar check.

1. Check your content against the advertisement. Go through your original notes from the job advertisement. Have you included all the key points they mentioned in the advertisement? You don't need to have covered everything, especially if you have gaps in your experience or the requirements for the role, nor do you have to evidence every point, but you should make sure you have mentioned the key components of the role and how you

match them. This is why, when you write your Covering Letter using this method, you don't need to stress about AI or keyword checks, as you're likely to have automatically included 75% of the skills required and will sail through the first sifting.

2. Don't repeatedly name check the name of the company(ies) you have worked for. It might be a good idea to mention once that you are working for a company or you worked somewhere that is very similar to them, but repeated use of other company names suggests that you might not be ready to move on. It could also indicate you'll bring a lot of baggage with you; especially if it is well known that a company folded or no longer exists. Sometimes when people start a new role, they are forever comparing and complaining (particularly if it is a company with a huge marketing budget, and you're now in a job with the marketing budget of a few pennies) and repeatedly saying things like, "Oh we didn't do things like that at my old company." Unless you've been brought into the company to make it exactly like your previous employer, don't do this. No one wants to work with someone who constantly references somewhere else.

3. Repeated words and phrases. The find and replace facility in any software is brilliant for identifying where you have repeated words and phrases. Use this along with a thesaurus to vary your language but be careful only to use words that you would use every day.

For example, I have a client who overuses the word 'currently'. Before we started work together, it was usual to find the word currently 22 times in one A4 sheet. Find words and check you haven't used them more than twice, unless you have a good reason to do so, and never start paragraphs with the same words. Also vary how you describe things; it shouldn't just read "I am", "I am", "I am", "I am".

It might read:

"I have", "I come with", "I've", "I am", "I'm". It is okay to start multiple sentences and paragraphs with "I", but vary the language immediately after it.

One of the main reasons for not repeating or overusing words is because WE WORK IN BOOK PUBLISHING; we will be working on other people's writing or writing about it. We need to demonstrate that we have a wide vocabulary. Can you imagine reading a marketing leaflet or an Advance Title Information with the same superlatives repeated all the way through?

4. The use of the word 'my'. How many times in the letter have you used the word 'my'? Again, the find and replace key is good for this. I recommend you aim to use the word 'my' no more than twice in any letter unless it is for a senior management or strategic role, then you might get away with using the word 'my' three times at most. But wherever you can, unless you clearly want to say 'this was my idea', avoid the use of the word 'my'. (The record number of times I have seen the word 'my' in a Covering Letter was 48.)

The reason is 'my' is a possessive word. It indicates that you are not a team player, and maybe you are not as collaborative as you say you are (it is okay if you are a team leader, but if you were a good team leader you would discuss 'our team' or 'the team', not 'my team').

If you want to indicate that you are a team player the good words to use are 'we' and 'our'.

5. Ensure you do a good editorial job on your Covering Letter and double-check there is no waffle. If you take a paragraph to describe one skill, you are waffling and the recruiter might think, "so much waffle. If this is how they write, how much waffle will they bring to an editorial meeting?"

6. Complicated words and exuberant vocabulary. Read your Covering Letter out loud; is there a word you stop or stumble over, or feels out of place? If so, change the word. Your vocabulary should flow and be in relatively plain English, using words you'd use every day.

7. Improving on your paragraph arrangement, sentence construction and phrasing. When it comes to Covering Letters, candidates frequently write the first thing that comes into their head and stick with it, as it contains all the key words and elements of what they want to say.

Or they stick rigidly to the order of the skills given in the job advertisement. However, taking a step back (usually leaving it for an hour and coming back to it later) can help you realise how to improve your letter further.

- Are sentences overlong?
- Is it engaging to read and will it keep the recruiter interested?
- Have you prioritised your letter, so that the points that instantly tie you to the publisher are in the first few paragraphs? Or are these buried at the end of the letter?

8. Stating you are their perfect candidate. You might feel you are their perfect candidate and if you want to say this, then do it towards the end of the letter not the beginning. This is how the brain works. If you tell someone that something is perfect for them, often they will spend the next few minutes trying to discredit this perfection and finding reasons why it is not perfect for them. When you start a Covering Letter, "I am your perfect candidate", unless you were specifically asked to say why you are their perfect candidate, the brain of the recruiter is likely to instantly read the rest of the letter thinking "no you're not", "no you're not" at every opportunity, and you don't want that.

What you want is for your skills and competencies to come across in a well-written letter, to get the recruiter excited when reading about how you match the role and come to the conclusion, all by themselves, that you are their perfect candidate. So, unless it is specified in the advertisement "tell us why you are our perfect candidate", I would avoid saying it.

9. Writing about a book. When you are asked to write about a book as part of your response to a job advertisement, you have a choice whether to include it in your Covering Letter or as an addition to your Covering Letter. Read back over the words they have used; this should be your guidance as to where to put this task. In the previous example the advertisement said, *"Please apply with a CV and Covering Letter, including 150 words about a book you've*

read recently." In this case I would add the paragraph about the book you have read in the Covering Letter.

Another job advertisement might say, *"in addition, please write 150 words about a book you've read recently".* This time, I would advise you to add it after you have finished your Covering Letter, as an addition, either at the end of your Covering Letter or as a separate document.

Publishers ask you to write about a book for several reasons. One is to partly reduce the number of applicants they get for roles where they are expecting a vast number of responses; only those committed to applying will follow all the instructions. The second reason is to see how you write about a book, how you discuss it, and whether you are talking about it in a way that someone else can easily understand.

Ideally, you should write about the book as though you are discussing it at a future editorial meeting, so the person reading your words grasps what the book is about, what makes it a good one, and may then want to buy it, as well as the components of the book you are talking about. For example, if you are going for a production role, and you have a print copy, the publisher might expect you to comment on the paper, typeface and production value of the book.

The third reason could be to see how well you read and understand instructions. It might be to check that you included the information about the book in your application and where in the application you wrote about it. This could be a key factor in how your application progresses. There is further guidance about discussing books in *Chapter Eight: Interview Questions and How to Answer Them*, in the answer to the question, 'What are you reading at the moment?'

TOP TIP
Your CV is a statement of fact showing where you have been; your Covering Letter says where you are going, why you want to work for the publisher and what skills you can bring with you.

Speculative letters

Sometimes in a job hunt it might be appropriate to write a speculative email, letter or enquiry, to see if there are any potential vacancies available or to put you in the publisher's mind if something comes up. The need for speculative letters has dramatically reduced in recent years, with publishers wanting to be more open about their recruitment processes to encourage inclusivity. Many publishers advertise on their career pages that they do not accept speculative letters. In the bookcareers.com Salary Survey we've seen recruitment via speculative letter drop from 4.7% of respondents in 2002 to 2.4% in 2021.

However, it is useful to know how to write a speculative approach letter. In any job search you might discover the publisher is launching a new imprint in your favourite genre, whether it is from an acquaintance, by recommendation or from reading in the trade press. In this case, you might want to make an approach for an informal chat, and this is the way to do it.

Email is the preferred way for a speculative approach; if you have their email address then it becomes easier. Otherwise, you can research their email or connect with them on LinkedIn.

Whenever writing a speculative approach it is always best to suggest an informal meeting or chat if there are no opportunities at present. This allows you to meet them face to face and pitch yourself, so that hopefully you become their number one candidate when a vacancy arises.

However, this is becoming far less frequent as, whilst someone may be willing to help, it may be against their company inclusivity policy. I've seen this a lot with the major publishers, where I used to be able to introduce non-standard candidates (such as someone with a disability or unique situation) to a Human Resources Manager, to discuss whether that publisher might be a good fit for a future career. Now these requests are refused on the grounds of inclusivity.

Here are a couple of sample ideas for writing a speculative letter:

Dear

I read in this week's edition of The Bookseller that you are venturing into Sci-Fi and Fantasy novels and wonder if you may have a future opening for an Editorial Assistant?

I've been a huge fan of (name authors, genres, details), and often attend ComicCon and (another event). I have already been an intern at (name other publishers) OR I have (your skills) and know that I would be a credit to your new list.

I appreciate you might not have anything available at present, but would it be possible for us to have a quick chat, so that I can learn more about your new imprint?

Yours sincerely

Dear

Adelaide Rose suggested I write to you, as I understand you may soon have an opening for a new Editorial Assistant.

I've recently completed a Master's in Publishing, where I received good grounding in all aspects of publishing and chose modules that specialised in editorial. As a result, I am professionally trained in proofreading and copyediting. I have top-notch organisational and time-management skills too.

Would it be at all possible to take 30 minutes of your time to discuss this further? I'm available most weekdays, so can fit in with your busy diary.

Yours sincerely

EXERCISE

If you know your favourite publishers, practise writing a 'I want to work for you because' paragraph that you may be able to update and use in a future Covering Letter.

ACTION POINTS

Review your past Covering Letters. Examine closely the ones where you got shortlisted and the ones where you had no response. How many of the following mistakes can you spot?

- Top and tailing
- Repeating the same information or skills
- Repeating names of past employers
- Spelling errors or typos
- Word repetition – which words or phrases do you overuse?
- How many times have you used the word my?

CHAPTER SEVEN

Ace the Interview Process

No matter what the selection criteria, or wherever inclusivity takes us, success at an interview will still come down to three things, that will never change.

1. *Can I work with you?* *
2. *Can you do the job?*
3. *Will you fit in?* *

Suzanne Collier

[* This is not an excuse to enforce prejudices or unconscious bias; read this chapter for the full definition.]

You've perfected your CV and Covering Letter and YES! You are invited to an interview and are one step closer to your dream job. Then you search online all about interviews and interview questions and understand that there might be a scoring system or hurdles put in place to ensure that the person with the right skillset is recruited. However, no matter what screening, scoring or positive discrimination might be taking place, the interviewer will rate you on three things – none of which should be used to enforce personal prejudices or unconscious bias; all three points relate to work.

1. Can I work with you?
- Do I like your way of thinking?
- Can I see unexplored talent in you?
- Do I think you'll do well in the job?
- Are you able to build rapport in a work environment?
- Do you understand the questions I am asking?
- Can you answer questions coherently?
- Do you sound like you take instruction well?

Throughout your career, you will probably spend more time talking to colleagues than you do to friends and family, so building rapport will be important, regardless of your background, race, religion or any other protected characteristic.

2. Can you do the job?

- Do you understand the job?
- Do you have the skills and competencies needed for this role at the right level?
- Do you know how to do the job?
- Can I trust you to do a good job?
- What training or support will you need?
- Will I need to spend a lot of time training you?
- Can you add value to the job?
- Are you already working in a direction that we aim to move towards?
- Will you let me down?
- What will my colleagues think of your skills?
- Will my colleagues think I have made the right appointment?

The interviewer will want to recruit someone who they can trust to do a good job. Whilst the interview is about your skills and competencies, and whether you can do the job, the interviewer's appointment will reflect on them; they won't want colleagues to think they make poor decisions about recruitment.

3. Will you fit in?

- Will you fit into the team?
- Do you have the skills the team is missing or replacing?
- Will there be any potential conflicts with colleagues?
- Do you fit into the company culture?

If you are used to working for a large corporation with huge budgets and other people to staff reception, send post, and share the workload, how will you cope in a company where every penny is counted and you are required to cover reception, despatch your own post and have no colleagues to share the workload?

That is it. Even if a different method of interviewing or scoring is brought in, it is likely that when it comes down to choosing the successful candidate, the answers to these three main questions will impact on any final decision.

There are lots of things you can do to help the interviewer decide that you are the perfect candidate; and it isn't only about answering questions posed at the interview.

Let's start by looking at the interview process and the theory behind interviews.

TOP TIP

How to impress your interviewer

Research the company
- Who are their competitors?
- What are they doing?
- What are they publishing?
- How can you help them do it better?

Understanding Interviews

To help you succeed at any interview, it is best to understand why interviews take place.

If everyone had the exactly right skills and competencies for the job on paper, an employer could simply offer the job to any applicant who matched these skills, without ever meeting them in person.

Many people believe that an interview is simply a question-and-answer session about your skills, yet it is so much more than that.

A job interview is a situation where you are meeting your potential employer, usually for the first time. It relies on you to be amiable, build rapport, discuss your skills, competencies and experience in a way that is truthful. Your answers should please your interviewer and give them confidence that you can do the job, want to do the job and you will stick at the job for as long as they need you and, thus, you will be an asset to the publisher.

At a bookcareers.com Job Club meeting, I asked the members, what the purpose of a job interview was. These are their responses.

Why do interviews take place?

- See how we communicate
- To discuss the experience on your CV
- To put a face to a name
- Whether they like you
- Whether you like them
- If you match your CV
- How you interact with them
- How you match their team
- Assess your personality
- To see if there are any gaps in your experience
- Check you are telling the truth
- If it is face to face, to see the office and meet the team

Interview Preparation

Your preparation for each interview is likely to have several components:
1. Research
2. Functional – including preparing for different formats of interviews
3. Questions
4. Tests

Interview Research

If you want to ace an interview, preparation is key. This section has been written so you can use this as a checklist for each and every interview.

1. **Re-read the job advertisement and your application**

    Go through each point on the job advertisement, writing down how your skills match, where in your career history you gained that experience, and how you performed the task.

    You might like to think of when you completed the skill well, if you under-performed the skill or did something badly when using the skill. Next, when did things go according to plan, when were they completely messed up and what were the biggest challenges you found within the task? If you aim to write your answers as a story, this will help you:

    E.g.
    Copy-editing, Proofreading and checking for corrections

    I've been proofreading and checking for corrections since my first job; the skill is now like second nature to me. In my most recent role at JB Publishing, I was required to do a major copy-edit of an 800-page scientific publication that contained a number of technical terms. From previous editing experiences, I already knew a lot of the terms and phrases, and I researched any words and phrases I was unfamiliar with to ensure they were being used in the correct context and the spelling was accurate.

    On one of the first books I edited I forgot to save all the corrections as I was working. It resulted in me having to redo two chapters again. As a result I've always saved my work continuously and I'm meticulous in backing up edits too.

    It could be you spend time doing this task for one job interview and then reuse it or re-read it when preparing for other jobs you're applying for, updating it as you go along. However, don't fall into the trap of thinking every role with the same job title requires the same skills and competencies – these are often unique to every single role you apply for, as an editorial assistant for one publisher may have different responsibilities to an editorial assistant in another publishing house.

2. **Research the publisher**

   Realistically, you should have done this before applying for the job, but now you are going to revisit your research and see things with a different eye.
   - Look at their website; is it user friendly?
   - Have you read their 'about us' and corporate pages?
   - Are there any recent company press releases?
   - What does any company news say about appointments, company structure or direction?
   - Is the company expanding or shrinking?
   - Have there been new appointments in the department you are applying to?
   - Is there a structured career resource section or a place where you can 'meet the team' (you can see who might be interviewing you)?
   - Is the blog up to date? How quickly are the pages loading?
   - What books are they promoting or giving prominence to?
   - Who are their major authors?
   - What formats do they publish in?
   - What prices are their products and how do they match the marketplace or their competitors' prices?
   - How do they categorise their books online?
   - Is it easy to navigate to see the latest or bestselling titles on their website?
   - How can you see the genres or subject areas they are known for?
   - Do they mention the marketing plans and promotional campaigns for their new books?
   - Are there competitions or giveaways?

- Have you already signed up for their newsletter?
- Read through their newsletter; what information are they giving and how often?
- Think about some of the vocabulary they use. Is it formal or over friendly; what tone of voice do they use?
- When you're reading all their promotional information, does it make you want to buy the books they are publishing?
- Outside of their website, what social media platforms are they using to communicate? Facebook? Instagram? Pinterest? TikTok? Something else?
- How often do they post on social media? When? Are the posts engaging or repetitive?

All of these items should help you answer questions such as:

- What do you think of our website?
- Did you sign up for our newsletter?
- What research have you done in preparation for today?
- What do you know about us?
- What do you think of our cover designs?
- What do you think of our forthcoming titles?
- Can you describe a marketing campaign for one of our books?
- If you were given control of our social media feed, what would you post?

Regardless of the department or area of publishing where you are aiming to work, knowing and understanding a publisher's marketing and editorial direction is equally important. What good is an Editor if they don't know how the books are promoted or what is selling well? What good is a Marketing Executive if they don't know about the genre, the authors and the books?

Also, when researching the publisher, learn about the key personnel. For example, who is the Chief Executive Officer (CEO) or Managing Director (MD), and can you find a photo of them on the internet? This is just in case you happen to bump into them in reception or in the lift. (This happened to at least one of my clients. They didn't recognise the CEO, and this led to an embarrassing encounter.)

3. **Who are the publisher's or company's competitors?**

   What other companies publish in the same genre, have competing lists or operate in the same marketplace? Visit the websites of the competing publishers, and go through the same actions, looking at format, price point, sales, market visibility. Do their competitors look like they are doing better or worse than the publisher you are interviewing for?

   Look at Amazon, both in bestsellers by genre, and by using the advance search by publisher name. See how the publisher's bestselling titles are listed online.

   - Does this match how the publisher promotes them or gives them prominence?
   - What books in the same genres are outselling them? Why do you think that is?
   - What is their metadata like compared to other publishers?
   - Are jacket covers missing?
   - Has the publisher added additional information, such as the contents page, national review coverage, or extra images?
   - Does the Amazon entry allow you to 'look inside'?
   - As Amazon sales are often a huge percentage of some publishers' income, do the Amazon descriptions feel like they are lacking in any way and hindering sales?

4. **Comparisons**

   Find three books from other publishers that you can discuss at interview, whether they are books from other publishers you wished you had published (and don't always say Harry Potter!) or three marketing campaigns that you thought captured the target audience.

   If it is a production role you might be asked about print and paper quality of other publishers, so again source three books from competing publishers and look at the quality of the print production, the typefaces used and check on the title page for the typesetter and the name of the printer, so you're knowledgeable about what their competitors are doing.

5. **Companies House**

   If you are going for an interview with a publisher, sometimes it is a good idea to check out their accounts on Companies House (UK) to see if what they've told you about their turnover compares with the reality. This is important if you are in a very stable role and looking to move to a company you don't know much about. Too often I see people jump ship and put themselves in a precarious position. Even I've been caught out by this – a small company who headhunted me were in dire financial trouble when I joined. A quick check with Companies House beforehand would have shown they were repeatedly issuing new shares and replacing their directors, demonstrating a potentially volatile environment. This might be something you'd like to go into, but at least if you do, go into with your eyes open.

6. **Search online**

   It is all very well looking at the publisher's website but when you do, you only see what the publisher wants you to see. Put the publisher's name in Google and see what comes up. You might add the words 'appointment', 'finance', 'results' and/or 'reviews' to see if you can get any more information about them, either good or bad.

   However, be wary of websites that give disgruntled employees the opportunity to write negative and misleading information about a company. I personally know of one person who has left at least eight negative reviews for the same publisher and it has proved impossible for the publisher to get these comments removed.

Also, understand that what happens at a particular time with one group of employees may not be representative of the true state of affairs at the time of your interview. At the very least go to the interview and make up your own mind; you could be pleasantly surprised and it will save you from missing out on a potentially smart career move – all because you took the word of an anonymous bitter ex-employee.

7. **Trade Press**

Look at the trade tress for current industry trends. What genres are selling well at the moment? What publishers, books or genres seem to be struggling? Is the trade press talking about the 'next big thing'? How are publishers responding to market forces such as new social media platforms, inclusivity, costs and price rises, and consumer focus?

This might help answer any questions at interview, such as, "What do you think is the next big thing in publishing?"

Search the trade press for reports about the publisher (these might not always come up on Google). How are any acquisitions or appointments being reported? Have their results been reported with added industry commentary? Are there any interviews with key personnel. For example, one client was applying for a job with a publisher and there was a two-page interview in *The Bookseller* magazine, that gave depth to the direction the publisher was going in and that provided key information for anyone applying for a role within their new imprint. You can find a list of the trade press at the back of this book.

8. **LinkedIn**

First of all, if you don't want your interviewer to know you have done this, ensure your privacy settings are set to

"Hidden". However, having your potential interviewer know you've looked them up on LinkedIn can often be seen as a positive.

Look up the person or people interviewing you. Firstly, you should be able to see what they look like, so when they join you in an online meeting, or you are greeted in reception, you know instantly who they are. View their employment history. Have they worked at any companies you have connections with? Is LinkedIn showing you how you are connected?

If you want to see who else works at the company, or who used to work at the company, then use the advance search feature and look for current/past employees. Maybe you have a friend who used to work there who can tell you more, such as whether it is a good place to work. Be wary though; sometimes a bad experience for someone else can be a good experience for you, and vice versa, and also be careful – maybe they don't want you to get the job or it may not be public knowledge that there is a vacancy. If a Recruitment Consultant is part of the process they might expressly forbid you from contacting any current employees; heed their advice.

9. **Social Media**

    You should have already been following the publisher and key employees on social media. But have you searched for the publisher on different social media platforms and seen what else comes up? Is there any other information you can glean? Look at the posts and replies; what are others saying about them? Are people constantly posting negatively or positively about them? How have they responded to any negative comments or criticism?

10. **Books or products**

    You've looked online at their books or publications, but what about in real life? Have you visited a bookshop or library and looked at physical copies? Ask yourself a few questions:

- What do the covers look like in real life?
- Do the books look like good value or overpriced?
- What is the quality of the paper like?
- How do the fonts look to you?
- Are the books easy to read or is the typeface too small?
- If it is a trade publisher and you're looking at their titles in a bookshop, how many titles from the publisher are stocked?
- How does this compare with the publisher's competitors?
- Are any titles front of store or in the window?
- If the publisher has said they are the market leader in their genre, does this carry through to the bookshelves?

Depending on who the target buyer or reader is for the titles, you might want to make an effort and visit more than one outlet. For example, if an Academic Publisher relies on their books being the required reading for a course, can you visit online or in person any academic or student bookshops, or check if their books are regularly recommended?

If it is a gift publisher, have you visited several branches and various stores in different towns see where their books and gifts are placed? Don't only visit the same chains (e.g. Waterstones), as the books are likely to have been bought at head office level then scaled out (the central buyer decides how many copies should be stocked by each branch). Look in your local independent bookshop too, or at a different chain.

11. **Look at recent campaigns from the publisher**

    Was a book recently talked-up very heavily? If it is a trade publisher, did you notice this follow-through in sales – did the book make the bestseller list? Where does the book rank on Amazon? Basically, do the campaigns the publisher invests in translate to sales?

12. **Look at people doing the role**

    Social media is brilliant for this. People often talk about their jobs on social media. You can usually tell whether someone is having a good day, a bad day, what someone had for lunch, and what interaction is going on with their colleagues. You could possibly find the person whose job you are going for and read all their historical social media posts.

    Although in today's society, people are far more guarded about what they post on social media (and, of course, you should never disparage your current employer), there might be some clues as to how the job will work out for you. Are they always saying, "working again this weekend", or "another late night in the office", or "got to go, crushing deadlines at the moment", or are they saying, "boss has just given me the afternoon off", "boss just bought yet another cake". All of these could be clues for what it is like working for a particular publisher.

If you do all this research then you will feel well equipped for knowing more about the publisher, as well as knowing how you could make a difference in the role, and if you still want to work for them. This information will equip you far better for an interview than if you only focus on the job advertisement and your skills.

Functional Preparation
All types of interviews

Check the time, date and place of your interview. Often people do not read the interview invitation properly and mix up the dates, or they are given a different time to one that was agreed, or it has been arranged in an alternative office or location. It might be that you were given the wrong date or information. Don't be afraid to double-check if the instructions appear incorrect or different but do make sure there is an error before you contact the interviewer. Aside from acknowledging you have received the email invitation for an interview and you are able to attend, it is best to keep contact with the publisher to a minimum before the interview, e.g. don't email three times checking the same information such as the date and time of the interview.

Plan what you are going to wear

It is recommended to have one outfit always ready for an interview, so even if you get called at short notice, you know that you have something suitable to wear.

This applies to both online and face-to-face interviews. You might think if you're in an online call that a smart top is okay, and not worry about what else you are wearing, but you could find you suddenly have to get up from the call (such as answering a doorbell), so don't take a chance.

There is a belief that if a company has a relaxed office dress code, then you should dress down, but this is often not the case. Never wear jeans to an interview; follow a smart casual dress code and you will rarely go wrong. There are lots of definitions of smart, so here are some guidelines:

- A shirt and trousers, jacket optional
- A dress, non-denim skirt or trousers, with a blouse or a smart top

Don't overdo the make-up and watch the jewellery. There is nothing more distracting than interviewing someone whose bracelet keeps rattling or who keeps playing with their necklace.

If you are wearing a jacket and trousers, a tie is not essential, unless you know the company has a rigid dress code. One way to find this out is to look at any meet-the-team or corporate company pages on their website; are there any images of staff? Only once have I heard of someone not getting the job because they wore a tie, but I often hear of people not getting the job because they turned up looking scruffy or in jeans. Being interviewed on days of extreme weather (hot or cold) is never pleasant, so dress to be as comfortable as you can without looking too informal; people do make allowances for the heat.

The whole premise of 'what to wear' for an interview is based on the fact that it is showing you scrub up well. In the publishing business you are forever meeting people from authors to buyers to customers, and it is important that the person interviewing you can see that you know how to dress appropriately and professionally.

If there is a reason why you aren't dressed as you wanted (for example, I had to wear trainers for one interview, because

I'd broken a bone in my foot), then explain it once and move on. Don't keep repeating the same negative fact and don't dwell on it. It is perfectly acceptable for these things to happen.

Remember that whilst it might be an interview, it is still a conversation. Don't talk too fast and have lots of natural pauses in your answers. Please do not go into a monologue when answering questions, and, even with a video interview, remember that silence is golden; you don't have to fill up all the space.

Do not interrupt the interviewer. Let them speak freely and listen fully to what they are saying before you respond. You might nod your head in agreement, but do not interrupt the interviewer; let them finish before you respond. Remember, this person is responsible for hiring you. When you are speaking, you only hear what you already know; when others are speaking, you may learn something new.

As with any interview, you are likely to be asked if you have any questions for the interviewer, but be careful that they aren't already things you have been told in the advertisement, during the interview or are not obvious things you should clearly already know if you are interested in the publisher.

Here are examples of questions that you might want to ask the interviewer, but may have already been answered when they were telling you about the company:

- *What titles are you excited about at the moment?* (there is a chance they may have told you this)
- *What is your next big project?* (they might have told you this; it could be reason they are recruiting)
- *How is the department structured?*
- *What will my first priorities be?*

However, good questions to ask could be:

- *I know you're really excited about this book / project, but what else is planned?*
- *I can see you've restructured recently. Is there more restructuring planned?*

- *You've mentioned my first priorities will be ___, what comes next?*
- *Will there be opportunities to add to my skills or take on additional responsibilities?*

Long gone are the days when the only interview you had was face to face. Here are some popular methods of job interviews and the additional functional preparation you should do for each.

Telephone Interview

The first and the most popular type of pre-screening interview is a telephone call. You might not be advised it is an interview, or the publisher might call you on the off-chance or phone you for any number of reasons. Look upon any contact with the publisher as an interview because at every stage they'll be thinking, "Do I want to employ you?" Will they be thinking "They sound enthusiastic and interested in the role", or "They didn't seem bothered about the job at all"?

When you are job hunting, always be ready for this type of conversational interview any time that you answer the telephone.

During the call you could be assessed on any of the following:

How you answer the phone and your overall telephone manner, particularly if the role includes taking telephone calls or any part of customer service. You might always answer the phone, "Yo Geezer", but now is the time to change your habits to anyone but your closest and identifiable friends.

A point of note – I've come across a couple of candidates who block all calls from withheld or international numbers or switch the facility to leave voicemail messages off. With the way telephone technology currently is, this could be a risky business, as for instance, my office number is withheld when I dial out, sometimes it comes up as International. I've seen similar things happen from recruiters who use VoIP to make calls or block their number if they are working from home.

By all means screen numbers, but if you are looking for a job, you need to be prepared to take calls from anyone as well as having a voicemail message facility. There is nothing more infuriating for a recruiter who is trying to set up an interview to be constantly faced with a voicemail message every time they call you, or even worse, have no opportunity to leave a message at all.

For example, a recruiter leaves a message; you phone them back, they say, "Let us call you back" (so they pay for the call; useful if you have a limited amount of credit on your phone)and they phone you back immediately, only to get your voicemail again. Infuriating!

Think too about your voicemail message; does it represent the professional person you are? The image you want to project? The person who sounds employable?

If you're in a shared house, think carefully about giving that number as your default contact number. Will the person answering the phone be professional? Will they take a message for you if you're not around and quickly pass that message to you? Very often recruiters have a set number of people to call for a shortlist. If they can't get in touch with you by a specified time, they sometimes cross you off the list and move on to the next candidate. Ruthless? Perhaps, but there may be no shortage of qualified candidates for the role you've applied for.

If the call is unscheduled, there may be a few issues. For example, you are at a train station and you cannot hear the recruiter clearly, or it is not a good time because you are in the Doctor's waiting room or about to go into another interview. In these cases, if it is anything more than fixing a time for a face-to-face interview, then let the publisher know it isn't convenient. A response such as, "I really want to talk to you, but I can't speak right now", should be adequate. In this case, take the name and telephone number of the person and call them back as soon as you are able. Don't go into detail why the time was not good; be friendly, polite and succinct. If the publisher asks you why it isn't a good time, then a default answer, "my battery is very low", usually works best; if there is a huge amount of background noise, then use that. It goes without saying that calling back at the first reasonable opportunity is an absolute must.

Sometimes, if the publisher has no intention of inviting you to a formal interview, but you have a connection to the company or are a supplier or business customer, they'll phone for a quick chat about the role. During the call they will steer the conversation in such a way that you will realise either the role is not for you, or your salary request is beyond their pay-scale. Therefore, at the end of the call, in the nicest possible way, you know you haven't got the job or will have withdrawn your application during the conversation.

This happens very often to personal connections who apply for roles, and, in particular, to buyers for bookselling chains who are looking for jobs in publishing. When I was working in a sales role for a publisher, I was as guilty of doing this as much as anyone else. Sometimes publishers call applicants who work in a particular role in bookselling for a face-to-face interview for the same reason. This will happen primarily because the publisher doesn't want to upset any buyer or bookseller, and have the bookseller bear a grudge against that publisher forever more.

For a scheduled telephone interview, here are a few essentials that will make it go according to plan and earn you an invitation for a face-to-face interview.

Your preparation should be similar to that for other types of interview but, instead, you have the luxury of having notes and papers spread out in front of you. Ensure you have the job advertisement or job description in front of you, with keywords highlighted. Maybe there are some key phrases you want to drop into the conversation, or a critical point you want to get across to make them want to employ you. Have these laid out clearly on the desk in front of you.

- For example, if the role asked for organisational skills for an event or conference, you might have a prompt written in front of you

    Organisation – organised the conference at so and so publishers
- Have a little sign that reminds you to 'Smile'. This will help relax you and also help you remain calm and breathe. Smiling uses far fewer facial muscles than scowling.
- Ensure you are somewhere where you can hear clearly, where there is minimal background noise, and you can talk freely without being overheard and without distractions or interruptions. You need to focus 100% on what is being asked or said.
- If you are able to, stand up whilst speaking. Your voice projects better when you are standing than sitting. It will also aid your concentration.
- If you cannot hear the interviewer, or do not understand the question, do ask them to repeat or clarify what they said as it is a conversation, after all.

- Don't relax too much and don't speak inappropriately. Although the person on the other end of the phone might sound like they want to be your best friend, they really aren't. Their job is to extract as much information about you as they can, so they can gauge whether they want to pursue your application.
- Always wait for the interviewer to finish the question before answering. Don't speak over them at any time.
- There might be a few leading questions during this telephone interview, such as, "How do you cope with boring tasks and repetitive work?" Whilst you might answer this question, it should also be a warning that if you struggle with boring repetitive work, then maybe this is not the job for you.
- At the end, thank them for their time. They might ask if you want to pursue your application, and if they haven't already mentioned it, you might ask: "What is the next stage?"

One thing to be on your guard for when a publisher calls for a telephone interview is for them to go into full-blown serious interview mode, even if the publisher says, "we'll phone for a quick chat".

Even an old hand like me got caught out by this once. A friend recommended me to a company. The senior manager got in touch and told me they would phone at a scheduled time for an informal chat about mutual contacts and whether we could work together, and then didn't call on time. The phone rang 90 minutes later, with the junior assistant on the line. Instantly, instead of having this nice friendly chat I'd been advised, they started going into full-blown, heavy competency-based interview questions. Needless to say, I didn't get the contract and, as a result, I will never allow myself or my clients to be caught out like that again. This is why I am sharing the information with you. Be warned.

Pre-Recorded Online / Hirevue Interviews

In recent years, a few publishers, such as Penguin Random House, have started using a pre-recorded video interview system, such as Hirevue, for first interviews. It is great for the publisher; they can see far more candidates for a role and involve a number of different colleagues in the selection process from an early stage.

From a publisher's perspective, it also makes the activity of interviews time-efficient, as the candidate usually picks and chooses the time the recording takes place. It also gives every candidate exactly the same interview, so, in theory, the publisher is assessing like with like.

From a candidate's perspective, if you have never experienced one before, you might find them far more stressful than a live interview. You have a fixed time to answer a set number of questions, and you only get one opportunity. You cannot re-record the questions and usually there is one question (the final one) that is designed to catch you unawares such as: "Tell us the most surprising thing about yourself," or "Who would you invite to a dinner party?"

However, there are huge benefits to candidates, such as not having to travel to an interview or take time off work.

Whilst the focus for the publisher is on the words and answers you provide, rather than a visual performance, those who are comfortable talking to a camera are likely to perform better. It also may disadvantage those with social disabilities or anxiety.

When you receive an invitation for a Hirevue interview, you'll also be sent some links so you can read more about them. These links contain some helpful tips about preparing. Do read them through and watch any preparational videos because, whilst different publishers may use the same systems, the process may vary from publisher to publisher.

Nonetheless, as someone who has coached hundreds of people successfully through Hirevue interviews, here is some guidance for how to prepare fully.

During your interview for a publishing related job, most of the questions are likely to be the type of interview questions you would expect; ones that focus on your soft skills for the role or the situations you have experienced in the workplace. Especially at entry level, they are likely to be general interview questions, not related to any special publishing-specific skills, but when you answer, see if you can tailor your answer so it relates directly to the role for which you are being interviewed.

For example, for the role of Editorial Assistant:

> *"Can you give me an example of when you've supported others in a team?"*

You could reply:

> *"when I supported the editorial team..."*

This would be better than:

> *"when I was at university, I supported the team who..."*

Even though the university team experience might be the one you are more confident speaking about, the supporting of an editorial team is directly related to the job.

Other sample questions could be:

> *"How do you organise your day?"*
> *"Can you talk about a difficult situation?"*
> *"Can you give me an example of when you've been creative?"*

Those might apply for absolutely any job.

As you go up the ladder you could be asked a higher level of question, yet they are still likely to be general questions:

> *"Can you give me an example of when you've managed a team?"*
> *"Can you give me an example of when you've dealt with a difficult author?"*

At a lower level, that might be:

> *"Can you give me an example of when you've spoken to a difficult person or dealt with a difficult situation?"*

Or a question such as:

"Why do you want to work here?"

This is a question that anybody could ask for any company, for any interview, but you should tailor your answer to the publishing company.

As you may have done for writing your Covering Letter, go through the job advertisement line by line and look at some of the key words they are using. For example: organising, deadline, challenging, team-player, multi-tasking, prioritising, editing, selling.

Then think of the questions they might ask based on these keywords such as:

- "Give me an example of when you were highly organised."
- "Tell me about a time you had competing priorities."
- "Can you tell me about a time you had to work to a deadline," or, "Can you tell me about a time when you missed a deadline."

Now you can work through each of the keywords, looking for evidence in your career history or education that you may want to use when providing your answers.

When you're doing this exercise, if you can, do it with a notebook and pen, then edit your words on paper. This is because a notebook and pen is more likely to represent normal speech and your normal thought processes. When you sit and type, your brain is editing your thoughts before you type. Equally, this is a task that is useful for face-to-face interviews and will be detailed in the next section.

As to the recording of the Hirevue, you will get one practice question that you can try over and over again. This allows you to familiarise yourself with talking to the camera, line yourself up and check your background.

Don't worry too much about putting on a performance; act as naturally as you can. The people who will review your interview at the other end know that you're not going to be natural; they know you'll be nervous. They know that you'll be tentative, and they know that you might lack confidence when talking on video, but they're not judging you on that. What they're looking at, or what they're listening to, is the quality of the information that you give about what is said and how much clarity is in your answer when they ask a question. As your body language will be limited by the interview, focus on your words. Just be aware that it is a recording, so try to stay focussed.

You'll usually be given 30 seconds in which the question is asked and you have time to gather your thoughts before answering. This is a plus if you usually suffer from interview nerves as it will help you gather your thoughts. Thirty seconds is actually a reasonable amount of time for you to do this (set a timer and see for yourself), especially if you've done your research and preparation for the interview. You can have a quick look at your prompts before answering. The time given to answer the question is usually between one and three minutes, but you'll find often you'll answer a question in one minute, maybe a little more.

A good way to practise is to open up Zoom and time yourself, but as part of the additional resources for this book, I've set up a mock interview you can use. Check the appendices for a link.

If you know you usually talk too fast when you're on camera, then it might be a good idea to have a Post-it note that says 'SLOW DOWN', or if you know you are prone to ramble, have one that says 'SHUT UP'.

One question I am always asked is how do you stand out as a candidate in a Hirevue interview? The good news is you don't need any gimmicks or to do a cartwheel in front of camera; it really is all about your words and how you explain your skills and competencies in front of a camera when you answer the questions.

Online Live Interviews (not pre-recorded questions)

When you are invited to an online live interview, usually the recruiter will determine which online system you will use (Zoom, Skype, Microsoft Teams, etc.), and this is a good indication of some of the software they use in house. But, in case they ask you for your preference, do have a clear idea which video call platform is your weapon of choice. If given a choice, using a platform that is familiar to you will take away some of the stress about being interviewed.

Check your internet or mobile phone signal. If you know your internet signal is patchy, or your mobile always drops out in a particular room, then aim to take the call somewhere where the signal is consistently good. Being somewhere with a bad or patchy signal can seriously hinder your progress in the interview process if the interviewer cannot hear key words or your voice is always cutting out.

Preparation

Before you take the call, check out your webcam or the camera on your phone and do a test video call to a friend. This is to familiarise yourself with the software and learn how it works, especially if you are using a video platform you are unfamiliar with. If you do this preparation with a friend, ask the friend to send you a screen capture of what they see, so you can adjust your background and seating position. Sometimes, a selfie screenshot is not accurate enough.

You need to ensure your best seating position where your face is central, and that the camera isn't always looking at the top of your head or elsewhere; be aware of the angle of your camera too. If necessary, prop up your computer or phone on books, so the camera is getting a clear view. For females, you should also be aware of how much of your décolletage is visible.

Check what is behind you in the room. Laundry on the radiator might be an essential part of how you live your home life, but a potential employer does not need to see this.

If you are able, it might be a good idea to change your background settings and use a background option provided by Zoom/Teams before starting the call. This could be wise if you are taking the interview whilst sitting on your bed or in a shared space.

Noises, distractions and interruptions

You are most likely to be at home with noise from another room, young children, or you might get interruptions from something like a dog or cat who is desperate to join you. Try to minimise these and use headphones where you can.

I know some of my clients are probably laughing here, as every time I'm on a Teams or Zoom call, Sam 9 the bookcareers.com cat, comes and joins me. But in an interview situation where you need to concentrate, whilst the interviewer seeing the cat might help to break the tension, it could also distract you too much when you're answering questions, and you really need to be focussed.

Have notes handy

Go through the job description carefully and think about what key points you want to mention, and then use either Post-it notes at the top of your computer screen, or other notes that are not in view of the camera but clearly in your view. That way, you can glance at them quickly without it being obvious you are reading them.

These notes might contain prompts to your answers for competency-based questions, or key words you want to drop into your answers. The idea with these notes is that they help you get your points across during the interview or support you if your mind goes blank. They are prompts and shouldn't be read verbatim.

Smile

I always recommend you have one Post-it note with a smiley face and the word 'SMILE' next to the camera. Every time you look at the camera, it reminds you to smile. This will help you to relax and make the interviewer feel you are pleased to be talking to them.

As with the tips for pre-recorded interviews, other key words on Post-it notes might be 'SHUT UP', if you know you ramble on, or 'SLOW DOWN' if you know you always talk too fast. If you know there are key words to the candidate profile they are looking for, you might want to write key words, such as 'organised', 'enthusiastic', 'flexible', on a Post-it note, so that when you answer, you remember these are the skills they are looking for, and you aim to incorporate examples into your answers.

Try not to have more than three Post-it notes at the top of your screen. Any more, and they will prove too distracting.

Taking notes

Have a pen and a notepad clearly in sight. When the interviewer asks you something or mentions something that you want to return to later in the conversation, you can jot it down and come back to it. This also means you can listen clearly to the question being asked before you answer it, exactly the same as you would in a meeting or any business conversation.

Face-to-Face Interviews

Face-to-face interviews are the pinnacle of the job search process; the Recruiter likes your application to the point where they want to meet you, and mostly, the decision whether to employ you will be in your hands.

Preparation is the key, not just in your research, but in your presentation for the day. We've all done it; we've opened our bag and millions of pieces of paper fell out. You didn't have a pen handy, or you pulled out a pen from your pocket, only for it to have a badly chewed end. Clear out your pockets/bags in advance, so that if you need to pull out a tissue it's a clean one.

Plan your journey

How long will it take for you to get there on the day? The best timing to turn up is no more than 10 minutes early, but that is cutting it fine if you are relying on public transport. It is best to leave yourself plenty of time in case things go wrong on your journey and stop a few minutes away to refresh your mind.

Make sure you are not solely relying on your mobile phone for directions: maybe print out a map so if, for any reason, you lose signal or your battery goes flat, you can still check the map.

Ensure you have the phone number of the publisher and/or recruiter, so if there is an unexpected transport problem delaying you, you can phone and let them know. If this is something you ever experience on your journey, apologise when you phone, apologise once when you get to the interview and then do not dwell on it or mention it again.

Always be careful when the publisher is in a remote location. You might be spotted from the window of the office wandering up and down the road trying to kill time. In the same way, I can remember an interview where at least four people were looking out of the window watching me try to reverse park into the tightest of parking spaces in the company car park.

The reason why 10 minutes is an optimal time is because frequently the interviewer is in another meeting, not necessarily an interview, and there is nothing more annoying than being interrupted by someone who has turned up way too early.

Bring your notes with you to read before the interview, either on the journey if you're travelling by public transport or stop somewhere on the way. These should be the preparation you've already done for the role – and re-read both your CV, your Covering Letter and the job advertisement. It is remarkable how many things about the vacancy and yourself you may have forgotten.

Arrange to phone a friend or colleague who knows your strengths and achievements for a pep talk before the interview. This can work wonders, as can imagining you are doing the job already. If you are trying for a promotion, or step up, then behave as you would expect your current boss to behave in that interview. However, you should never lie or exaggerate your skills or experience.

At the interview

You may be monitored from the minute you approach the main door to when you finally see the interviewer. If you are in reception, look at the books on display, pick up a catalogue if there is one on the table or a shelf (if there is a pile of them, ask if you can take one, and take it into the interview) but, most of all, be polite to each and everyone you speak to ... and smile.

During the interview make eye contact. If this is difficult, then focus on something like the interviewer's ear, so it appears you are looking at them. But at all times, if your culture allows, look at the interviewer and their face. In the UK, people sometimes assume that looking away indicates that you are lying; however, in other cultures it is believed that looking directly at someone's face is disrespectful.

Body Language

It is all very well coaching you on the words and phrases to answer at interview, but 80% of communication is non-verbal; it isn't all about your words.

As well as focussing on what you are saying, you also need to focus on your non-verbal clues: your posture, hand movements and the tone and speed at which you talk. In addition, see if you can notice any other interview behaviours about yourself. For example, does your posture change if you are asked a question you like versus a question you don't like?

One of the clients I worked with always had a habit of leaning forward when it was a question he liked and pulling back when it was something he didn't really want to answer. These postural changes were clear to anyone interviewing him, so he was getting turned down for roles that he should have been offered. Once I pointed this out to him, he modified his behaviour and, yes, got a job he wanted.

Your arms and hands

Most of us gesticulate when we talk; we use our hands as part of the conversation. This is fine, but often clients ask what they should do with their hands in an interview. Your hands need to be either on the desk or in your lap, lightly clasped with your palms turning up, that shows you are open to new things. The worst thing to do with your hands is to fold your arms, as to many that instantly signals that you have put up a barrier.

Mirroring and matching often happens naturally in job interviews. This is when you create a mirror image of the body position of the person you are talking to, or you match them. So, if they are leaning forward with their hands on the desk, by mirroring them you could be building rapport. In an interview it is best not to mirror or match completely, as firstly, it is so obvious and, secondly, some of the mirroring could be deemed inappropriate.

In the same way, you might be able to use non-verbal clues to gauge how the interviewer is feeling, or what they are thinking as you give your responses. You might be able to see how the interviewer is feeling by looking at their posture, and you might modify your answers accordingly.

For example, many clients talk too much at interviews! Yes, it is possible to talk too much at an interview. Your answers might be overlong and you find yourself waffling (you should be able to cut down on this problem if you complete your interview preparation properly), but look at the interviewer when you speak. Are they looking interested or bored? Are they doodling? Looking at their email or watch? Maybe they are looking for an opportunity to get a word in edgeways because you have gone on so long.

Silence is Golden

There is always a tendency, during an interview, for the interviewee to feel that they have to fill every single silent moment with speech. This is not the case. Silence is Golden. If you've finished answering the question, stop and shut up. Let the interviewer ask you another question, either a question in response to your answer, a supplementary question or a question on a different topic.

> **TOP TIP**
> If the advertisement says the role requires a particular essential skill that you don't have, and you are still invited to interview, don't think the publisher has made a mistake in selecting you. It could be that you have strengths in areas that they are looking to expand in, or they will reorganise the work to play to your strengths.

Dealing with interview nerves

A number of the clients I've worked with have terrible nerves before an interview. They panic, sweat and the moment they sit down in front of the interviewer, their mind goes completely blank, especially in a face-to-face interview. One way to help you cope with this is to have an interview pack in front of you. This is a clear plastic folder into which you put all your notes and research for the role in question, as well as a copy of the job advertisement or job description, your CV, Covering Letter and the directions. In addition to this, have at least one A4 sheet with some simple prompts to remind you of your skills and experience and any questions you know you want to ask about the role.

Personally, I have two sheets, folded over so I can still see the start of the key points of text.

You are not intending to sit and read this or refer to it all the way through the interview, but it is designed so that in a split-second of panic, you can briefly and surreptitiously glance down and see a few words to remind you of your skills. Hopefully, this will calm and reassure you.

For example, when I was a Sales Manager, and was asked about the key accounts I had called on, I used to say one or two names and then my mind would go completely blank and I struggled to think of anyone else. But when I had an interview pack with its prompt sheet, I could quickly look down for a millisecond before I answered and all the names came back to me. I could then answer confidently about which accounts I had managed.

Sample of A4 sheet

Questions to Ask

- How many days in the office?
- Structure of the dept – how does it work?
- What support is there?
- How good are other departments in keeping to the critical path?
- What are the immediate priorities?

Experience

- JB Publishing – Such a good opportunity working with bestselling titles
- Other experience – working for CJ Publishing, researching children's book, slush pile
- Forecasting and projections, budgets vs actuals,
- Marketing campaigns

Seeking out new opportunities

- Give example of KG notebooks
- Marketing and publicity
- Analytical mind – market research on customers
- Budgeting – always underspend/under budget; never over, constraints
- Team player – Star Wars book
- Future plans – more of the same

Likewise, I coach clients who have varying degrees of special abilities (such as being neurodiverse, anxiety, panic attacks), and they find having an interview pack, with all their preparation, helps overcome any moments when their fear takes hold. They know during a face-to-face interview they can pause at any time and say, "Please can I refer to my notes?" Even having this reassurance, whether they use it or not, helps their confidence level when talking about their skills and experience.

There is nothing wrong with doing this or taking an interview pack into an interview. You wouldn't go into a business meeting unprepared, so why would you go into an interview empty-handed? Be ready to go through your folder with the interviewer if they ask; this has happened to clients on more than one occasion. What you'll then be able to demonstrate quite clearly is how much you want the job, as you'll be able to show your notes (of course, ensure they are suitable to pass over if asked) and the preparation you undertook. Nothing says 'I want this job' more than having spent a few hours researching the publisher and their books.

Interview Assessment Centres

If a publisher has a number of vacancies at the same time, particularly at entry level, it is not unheard of for them to use an Assessment Centre. Examples might be, having four vacancies for a Marketing Executive and 80 applicants who would make the overall shortlist or five entry-level vacancies across the publishing spectrum.

An Assessment Centre, for most people, is hell. It is like being in a bad episode of *The Apprentice*, where maybe 100 candidates are gathered in a day-long interview, all vying for that elusive permanent job, and you are given tasks to perform, both as a team and individually.

Those who perform well in the tasks are called off one by one to face an interview with a panel. Personally, Assessment Centres do very little to help inclusivity or diversity – disabled or culturally different candidates usually struggle – and many who might have the right skills for the job may not perform well in such a pressurised environment. "Oh, they are not like that", I hear the organisers of such centres say. "Oh yes they are", I reply. Even in the most well-thought-out Assessment Centres, individuals might find themselves intimidated or isolated by dominant characters and their participation limited.

If you find yourself in an Assessment Centre situation for a job you really want, here are some guidelines as to how you survive and hopefully win.

1. As part of your preparation for the day, refresh yourself on the key points of the job that this assessment is for. Go through the key skills and understand that those are some, if not all, of the skills you need to demonstrate on the assessment day.

2. When you arrive, be friendly and approachable to everyone. Smile and look pleased to be there, even if you feel like it is the worst day in the world. If there is an issue, such as the organisers not having the room set up, or they tell you that not all the interview panel will be in attendance, remember this could be part of the test. Offer to help and take whatever negatives are thrown at you without complaining or being thrown off balance.

    Employers usually want to work with people who have a pleasant disposition and who shine in the face of adversity. In the same way they also may not want to necessarily work with people who are annoyingly happy, so be careful not to overdo the cheerfulness.

3. Choose your friends wisely. The awkward person in the team task might be part of the process; and the assessment is seeing how you communicate or work on a group basis with someone with different skills to your own. Ensure that when you are working as a group, everyone is included and different voices are heard, not only those who have the confidence to speak out.

4. If the group task is not going with your ideas, you still need to work with the rest of group regardless. That is how publishing works; sometimes our ideas are not pursued and we have to go down a different route. If you think the group is doing something wrong, then yes, point it out, but don't harp on at it, unless it is critical to the success of the task (such as the plan going over budget). Not having your idea selected, or the group not succeeding in the task, doesn't mean you won't get the

job; it all depends on how you cope with the knock-backs and present your ideas.
5. Remember that everything you say or do is being watched or monitored. The gossipy conversation you have over lunch (or even how you behave if someone jumps the lunch queue), is all being observed. So if you are saying inappropriate things, like you are not sure you want the job because you heard bad things about the employer, someone might be logging your comments. In the same way, if someone gossips with you in this way, don't join in the negative talk. Either change the subject completely or move away from them.
6. In the group task it is all about teamwork; you might be allocated a role to play, an idea to pursue or provide part of the jigsaw. You are being tested on a variety of skills, all pertaining to the job and successful employment.

The competencies they will be assessing, regardless of the role, are likely to be:

- Your ability to read and understand written information (remember that from *Chapter Four: Recruitment Practices and Selection*?).
- How you listen to verbal instructions and act upon them.

    Remember the tasks you are set for the day are all going to come from instructions, either verbal or written.

- Whether you read through the whole task before acting upon ANYTHING.

    Did you ever get that handout at school, numbered 1 to 10 with different instructions, such as 'underline the words in point 3', only for point 10 to say, 'ignore all points 1–9'? The task at the Assessment Centre might be very similar.

- Your approach to the task; how you plan what you are going to do and how you organise yourself whilst you work.

Think about the small things, such as all the papers on the table in front of you being in tidy piles, or laid out well, or whether the whole table looks a mess.

- How you communicate with the rest of the team; how inclusive you are and accept other people's opinions.

  Are you excluding anyone who might not have the same social skills?

- How respectful are you? Do you constantly talk over other people, shout people down or raise your voice in order to be heard?

  In the same way, if you are working in a team with others, then it is important that your voice is heard too.

- Your role within the group, whether you are the leader or a follower, whether you come up with ideas and correct and support others, or whether you prefer to work alone.

- Your creative skills! Let's not forget this is likely to be a creative task; for example, a new list is launching.

  As a team, you could be asked to put together a comprehensive marketing plan, design an advert, pick the three lead titles from the list given, write the final campaigns for each and deliver as either a group or individual presentations later in the day.

- How you approach challenges and problems and solve them.

  The task is likely to include hindrances or barriers to prevent a straightforward outcome. Are you using the opportunity to think in a new or different way?

- Your presentation skills; how you talk about the books or the project you have been assigned.

At the interview your questions might be led towards points that the interviewers have observed, such as group members being isolated, your ideas being ignored, or the annoying person in the room. The key here is not to completely pretend that these things didn't happen, but to acknowledge them and move on.

For example, the annoying shouty person in the group might draw you into denigrating the person, such as, "Jay was really annoying; we kept noticing that they were repeatedly talking over you." Instead, you might say, "Yes, they did have a particular way of trying to get their point across, but I am used to working with people of different personalities and feel I still managed to get some of my thoughts and ideas across."

In another example, the interviewer says, "We noticed that your brilliant marketing idea was ignored. How did you feel about that?" "Obviously I was disappointed, but I went along with the group decision anyway and enjoyed the task. I always have lots of different ideas and enjoy generating them."

If you had spotted a mistake and you pointed it out but your comment was ignored: "We noticed you picked up that the marketing plan was over budget, yet your comments were ignored. Why do you think that was?" Then you might reply: "I pointed it out and mentioned it in a few places. I'm not quite sure why the rest of the team didn't pick up on it too; maybe this is something I need to work on."

The interview might also focus on competency questions, but with examples used from the group task. For example: "Tell me how you organised yourself during this task." This is to gauge how you might think on the spot too, as they know you haven't got any pre-rehearsed interview answers ready!

All in all, it can be an intense day, and even those who were successful and got a job via an Assessment Centre have described it as a tough experience. I hope it doesn't catch on too much.

After the interview

Whatever format your job interview has taken, on the day of the interview, email the Recruiter and tell them you really enjoyed meeting them and you are still interested in the role. This is also your immediate opportunity to pick up on a concern they mentioned, or ask a question or make a comment that you wish you had made at the time.

For example:

You asked me about how I would cope taking work off four different people, and in the moment I'm not sure it came across that I gained experience in this during the six-month placement at Zy Publishing. There were four directors, and each had different responsibilities and deadlines. I organised my work and priorities to accommodate all their requirements.

Or

I had a quick look at the cover illustration you mentioned. It is gorgeous; I love the way the blue and purple blend in places to give a 3D impression. I will definitely buy the book when it is published.

TOP TIP

One of the most important things to do immediately before an interview is to go through the job advertisement and description again and write down how you match the role.

Even though you may have done this as part of writing your CV and Covering Letter, doing this again can be critical to you acing the interview, because the role will be fresh in your mind, along with any key responsibilities or functions. Knowing the job in detail and how well you match it, should give you confidence for the interview.

Second (or third) interviews

You apply for the job, you make it through the first interview and then they call you back. Fantastic, you made it through to second interview. Now what?

Imagine, when you meet someone for the first time and you think you really hit it off. You arrange to meet up again and when you do, you're either 'this was such a good idea', or 'oh, what was I thinking'. That is what a second interview is like; it is about meeting someone for the second time and scrutinising their skills and competencies further.

One of the main reasons there is very little written about second interviews (and beyond) is because most of what happens at a second interview is building on the discussions of the first interview. So for the second interview you should expect more of the same.

What this means, in real terms, is whatever way the discussion went at first interview, you need to take that discussion and research it thoroughly or act upon what was said. Say the discussion went around a computer software programme of which you had no prior knowledge, or was something popular, such as InDesign, that you had never used before.

In between first and second interviews you should find out more about the software. If it is specialist publishing industry software, look up the software producer's website, see which other publishers are using it, read the company's PR and understand the principles of it. Is it similar to other software that you already know how to use?

If you haven't used InDesign before, but know that you'll be using it in this role, then download the seven-day free trial and see if you can teach yourself some basics with the help of the free tutorials on the Adobe website, YouTube or elsewhere on the internet. (A basic level of InDesign should mean you are able to create or open a document, resize text and graphics, import text or graphics, and finally safely save and close the document.)

Say, at the first interview, you were discussing a big marketing campaign that was in process. You need to hunt out this marketing campaign and follow everything they are doing on every platform with it. Read every social media post, look at the vocabulary they are using, and how they are engaging with their audience and interacting with their followers. Are there any interesting comments or posts you can use in your next discussion?

Examples of this in practice

If it is a publisher of Personal Development, for instance, and they've told you the book they are so excited about is coming from an author they describe as the 'Next Wayne Dyer'. And be honest, you have never heard of Wayne Dyer but in the first interview automatically nodded in agreement. The action to take after the interview is to research Wayne Dyer and you find out that, sadly, he is no longer with us. However, his audience and followers are there for the taking – they are looking for the 'next Wayne Dyer'. So you look through Wayne Dyer's back catalogue to see what books he wrote and where they were positioned in the marketplace. Then you research the author the publisher mentioned at your interview and see what they are up to. At this point, you might compare where the new author's fans are against where you might find Wayne Dyer's fans.

You're being interviewed by an Academic publisher and they mention that they are building a platform in the same manner as Science Direct, and it will host all their journal articles. However, they are debating the layout, whether they want it to be more like Publisher A or Publisher B. You need to go away and research all they mentioned – look at Science Direct, look at Publisher A and Publisher B, so you have some thoughts and discussion points that can raise at your second interview.

Your second interview is with Pan Macmillan and they were very excited, not only about the hardback edition of Mariah Carey's autobiography but also about the paperback publication of Elton John's autobiography, that is being sold with a new additional chapter. In this case, make sure you check all their social media platforms to see what material was in this new chapter, and how they were marketing it. Then you are able to comment on this being an inspired piece of marketing that encouraged hardback customers to buy the paperback edition too, just for the new chapter.

These examples should give you an idea of what signposts you should follow from your first interview. Whilst the questions you can expect within your second interview will be similar to the first one, the opening question of a second interview is likely to be: "So what have you done since we last spoke?", or: "Have you learned anything since your first interview?"

You can then wow them with your answers, as a direct result of undertaking this research. It demonstrates that you are genuinely interested in the role and the publisher, and you know that you would make a great employee.

The rest of the questions are likely to be along the same lines as the first interview but may be more conversational in style. If you're limited on examples or scenarios, it is okay to use the same ones you discussed in your first interview, but this time you might go into a little more detail in your response. Do not feel you're repeating yourself, or feel aggrieved that you are answering the same questions again. Last time they were skimming the surface; now they are looking in more depth.

And remember, that for a second interview, you are probably in the final two or three candidates, though it is not unheard of for a second interview to involve five or six candidates.

Once again, after your second interview, send a thank you email and re-enforce your interest in the role.

All being well, you will have wowed them so much, they will offer you the job.

But if not, remember there is a job somewhere with your name on it. You just need to find it.

ACTION POINTS

- Have a think about the reasons given at the beginning of this chapter why we have job interviews.
- Are there any points you'd add, or you think are not valid?
- Think about your body language when you speak to someone else. Do you always pause if it is a question you don't like as opposed something you are happy to answer? Can you spot any patterns in yourself?
- Try this exercise with a friend or colleague. Watch their body language and see if you can read what they are feeling by the position of their posture and hands when they talk to you. Sometimes it is a simple as thinking: "How do I feel when I am leaning on the desk with both hands holding my head?" "How do I feel when my hand is covering my mouth?"

CHAPTER EIGHT

Interview Questions and How to Answer Them

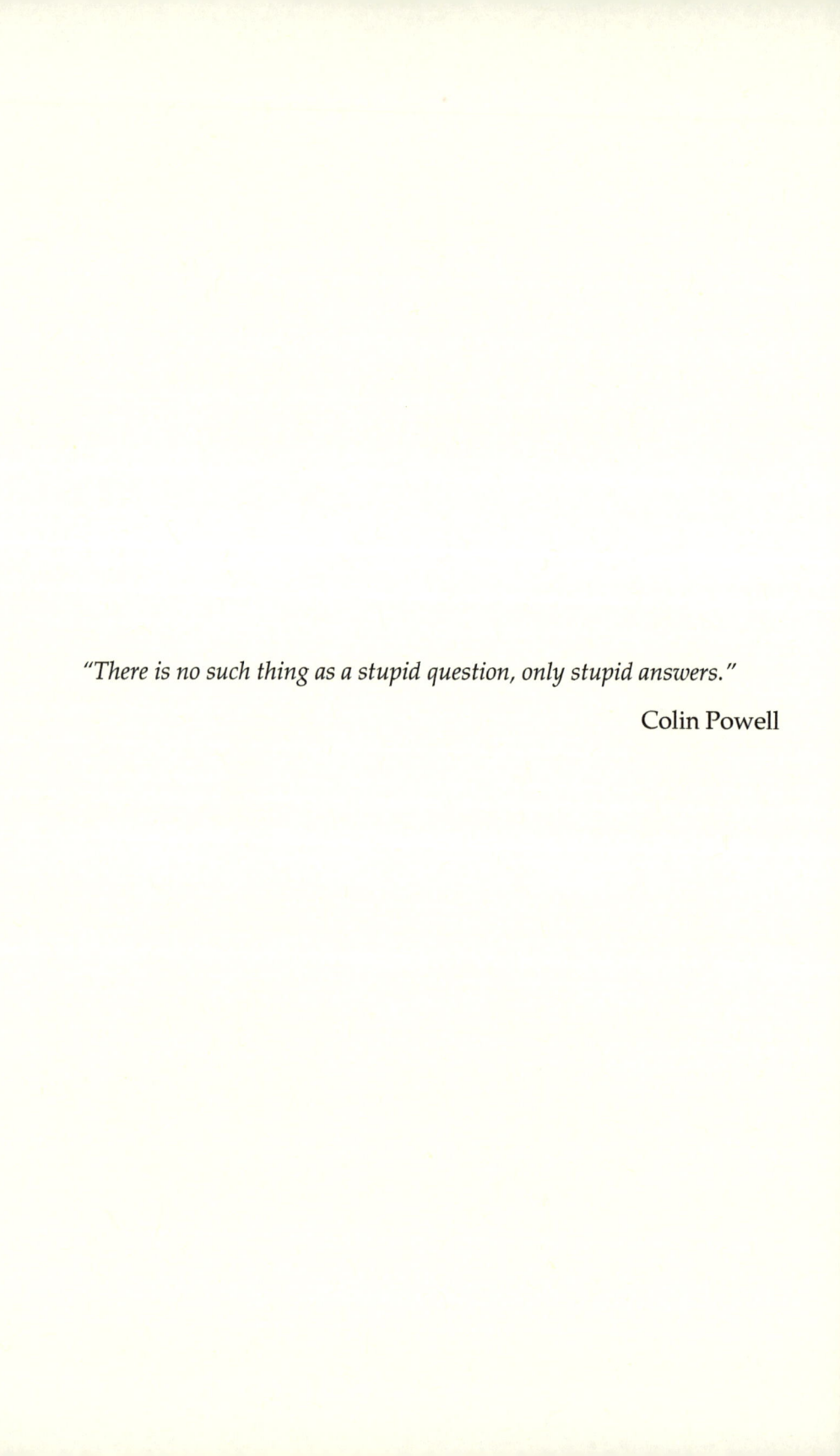

"There is no such thing as a stupid question, only stupid answers."

Colin Powell

When it comes to the interview, there are different kinds of interview questions, and each should give you an idea for the response expected. These are the types of question you might be asked:

- Open Questions
- Closed Questions
- Probing Questions and Supplementary Questions
- Hypothetical Questions
- Leading Questions
- Multiple Questions
- Competency, Situational or Behavioural questions

Open Questions

These questions often start with Who, How, Why, When, Where. For example:

- "Why do you think we should employ you?"
- "What has been your greatest achievement?"

These questions allow you to answer as you wish and are intended to find out more about you, your skills and experience.

I'm often asked as to how long your answers should be. I would guess from one second to 1 minute, 30 seconds. However, don't go on too long and don't ramble – do not feel you need to keep talking, and do not feel you have to fill any silences. Look at the body language of the interviewer and read the non-verbal clues mentioned in the previous chapter.

Closed Questions

These questions require a Yes/No answer. For example, "Can you start Monday?" "Yes."

However, they can also be leading questions in that they guide you towards the answer. For example, "Would you say you were pro-active?" is actually a closed question, as it requires a yes/no answer, but it is leading you towards saying "yes", as the role you are being interviewed for probably wants someone proactive.

Probing Questions and Supplementary Questions

These are very often **challenging questions**, ones that reflect on statements you may have just made. Sometimes they are targeted to see how you react when your opinion is challenged, the same way it might be challenged in a meeting with colleagues.

- "Why do you think that scenario happened?"
- "What would you have done differently?"
- "You say you were unhappy with the book jacket, why?"
- "Why do you think the authors always delivered late?"

Hypothetical Questions

These are designed to give the interviewer an insight into your thought process and actions.

- "Say I offered you this role, what would be your first priority?"
- "Say you were given three tasks all with a high priority, which task would you do first?"

- "What would you do if you were about to miss a deadline?"

(The last one can also be a trick question because your answer might indicate that you always miss deadlines!)

Leading Questions

This is where the interviewer is leading you to the answer:

- "I said this job involves a lot of admin tasks, are you okay with that?"
- "This job involves a lot of travel. I take it that won't worry you?"

Very often, whilst you might agree with the interviewer that all is well with the suggestions of lots of administrative tasks, travel or something similar, if after the interview you are quite worried about how they emphasised these facts, then that is a sign the job is not for you.

Multiple Questions

This is where they fire several questions to you at the same time

- "What about your last job? What did you do? How did the team work?"

As well as wanting to know your answers, this is also to see how you work through multiple priorities. Do you answer them in order or do you start with the last one first. It is always best to start with them in order, and work through. If you've forgotten the final question when you get around to it, do ask them to repeat it.

And then we come to everyone's favourite

Competency, Situational or Behavioural questions.

Competency-based questions live under the belief that past behaviour equals future behaviour; that how you reacted or dealt with a situation in the past could be indicative of how you will react in a similar situation in the future. Your answers can also show growth, learning and understanding, as we tend to learn from situations that haven't gone according to plan.

These are the questions that are often scored and then the scores of each candidate are added up at the end, to ensure that the process has been fair and non-discriminatory.

The questions might start with:

- "Tell me about a time when ..."
- "Give me an example of ..."
- "What would do you if ..."

One way to answer these questions is to use the STAR formula to ensure you have included everything. The problem with the STAR method is whilst it can be great for helping you to organise your thoughts or scenarios, in reality, too many people take it literally and their answers are mechanical, boring and monotonous.

Candidates tend to stick to the STAR method rigidly, and when asked a question at interview, give a formulaic answer, sometimes vague in its detail, and it sounds like they have learned a script, rather than having a natural conversation. Instead, the best interview answers are authentic, help build rapport, and have depth, clarity and detail.

This is the STAR method.

- Situation – The situation, what was going on?
- Task – What was required of you?
- Action – What you actually did?
- Result – What was the end result?

Here is an example of how the STAR method works in practice. It will help you plan an answer to a question that may relate to the skills of the role

SKILL HEADING   Organisation
SITUATION (Describe the situation)   We were organising a sales conference (expand on this)
TASK (What was required of you)   It was my responsibility to confirm the booking, ensure that everything ran smoothly on the day and that all the delegates needs were met
ACTION OR EVIDENCE   (What did you actually do? Describe the details of what you did.)   I met with the venue's conference manager and laid out precisely what we needed for the day, particularly in respect of audio-visual equipment. I liaised with our department manager and ensured that everything was taken care of. This included the arranging for delegate badges, the sales kits (with contributions from every department), the PowerPoint presentation, the menus, including any food allergies, and our guest authors. I turned up an hour early to make sure that all was in place as well as did an extra run through of the presentations, to check everything was flawless.
RESULT (What was achieved as a result of your actions?)   Everything ran so smoothly. The Managing Director said it was the best company sales conference he had ever attended, it was so well organised. As a result, they have given me the responsibility of organising all future conferences, as well as our attendance at other external events.

STAR: Situation / Task / Activity / Result

Here is a blank STAR form for you to work with, if you choose. You can also download this from bookcareers.com

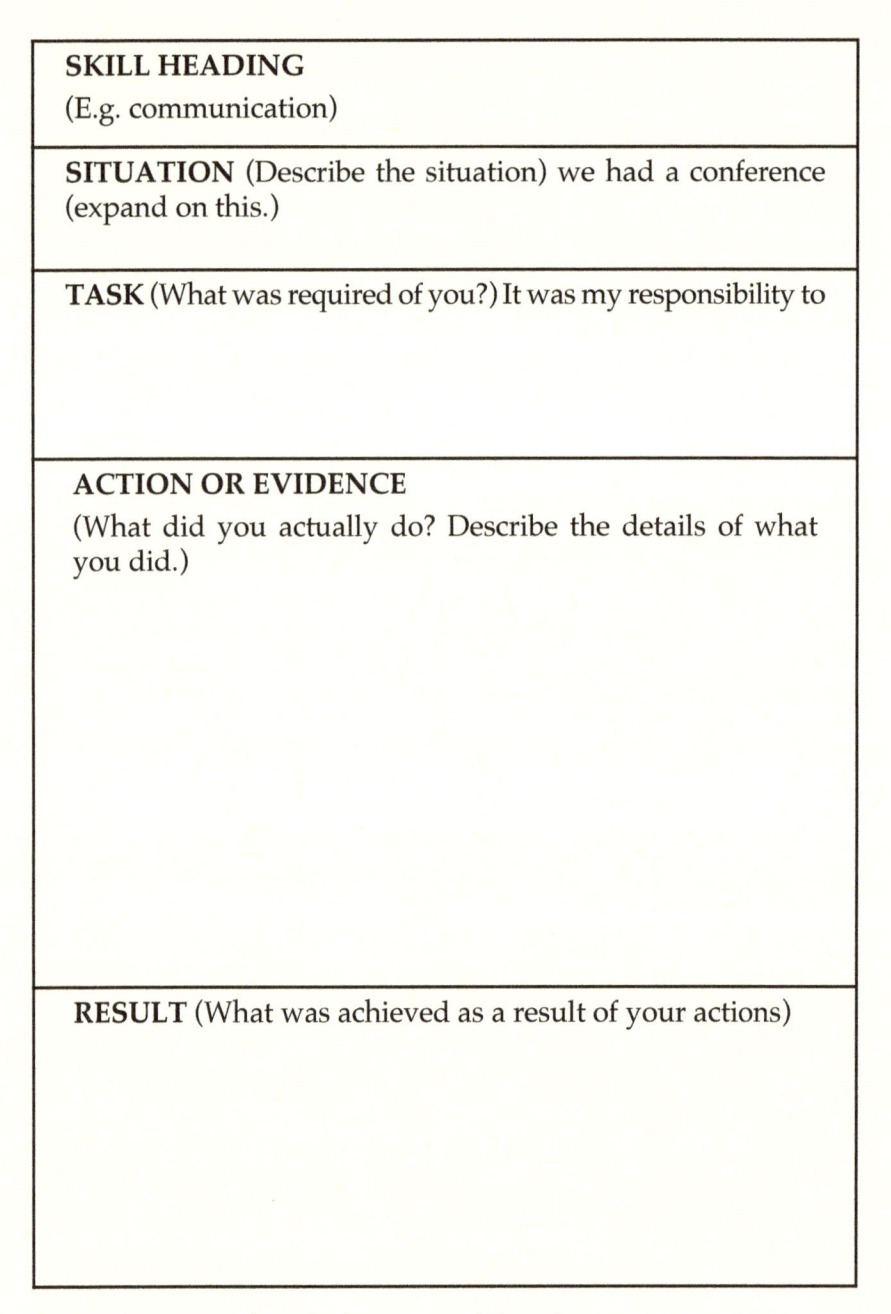

SKILL HEADING (E.g. communication)
SITUATION (Describe the situation) we had a conference (expand on this.)
TASK (What was required of you?) It was my responsibility to
ACTION OR EVIDENCE (What did you actually do? Describe the details of what you did.)
RESULT (What was achieved as a result of your actions)

STAR: Situation / Task / Activity / Result

However, to prepare yourself fully for any kind of interview question the best preparation is to get a notebook and pen, as you would have done for your Covering Letter, and go through every single word and phrase of the job advertisement and in response, write your career experience in relation to the job, giving a success, mistake and challenge.

Sample job advertisement

Acclaimed independent publisher bookcareers is looking for an Editorial Assistant to join our team. This exciting and busy role is an opportunity for someone who would like a grounding in publishing to work with our editors across bookcareers adult and children's imprints developing editorial skills as well as providing key administrative support.

Responsibilities include:
- Supporting editors working on a variety of fiction, non-fiction and children's titles, and working closely with the Managing Editor, as well as liaising with the sales, design, marketing and publicity teams, authors and translators
- Proofreading, copy-writing, proof checking and clearing permissions
- Writing AIs and maintaining the BiblioLive database
- Prize and translation grant administration
- Overseeing the eBook publishing programme
- Administrative tasks including minute taking, phone and email queries, post
- Reading and reporting on manuscripts

Essential skills include:
- A voracious reader with demonstrable interest in bookcareers publishing
- An energetic and flexible approach to work, self-motivated with excellent organisational, time management and planning skills

- **Excellent verbal and written communication skills and meticulous attention to detail**
- **Strong IT skills**

We publish around 70 titles per year across our imprints.

Please apply to us by Wednesday 10th July with a Covering Letter explaining why you want to work at bookcareers and CV. Salary dependent on experience.

Here is a sample sentence from job advertisement marked up with success, mistake, challenge

Supporting editors working on a variety of fiction, non-fiction and children's titles, and working closely with the Managing Editor, as well as liaising with the sales, design, marketing and publicity teams, authors and translators

Success

It is my responsibility to keep the publishing database up to date, and check that sales, marketing and publicity have all added their contributions so our catalogue and website have the fullest of information. This used to be done twice-yearly, which made a lot of work for everyone, and sometimes they didn't have all the information to hand. I came up with the idea of doing this monthly instead. After discussing this with the Managing Editor and the wider team, I added this task to the critical path, and it has become an ongoing process. As a result, as a company we are never far behind, and it has been far easier to track the information. The other departments seem to find it easier to keep on top of too.

Mistake

When I first started I didn't know how to pronounce the surname of our bestselling author as it didn't sound like it was spelt. I welcomed the author into a big company-wide meeting, mispronouncing their name, and they were very upset and suggested to the Editorial Director I wasn't up to the job. I sent a personal written apology and some flowers to the author, and they accepted my apology. Ever since then, if an author is coming in for a meeting, or if I have to introduce anyone or I am unsure about how to pronounce their name, I will always ask how they like to be introduced, so this does not happen again.

Challenge

I really enjoy supporting editors and it is a very busy department where often the Managing Editor has tight deadlines and needs to chase authors. I keep a diary of when to chase so that nothing slips through the net. There was one time where the author was so late with the photographic images that they didn't have time to scan them in, so I arranged for them to send the original prints and scanned them in myself, staying late in the office, in order to speed up the process and meet the deadline.

Whilst this example is only one sentence, by doing this for every single point and sentence of the job advertisement, you will really learn the detail of the role, what is involved, and how your experience directly or indirectly matches the criteria. Even if you are unfamiliar with the job itself and you do not have the full experience the role requires, you should be able to reference other situations from your career history that demonstrate similar skills. You are also likely to discover the best scenarios and examples from your career history to choose to discuss at interview. For example, the success answer given here, could also be used to demonstrate how you would *keep the BiblioLive database up to date and it proves how you are self-motivated with excellent organisational, time management and planning skills.*

I recommend that if you are starting out you find at least three scenarios you can talk about. These should relate to work experiences or situations you have been involved in. It is fine to use examples from the student newspaper, university societies or other voluntary experiences, where the situation mimics something that might go on in a publishing house. However, do be wary of constantly using these experiences throughout, as it might indicate how little real-life work experience you have and lead you to get the rejection letter "we've chosen someone with more practical experience". Always aim to prioritise employment scenarios over educational ones, unless the educational example is directly related to book publishing, such as editing a student newspaper.

If you are looking for a job at manager level, or above, aim to have at least six scenarios you can talk about.

However, regardless of your level, if you have a scenario that you can use for each of these situations you are likely to be able to answer a high percentage of any competency-based interview question which is thrown at you. This is because one scenario can answer many questions.

1. Your greatest success or something you are proud of
2. A mistake that you made and the consequences
3. The worst situation you have ever been in
4. When you worked with others as a team
5. When you've had to communicate with others
6. An example of being organised, how you prioritised work or practised effective time management
7. A time when you have been creative
8. A time when you have solved a problem
9. An example of when you have had to persuade someone to change their mind
10. And for a senior role, a leadership and management example

Let's discuss each of these scenarios further. I have used my personal experiences throughout this chapter so they seem far removed from your own experiences or any scenario you may use at an interview. Even though the incidents may be from some time ago, the principles and how to answer the questions are up to date.

Imagine at an interview there is a shovel in the middle of the desk, in between you and the interviewer. Every time a question is being asked the interviewer is passing you the shovel. You can either use it like a tennis racquet to bat the answer back, or you can use it to dig a hole for yourself.

This is what the challenging, probing, negative and competency-based questions do; they show you have precisely the right skills for the job or give you the opportunity to bury your chances of ever getting the job.

1. Your greatest success or something you are proud of

This could cover any question that needs a positive answer, whether it is working well under pressure, being organised, dealing with a difficult person, or overcoming a hardship or difficulty. It is often best to pick a success story that mimics at least one of the key skills for the role, for example, if the role involves lots of deadlines or multitasking, aim to find a scenario where you were doing just that.

2. A mistake that you made and the consequences

This is definitely a shovel question, one where you could end up digging yourself the deepest hole.

I would recommend you choose a scenario that answers a mistake question and then do not use it elsewhere in the same interview; only use it for a direct 'tell me about a mistake' scenario. Also, always pause before answering this question, as if you are struggling to think of a time when you made a mistake. If you instantly jump in with the answer, then one might assume that you are always making mistakes.

When looking for potential answers for negative questions, aim to find a scenario that was a while ago, one that didn't cost the company (or anybody) money, and that you learned from the experience. You would always end by saying, "and that is why I am now so good at... because I always..."

Never blame another person, particularly never blame another colleague, although sometimes it is acceptable to blame authors, providing you had given them clear instructions and already prepared them for every eventuality beforehand (we do love all authors, but in some situations, they can make life tricky). In every circumstance, never say you weren't briefed properly. Always accept responsibility for your actions and own your mistake.

This is a sample answer where others are blamed:

When I was working at Andre Deutsch we were producing our first catalogue order form – a complete order form of all the titles we had in stock. We had no prior document to go on or refer to for guidance. It was a mammoth task, beset with problems – we'd had an issue where the typesetter had read all the ISBNs a line down, and we had to spend three days calling back ISBNs to each other to pick up any errors. It was already running late and just as I was walking out of the door to take it to production, the Sales Director stopped me and told me that she wanted a template on the back, with numbers 1–20 to represent the page numbers, so the reps could circle the page numbers they used. I got some Sellotape and stuck the template she had given me on the back page, doing as I was told. It was the Sales Director's mistake. There were actually 48 pages to the catalogue. But I always check now things like page extent.

This is how it should be answered, taking full responsibility:

When I was working at Andre Deutsch we were producing our first catalogue order form – a complete order form for all the titles we had in stock. We had no prior document to go on or refer to for guidance. It was a mammoth task, beset with problems – we'd had an issue where some of the ISBNs had shifted a line down in formatting, and we had to spend three days calling back ISBNs to each other to pick up any errors. It was already running late and just as I was walking out of the door to take it to production, the Sales Director stopped me and said, it would be a good idea to put a table on the back so that the reps could circle which pages they had used. She gave me the template she had drawn, numbers 1–20, and without thinking I got some Sellotape and stuck it on the back page. There were actually 48 pages to the catalogue, and the reps had a good laugh about it. This is something I learned from. Ever since, I have always checked finer details on any project, such as ensuring page numbers correlate throughout, no matter how urgent the task is.

Do you see the difference in the examples given of the same circumstance? In the first the blame is going on other people – the typesetter and the Sales Director. In the second example, I haven't blamed anyone else; I was the project owner for the catalogue – it was my responsibility to get it right. Also, in this example, whilst it was a printing mistake, there was no money lost. There was only the embarrassment of someone daft in the company (me) not counting the page numbers.

Even if you have made a serious mistake at work, one that was costly to the company, or you are unfortunate enough to be constantly making mistakes, do not choose these examples for job interviews. Aim to choose a different example that whilst demonstrating something went wrong, you actually didn't come out too badly from it. Remember, an interview is not a confessional; you want to be seen in a good light.

3. The worst situation you have ever been in

This has the potential to be a shovel question. It could be, like me, you don't see things as 'worst situations', they are more 'difficult' or 'uncomfortable'. Nevertheless, you might say this and then plump for an answer.

This is definitely a scenario that should answer lots of different interview questions and, if you have limited experience, it is fine to refer back to this later on when asked a question that relates to your skills.

Again, ensure that you do not blame a person or the team. Find a circumstance that you can talk about. If you're already in the industry, often it could be something like, "we had a deadline and the server went down" or "an author event and the trains were cancelled". Don't choose an author event and say the books didn't turn up, because you would be expected to be prepared for the books to turn up and taken every precaution to make sure the books were there.

For example:

On the day of the 7/7 London bombs I was due to visit Gardners in Eastbourne (a major account for any publisher) to present November titles, some of which had huge targets. As I go in the opposite direction to the traffic and have a variety of ways to get there, I picked up the travel report as I left home, and heard there had been a power surge on the underground. I switched the radio to a news channel and for the next two hours listened as the news unfolded.

By the time I got to Gardners I knew there had been four bombs and a major loss of life. I was deeply worried about friends, family and colleagues. When I arrived, I was presented with a new buyer, and we had no existing rapport, but we quickly built it as he was just as worried about his friends and family. I said we need to do some work, switched on my laptop and started the presentation.

The first title that came up was Worst Case Scenario Extreme Edition, and I wanted to burst into tears and fall through the floor. I had a major target to achieve, and it was now no longer appropriate for me to talk about the title. It was no longer appropriate for me to ask questions from my sales pitch, "is it better to be bitten by an alligator or a shark?" and "how do you stop a runaway train?". Instead, I told the buyer how many copies I was looking for, and what we could do to support an order of that size in promotion and advertising. I left the information for him to come back to me in a few days, which he did.

* *It is better to be bitten by an alligator than a shark. You are more likely to survive an alligator bite than a shark bite.*

Now I'm not suggesting that you find a scenario with as much drama in as this, and one has to be careful when talking about things so emotive as the London bombings. You do not know how the other person on the side of the table might have been affected on the day, either by being close to one of the bombs, or by losing a loved one. And whilst I describe this as a Worst Situation, many other people had far worse experiences on that day and my heart goes out to them all.

Nonetheless, can you see, in this extreme scenario, how it would be useful for many other interview questions too? Here are some examples:

- Tell me about a difficult circumstance
- Tell me about a time you built rapport with a new buyer
- Tell me about a time you had to think on your feet
- Tell me about when things didn't go according to plan

4. When you worked with others as a team

Think about a time when you've worked with others on a project or idea, and it came to a successful conclusion. The chances are that if you already have some employment experience, you have regularly worked with others as a team. What a recruiter is looking for in your answers are signs of teamwork and collaboration.

If you're early in your career, this question, and the next, might present themselves as "What role do you play in your group of friends?" This allows the recruiter to discover the dynamics of how you behave with others. When presented with this, obviously think about how you are within your group of friends and choose a skill that is key for the role you are going for.

For example:

- "I'm the one who always organises everything."
- "Some of my friends don't see eye to eye, but I'm the one who brings us all together,"
- "I'm the one who has the sense of responsibility and always checks everyone gets home okay,"

5. When you've had to communicate with others

Again, if you have employment experience the chances are you regularly had to communicate with others. If this is the case, always say it. When looking for a communication scenario you should find an example where the communication relationship is the same as, or similar to, the one for the job you are being interviewed for. Examples of these relationships are:

- Editorial to sales
- Production to supplier
- Sales to buyer
- Cross-department
- External relationships
- Social media posts

Example

I have to communicate every day, with colleagues across all the publishing functions as well as authors. I'm the first point of contact for the department and manage the department inbox as well as the incoming calls. With the telephone it is really important to answer everything promptly and professionally, as you never know who might be on the other end of the call. Usually the calls are from prospective authors who haven't read the submission guidelines on our website and they are asking specific questions about how to submit their manuscript, which I am happy to answer, although the answers are available for them to read online.

6. An example of being organised, prioritised work or practised effective time management

This scenario may present itself in many different ways, and it is a critical question for anyone, especially if you are seeking an entry-level role.

With these, interviewers are looking for long-term and short-term organisation and time management examples. Think about how you plan your day with short term tasks and how you keep up with long term tasks, or tasks that you have to bring forward.

The answers the interviewer is likely to look for include keeping a daily list, that you write before you leave the office the previous day, adding anything urgent from your emails the next morning and maybe keeping a bring forward folder, diary or long-term task list so nothing gets lost. What they are looking for is the note keeping, the diary management and a task list.

It is no good being vague when answering this question; specifics are very important, whether you are using a computer, an app, a bullet journal or pen and paper. Clearly spell out to the recruiter how organised you are and how you always know your deadlines, explain what system you use for reminders or bringing things forward; all the time aim to show how nothing slips through the net.

Example

I'm used to having a heavy workload and juggle more than 500 customer accounts of varying sizes. I use tools, such as Outlook for reminders of tasks to bring forward, and an Excel spreadsheet that is a full list of things to do. At the end of each day, I write a to-do list with pen and paper that I can update wherever I am. My Excel spreadsheet is colour-coded and has a number of formulas so I can easily sort and filter all the work into different tasks. For example, one colour shows all the people I need to phone, if I have spare moments; another has the people I have to email, if I am in the office.

7. A time when you have been creative

This is a very important scenario to have if any of the role involves some sort of creativity, whether it is writing jacket blurbs, creative copy or social media posts, copywriting, designing anything including marketing collateral. Creativity doesn't mean you are the next Picasso, but the scenario could be when you've used your imagination, either in a work or personal space, for professional gain or personal pleasure. If you can find a creative work example, all the better, but don't worry if not. Aim to answer so the creative example you give matches the creativity involved in the role you are being interviewed for.

Example

One of the most creative things I have done was to help with the redesign of our university music society website. We had a limited budget so I downloaded several different website templates and undertook some market research as to what layout and colours students preferred. Then I modified a commercial template so it had a funky, appealing and readable look, where students could easily locate the information, whilst ensuring the website was accessible. I then designed some posters for our music events that matched the website design and displayed them across campus.

8. A time when you solved a problem

Even the most junior of roles can involve you solving problems for the wider company. This might be through the administrative tasks you've been delegated or a publishing function that you are responsible for. It could be a simple problem solve or something far more complex.

Example

I was responsible for ordering all the free sample copies from the warehouse for every department. Colleagues would send me requests at all times of the day demanding immediate delivery, that always came at a premium, and our additional warehouse costs were huge as a result. Our distributor was getting fed up with the constant sample requests too. I spoke to my line manager to get their approval, then approached each department to organise a new system. I'd automatically order a set number of advances of all new titles as soon as they were in the warehouse. All additional sample orders would only be processed once a day before 10.00 am and that immediate delivery was only for exceptional circumstances. By doing this, our warehouse costs dropped to a manageable level.

9. An example of when you have had to persuade someone to change their mind

This is the negotiation scenario and it is key if the role you are interviewing for has involvement in buying, selling or negotiation. Think of an example where you manage to get what you want out of the situation but also make the person you are negotiating with feel like they also have won.

Example

Part of my current role involves negotiation as I am always having to negotiate with international publishers over contracts. We have our set contract, but often the international publisher wants us to use their contract, with less favourable terms. I try to use our contract but amend any clauses where we can. This keeps our Contracts Director happy, as our contract has other clauses, such as the use of AI, which the international publisher's contract doesn't. There are one or two sticking points, such as the number of advance copies, but I often let the publisher win one or two of the small things, which don't cost us much, if anything, so they feel they've won overall, but maintaining our position on the bigger picture. *This way the other publisher feels they are in a partnership with us, which is very important as we want to sell them more titles.*

10. And for a senior role, a leadership and management example

Again, it is really important here that in your scenario you demonstrate the skills you have that relate to the role, whether it is team leadership, staff management, or publishing management. Aim to be as specific as you can, so the recruiter will be confident you can handle challenging situations at a senior level.

Other interview scenarios you may face:

Questions about conflict:

"Tell me about a time when you had conflict with your colleagues."

or

"Tell us about a time when you've had a difficult member of staff and how you resolved it."

This is a shovel question, and you have the opportunity here to dig yourself into a big hole. How long you take to answer it relates to how deep you are digging the hole for yourself. You need to answer swiftly: You do not have conflicts with people. The recruiter might press you and say, "Surely you've had a disagreement with somebody", but please don't fall into their trap.

Depending on the role, you might add you have to deal with challenging situations or people all the time, but you're calm, give the person the opportunity to be heard, and then carry on. It is not in your nature to be anything other than a peacekeeper. You might respond you get on well with everyone; you are known for being easy to get on with. This could be true, but if you are further up in your career, the chances are you have had to resolve a situation like this. It could also be a warning sign that there are difficult people in the department, so if you are a sensitive soul, you might not want to work in such an atmosphere.

The best way to answer this question is to say that you tend to get on well with everyone. However, as in all publishing companies –

and all businesses – there are personalities who from time to time like to make things challenging, but you don't find this a big issue. If asked, be prepared to give an example of how someone has been challenging, but don't volunteer this information willingly and don't name the person. The challenge could be: "They always demand their titles are given priority, no matter what the other deadlines or budget. I give them confidence that their issues will be dealt with, then go on to complete the tasks as originally agreed; they don't seem to notice."

Giving away company information and secrets

As book publishing is a very insular industry, if the publisher interviewing you is a major competitor of your current employer, it could be that the interviewer is only interviewing you to pick you brains.

This will occur less if you are working for a small or medium publisher with no ragingly high profile, but if the imprint you work for is a market leader or has taken the publishing industry by storm in a particular genre, niche or way of marketing, it is something you should be aware of. It is more likely to happen if you are working for a big publisher and interviewing for a small publisher.

Of course, it is important that you still talk about your job and scenarios, but you might not give all the specifics (like not giving the name of an author, customer, or any financial information). What you don't want to do, is to give away anything that could be classed as company information or secrets. As much as you want to sell yourself in the interview, think for a moment if you don't get the job, would you be happy with the information you shared? Don't get carried away, and if at any time you think the recruiter could be crossing a line, you can always say: "I don't feel comfortable sharing company confidential information." They won't hate you for it, if anything they might respect you more.

What would you say to the MD/CEO if you met them in the lift?

This could be a trick question to see if you would be outspoken, say something political, or pitch yourself, or say "I'd tell them what was wrong with this company", or ask what football team they support.

If you've done some research on the company, you might have a question you want to ask them, maybe about the company structure, an acquisition or a new genre that is up and coming. You don't have to be clever with this question, just ensure you show that you are interested in the company and what they are publishing.

Questions that you might have researched before the interview

How does digital publishing affect children's publishing?

This is where having an interview pack that includes your research may help you, especially if you did a lot of preparation on this before the interview and your mind has suddenly gone blank. Ask the interviewer if it is okay for you to refer to your notes as you did some work on this beforehand, and if they say okay (it is unlikely they will refuse, but always be courteous and ask anyway) then refer to your notes. Be careful not to do this more than once in an interview; you do not want to look like you are reading a script.

What are the main issues facing this publisher?

If you've done your interview prep properly you might have seen one or two areas of concern. Especially if you've signed up for their newsletter and the newsletter of their competitor and followed both on social media. By reading the marketing output of each publisher it would make you aware of what the issues are.

For example, you might have noticed that their nearest competitor is publishing a very similar list, slightly cheaper or offering a free eBook version with every purchase.

It is okay to say what you think might be an issue, but be wary about how you phrase your thoughts. For example: "I can see you are likely to be hit hard by the new books coming from X publisher", won't necessarily go down as well as "I can see that you've now got competition coming from another new publisher in the same marketplace."

You've got a lot of experience in Editorial, why do you want to work in Sales (or vice versa)?

One of the things that a publisher doesn't want to do is recruit someone who wants to work elsewhere, or who would always be hankering after an editorial job. So, if you've already got editorial experience but have decided to refocus your career in Marketing, then make it clear that you don't want to move back to Editorial. If you are only applying for the marketing job because you can't get an editorial job, then it might be better to apply only for jobs you actually want.

If you seriously want to move from Editorial to another department you might say something about the culture of an editorial department, perhaps you found it more suited to an introvert, and you consider yourself an extrovert, so Sales/Marketing always seem to be better fits for you.

What has been the most enjoyable aspect of your job?

Whilst you want to be genuine about the parts of the current role you enjoy, you also need to ensure that the skills you enjoy using are a key part of the role you are being interviewed for. For example, if you enjoy customer service and talking to people, and the role you are being interviewed for is a very insular one, with little communication to the outside world, the interviewer may assume you would be unhappy in the new job.

What is more important to you – working in publishing, or working with the skills for this specific job?

There is no real right or wrong answer to this question; it is more to discover a little bit more about you and what motivates you in the world of work. Alternatively, this question might appear in an interview for a big conglomerate that has a variety of companies in non-publishing sectors, and they are testing whether you want to keep to the publishing career path or be happy in any career path, as long as you were in marketing, for example. It doesn't necessarily mean they will rule you out as a candidate, but they ask this question to understand your motivation.

Tell me about yourself

So many clients tell me that they hate getting this question as they don't know how to answer it.

Many people start by answering this question as a complete historical walk-through of their CV and every job and every single career decision they made (good and bad). Then they wonder why they feel bored and the interviewer looks like they are losing interest too.

But "Tell me about yourself" is the creme de la creme of interview questions. It is the BEST interview question to be asked. It is the question where you are standing on a stage, the spotlight shines on you, the interviewer gives you control of the shovel, and you get to pitch yourself for the job. That is right, you steer the "Tell me about yourself" to talking about your career history, skills and experience but ensure you keep it relevant for the job you are trying to get. For example, the job advertisement said they wanted a Rights Assistant who was organised, methodical, and could juggle multiple projects, and languages would be a bonus.

Example

I'm a language graduate who is fluent in French, Hungarian and Spanish (you might say, Bonjour, Szia, Hola) who is really keen on international rights. I've been busy working in a coffee shop and local bookshop whilst studying at university and this has given me great customer service skills and a good knowledge of what the company publishes, as well as lots of self-discipline, as I had to organise and prioritise different shifts around lectures and writing a dissertation.

I got the opportunity to go to the London Book Fair and spent most of my time walking around the stands of the international publishers and looking at what books they were promoting. I find Rights a fascinating area of publishing as you get to understand so many different cultures and countries and how the tastes and demands change according to the location. I also enjoy travelling and I hope one day to be in a Rights role which involves international travel.

This answer is almost like playing interview bingo. Can you see how it has incorporated so much about the skills for the role, and added informal knowledge about the publisher and international rights? Any Rights Manager looking for an assistant would be really keen to see and hear more from this candidate, regardless of their other experience. And if they are comparing this interview answer alongside a candidate who gave their career history and a walk-through of their CV, you can see which candidate would score higher.

Can you tell me about your current position and your other experience? (or Talk me through your CV)

I recommend you rehearse your answer in advance for this. It is another question where you need to be playing interview bingo – tailoring your response so you match the skills you already have with the skills the interviewer is looking for in the position.

For example, for an Editorial role, that asks for proofreading, copyediting or reporting to different directors all with varying priorities, you want to ensure you cover these points in your response, even if you've only recently graduated. Talk about the times when you've edited documents, maybe thesis of other students, and worked to different deadlines, or when you volunteered for a student society.

You might be thinking, this will show I have no real experience to do the job, as the examples are all based from time spent in education, but if they really believed you had so little experience, they would not have invited you to interview.

Why are you looking to leave your current role?

This is clearly a shovel question! These are acceptable reasons for leaving your current job:

- Career progression
- You weren't really looking but this seemed too good an opportunity to pass on
- Your contract is coming to an end, or you want to focus more on a particular area.

What you do NOT say is anything detrimental about your employer, the people you work with, or even the work you do, unless you are currently employed in a frozen pea factory counting frozen peas. You must remain professional at all times.

If your job has been made redundant then the vocabulary to use is, "My job has been made redundant", not, "I was made redundant". It is worth knowing jobs get made redundant, not people. Don't dwell on this and shut up. The recruiter might want to pry but more often than not they will already know the reasons for redundancy (publishing is a small industry; it is likely there has been an announcement in the trade press) and should move on to the next question.

The reasons you are looking to change job are you want fresh challenges, to work on different skills, genres, departments, with a team you admire, or anything positive or exciting you have researched about your potential new employer.

What part of the job do you think you will struggle with?

This has the potential to be a shovel question. Of course you might struggle with something, but the way you respond to this question can make or break the job offer. There is a tendency to joke and say, "all of it", or, "getting up in the morning". However, you should never make this type of joke at an interview.

If it is a job you are familiar with you can honestly say that you wouldn't struggle with any of it; it all seems relatively straightforward. However, if it is a promotion or your first job, you might want to pick something relatively minor or insignificant but turn it into a positive. Whatever you do, don't pick a key element of the role or anything organisational or time management based.

For example, "I can't really see that I would struggle with any of the role, but I know whilst my InDesign skills are good, and I can work on documents with integrated illustrations without issue, they could always be better, but that is probably because I'm not complacent."

Where do you see yourself in five years?

Whilst this might seem a straightforward question as to where you want to be, it is also where you might talk yourself out of the job. For example, it would not a wise decision for you to say you wanted to be a published author, running your own publishing company or to work on a part of their list that they are reducing and retiring.

What you should talk about is your future within the job, role, company or something similar. That you hope to have progressed on to a more senior role and maybe managing. If it is a small publisher and they've made it clear there is no room for progression, you might add, "I appreciate I might have to move on from here, but I know I would love to do it within this company." This is because they might turn you down if you still think you are going to get a promotion when they have made it clear there is no room for promotion. Within a big company it is fine to say about staying and progressing and that would be expected.

What are you reading at the moment?

Questions about books and reading are designed not only to find out about what you are reading but also, and more importantly, how you describe a book, and we partly discuss this in *Chapter Six: Covering Letters That Work*. No matter what your role, you are often going to have to pitch titles to someone, or discuss them in a meeting, or present them to colleagues. It's no good saying 'I'm reading *Loose Connections* by Esther Menell', and then stop. It is about saying "I'm currently reading *Loose Connections* by Esther Menell, which is about the author's early life in Estonia before World War 2 through to her career in publishing where she worked alongside Diana Athill. As well as the historical importance, it is an interesting insight into the editor and author relationship, especially as she worked with names such as Jean Rhys and Simone de Beauvoir."

The way you describe the book should make the interviewer want to read it themselves.

I suggest is that you always have at least three books you can talk about at interview. Now, it isn't for me to say you have to be reading them right at the time of the interview, because unless you've actually got a book in your hand, the interviewer isn't going to know exactly what you are reading. So have three books you can talk about at any time and be prepared to answer the following questions about them:

- What influenced you to buy/read the book?
- Were you persuaded by a great marketing campaign, for instance? If so, describe the campaign.

- Was it by recommendation? If so, who recommended it to you and why?
- Where did you purchase it?
- Who is the publisher? Have you read any of the author's other books?

You do not need to say you are reading one of the publisher's books, unless of course that is true. But be warned, if you are reading one of their books, it is likely the conversation might go far deeper into the content, as well as what you think of the author's style, the jacket, the price point.

You also need to think about your favourite authors, when you last read one of their books and know not only when their next one is coming out and who is publishing it, plus any additional information. This could include events where you've heard them speak, their social media channel, and maybe how prolific they are (a book a year, for instance) or how long it takes for a new title to come out (a book every five years). These are meant to be authors you love, so when you talk about them, let the passion for their writing show in your voice.

Do you have any favourite illustrators?

This is to see how much knowledge you have of the genre, particularly in relation to children's books. Do your research before the interview.

Do you know any of our authors? Could you describe our list?

This is where the research you did before the interview comes into play. You will be surprised how many interview candidates are unable to answer a few basics about the publisher's authors and their list. They are not looking for assumptions or necessarily a critique, but they want to know you understand what they publish, perhaps if the genre is not a popular or fashionable one, that you'll be okay working with it.

Unless the job specification has mentioned writing books (for example, some publishers create their own titles), do not mention your own writing and wanting to publish your own books. Whilst

> **ANECDOTE**
> When I was interviewed by Ian Allan Publishing, at the time a major publisher of transport books – books about steam trains, buses, aircraft – for the role of Sales Representative, I was asked at the interview questions such as, "Do you understand what we publish?" And then "How do you think you will cope selling this type of book?" To this question, I laid down my trump card, replying, "Would it help if I told you I used to be a bus spotter?" The Publishing Director jokingly replied, "Get out now!", and pointed to the door. Yes, I got the job, but a large part of that was down to me having a knowledge and enthusiasm for what the company published, as whilst I had worked in sales, I had never been a sales representative.

many people in book publishing are now published authors, it can be one of the worst things to mention at interview for an entry-level role, as the recruiter will perceive that you only want to work there to get your own book published and are not really interested in working on other people's. It can also be mightily frustrating for an unpublished author (you) to see others hit the publishing jackpot so merrily. Whilst writing and publishing might seem like they go hand in hand, the reality is that often the best publishers are not the best writers.

Off-the-wall questions

Sometimes you might find that with any interview you get asked a question that is off the wall, such as, "Tell me how many jellybeans will fit in a car?" As well as trying to catch you unawares, they also may give the interviewer an extra insight into your thought process.

So if I asked you now, "How many jellybeans will fit in a car?", what is your answer?

Did you say 6 million? 2 million? 1 million? Maybe you might joke back, "Not that many; I would have eaten them all first." Or maybe you answered the question with questions, "How big is the car and what size are the jellybeans?" Often there is no right or wrong answer, but how you answered the question might demonstrate how you may react in a situation where you are asked a question that you don't automatically have the answer for.

Here are five shapes, tell me which shape(s) you are

Thankfully most publishers don't play games in interviews. This isn't so much a trick question but to see how you cope when something unexpected is sprung on you, and also how you describe the shape. No matter if someone tells you that picking a particular shape has a certain meaning, pick the shape(s) you prefer and then justify your choice.

Find me the adjective in this sentence

"The quick brown fox jumped over the lazy dog."

Editors should always be ready for these kind of grammar questions, especially ones asking about conjunction and sub-conjunctions, and educational publishers are sometimes the most particular about this at interview. There is a belief by some that you need to understand the structure and formation of the English language before you can be responsible for editing any books.

Tell me about a book you didn't like

One would hope that the recruiter would spend more time talking about books you do like or are interested in, as well as the books they publish, but sometimes, they throw in this question to see what your reading tastes are like. I suggest you always have one book to discuss you don't like, but make sure it is not comparable, or of the same subject area as the books on the publisher's list you are interviewing for.

This may be because that the publisher has just secretly signed the author whose book you didn't like, and it hasn't been announced. It could also be, if you forget and choose one of the publisher's current authors, that you have talked yourself out of the job if the author has another 10 books awaiting publication.

But do answer this question. In publishing you are entitled to have opinions about things, whatever role you are in, and you are likely to have a forum (such as an editorial or marketing meeting) to voice how you feel about certain books and campaigns.

Example

Probably the most memorable book I didn't like was Martin Amis's London Fields. I read it at the time it was first published, and it had review coverage everywhere, mostly mixed. I found the further I read into the book the more frustrated I got with the characters of Keith Talent and Nicola Six, so much so I wanted to throw the book away, but I persevered to the end!

I guess it says a lot about the way Amis draws such strong characters, that even though I can't remember the plot of the book all these years on, I can still recall the characters names and remember that they were annoying. Talking about it again now almost makes me want to re-read it to see what it was I didn't like, but life is too short and there are so many other enjoyable books I need to read.

Sell me this pen...*

Hopefully you won't get asked that question in a publishing interview. It is lazy and flippant. But what you need to do is to start by saying, *"I am going to show you something that you can't live without"* and then go on to say why the interviewer can't live without a pen, describing all its uses and why it is better than a computer or phone.

*Although I have been asked that question!

Do you have any questions for us?

I hear lots of conflicting views about how it is compulsory to ask a question in this section of an interview. My view is that it isn't. A good interview is one where it becomes a conversation; you are asked a question you respond and maybe ask a question or for something to be clarified in return. If you've been in a situation where the interview flowed, you will probably find that all the questions you had prepared in advance have already been answered and you have nothing left to add.

In these circumstances you might feel tempted to quip "when can I start?" to show you are extra keen. It is fine to say clearly, "I've asked so much already, and I think you've answered everything. But, if it's okay, I will just check my notes." and then go to your interview pack, find your page of questions you wanted to ask, and say, "No, thank you. They've all been answered." The interviewer might ask what your questions were, so be prepared to tell them.

If you are struggling to find questions to ask at interviews, here are a few good examples; remember these will all depend on the role and what had already been said:

- You mentioned what the first priorities will be, what comes after that?
- Are there any additional challenges coming up?
- Aside from the books we've already discussed, what else are you excited about?
- What do you like about your job?
- What do you like about working here?
- How good is each department at sticking to the critical path?
- How will I know if I am doing a good job?
- I saw you have started publishing in this field, is there more to come?
- What is the next stage in this process?
- You mentioned InDesign, what other software are you regularly using in-house?

Interview Panels

Very often you will find you are interviewed by more than one person. In large companies it is common to have someone from the recruitment team or a Human Resources person either interview you before the department member or to sit in on an interview. As well as ensuring that the interview is being conducted fairly, the main purpose of the Human Resources professional being present is for them to assess whether you are a good fit for the company, and whether you will fit into the team. When answering a question, the trick here is to make eye contact with both interviewers. You might start by addressing the person who asked the question then, whilst still talking, glance at the other member of staff before returning your eyes to the person who posed the question.

If it is a large panel of four or more people, you might think they are playing good cop, bad cop, but this is becoming less common.

It is more than likely a different panel member is assessing a particular area of your experience or company fit.

When positioning yourself to the panel, face centre but when answering a question turn your body slightly to the person who asked the question and start your eyes on them, but as you talk make eye contact with the whole of the panel. Don't only look at the person asking the question. Think of it as being in a meeting with several members of a team. You might start by responding to the person who asked a question, but you make everyone else feel included. It isn't a one-to-one – it is a group discussion.

The Salary Question

No matter who you ever want to work for, salaries come out as overheads and are taken off profits and, as they are a repeated annual expense, it makes sense for companies to keep them within a budget.

When it comes to salary negotiation at an interview this should be the last thing that is discussed and you, as the interviewee, should never raise the subject first.

> **TOP TIP**
> Prepare, prepare, prepare, the more preparation you do, the better the experience will be.

What needs to happen is for the publisher to decide first that you are their ideal candidate, the perfect fit and they really want you, because then when they offer you the job, you may find a little more flexibility in salary than perhaps they wanted to give. This doesn't work all the time but let the decision to employ you be based on your skills and competencies and not because they can get someone £1,000 cheaper to do the job.

Very often publishers ask in advance, "What salary would you require?" This is to give them a guideline as to what you would expect to be paid. If they asked this at application stage, and you told them a figure, and they still interview you, the chances are they can afford to employ you on that salary. If you were way above their salary budget, it is unlikely you would be interviewed, unless you worked for a major customer, client, or competitor and they didn't want any bad feeling or wanted to learn more about what was going on with your current employer.

If they ask you in an interview, "what salary are you expecting?", you then might say a number of things, but if you want to lose all power in negotiation, then give them a figure. Once you've said this figure you could find it impossible to go any higher, but they might try to get you to negotiate a lower figure, or stagger the salary, with your full salary requirement being given after you have passed your probation.

You might reply, "what salary are you offering?", then you can see if they can give you a ballpark figure. The response could be, "the salary we are offering is between X and Y." As the higher figure, is what you were looking for, and you didn't want to work for the lower figure, reply by saying "I'm looking for around (the higher figure) because ..." and explain why you are worth paying the higher figure.

After the interview

Within 24 hours of your interview send a follow up email. If the job came to you via a Recruitment Consultant, then email and ask for them to forward your email on to the publisher.

A good follow up email will:

- Thank the person for their time and tell them how much you enjoyed speaking to them.
- Confirm that you are still interested in the role, perhaps mentioning how keen you are to work on a project that would be a key part of your job.
- Ask a supplementary question to something they mentioned or adding a further comment about a point that you feel you might not have mentioned.

When to chase

The whole process of going through applications, selecting candidates for interview, second interview and then deciding who to appoint, is a slow one. It is not unusual for it to take three months from the closing date of the advert to when a job offer is made. Most of the time, the recruiter is keen to make an appointment but finding the time to recruit, on top of their usual daily workload, can be difficult.

At the end of each process, such as an interview, I recommend that you ask when you might hear from them next, or what the next stage will be, so you have an idea of timeline. Bear in mind people take holidays, might be off sick, priorities change and, of course the job itself can change too.

If you've asked at an interview and they say, "we'll be making a decision in around two weeks' time", and then you don't hear anything, you might instantly assume you have not got the job. However, whilst this could be true in about 50% of the time, the other 50% of the time the publisher is being incredibly slow. Sometimes, they offer the job to another candidate and the candidate turns it down. This is why a quick rejection letter is not always forthcoming. They aren't going to tell you that you haven't got the job until a candidate has accepted their job offer.

Often this leads to unfortunate circumstances, where you see someone else announcing their new role on social media, before you receive a formal letter of rejection. It doesn't feel nice when this happens, but it is more a foible of social media rather than any conspiracy or deliberate attempt to upset you.

If, however, you do want to chase, a friendly reminder a week or two after they said you would hear from them, when you think the interview went well, and once again reinforcing your interest and commitment in the role, is acceptable.

If they reply and let you know you've been unsuccessful, do respond politely and let them know you still enjoyed the discussion and hope to be able to work with them at some point in the future. You never know, it could be sooner than you think. Even if another candidate starts in the role, they may not make their probation.

It has happened to me on one occasion, for a job I was certain I would get. I knew all the people, knew the list, had huge connections with the company and the experience. In my mind I was just who they were looking for. I could probably perform the role standing on my head, However, I was rejected because the Managing Director thought I would be too bored typing correspondence. The successful candidate was a friend's relative instead, who had far less experience. Six weeks later the Managing Director wrote me a most apologetic letter, stating he had made a mistake with his choice and offered me the role. He also admitted it wasn't the first time he had made that sort of mistake either; as he had done something similar in the past, when recruiting one of our mutual acquaintances. Like me, the mutual acquaintance had been rejected, and then offered the role six weeks later after the initial choice of candidate didn't work out. Anyway, I started work there and stayed for four years before moving onwards and upwards.

Feedback

It is a current trend for unsuccessful applicants to ask for feedback from an interview, to see if there are any learning points you can take forward. I'm afraid that most of this feedback should be taken with a pinch of salt; it could be misleading, ambiguous, and what didn't work well for one publisher might work better for another. The feedback also relates to a particular job and skills requirement at that moment in time, with a specific team; it is unlikely to be a generalisation, such as, "this is what you are doing wrong".

For example, you have an interview with Publisher A who turns you down and tells you the reason you didn't get the job is because you are too ambitious.

You then modify your behaviour for Publisher B, who turns you down and tells you the reason you didn't get the job is because you aren't ambitious enough.

Feedback is always likely to be vague or computer-generated from a test you may have completed.

So, even then, if you are still keen to work for the publisher then ask for feedback, but don't take it personally.

Application questions

The reason I have listed application questions in the interview question chapter is because most of the time application questions need interview-scenario type answers, not bullet points and not cutting and pasting from a CV or Covering Letter text. You need to construct full and well-written answers, including, where you can, specifics of the skills and competencies that you used and that are key to the role for which you are applying.

Candidates who fall down on application questions often have not read and understood the job advertisement or question properly or have not stuck to the word count. If a word count is given, then do not go over it.

The best way to answer these questions is to log in to the publisher's system, get to the point where you find the questions you need to answer, copy the questions, plan and write your answers offline, away from their system. Go through the job advertisement again, line by line, as described elsewhere in this chapter, finding your best scenarios to use. When you have perfected your answers, log in again, copy and paste your answers and complete your application.

Here are some examples of full answers to application questions:

What attracted you to this role? (120 words maximum)
I have always wanted to work with crime fiction and am a passionate reader of all crime books, be they police procedural, cosy crime or thrillers and have read a lot of JJ Publishing's authors (name a couple of authors here). I'm attracted to this role because it enables me to bring all my skills and experience together. I have passion for being organised, multitasking and working to deadlines, and have been working in a busy team during a publishing internship, where I have to constantly ensure tasks are completed at the end of each day. I enjoy copywriting, and have contributed a number of reviews to Goodreads and via my bookstagram account, as well as the crime fiction community.

Please give an example of how you have been creative either in the workplace or outside of work? (150 words)
I'm lucky in that, even though I currently work in hospitality, I am able to be creative every day. A key part of my day is planning and creating social media posts. I keep a marketing plan of up-and-coming themes, such as different days and events, and write posts accordingly. We've had summer cocktail hours, Equinox days, as well as the traditional like Halloween. My favourite time where I was creative was when I designed a cocktail event for those who didn't have tickets for the local town show. I wrote a social post that allowed us to jump on all the hashtags, and created a reel that I posted on Instagram, and Facebook. I jumped on to TikTok too, and we had a packed event as a result. 'Life in town isn't fun when you don't have tickets for the gig. So why not join us instead?'

Tell me about a book that you perceive to be a game-changer in publishing? (250 words)

The first big trade book that had a marketing campaign and that was a real-game changer in publishing terms was Julie Burchill's debut novel AMBITION. It was published in June 1989 by Bodley Head. At that time debut fiction was always published in January and February, as book reviewers had fewer big names to review, so new authors were often featured. No publisher would ever publish new fiction in the summer as everyone was going on holiday; it was a belief that fiction would get buried and forgotten. AMBITION had a huge marketing campaign and every bookshop you went into there was a full-size cardboard cut-out of the female from the cover with the strapline 'The only thing she can't hold down is her own ambition'. The book itself was the first to be described as a 'sex and shopping novel' at a time when, aside from Harold Robbins and Jackie Collins and one or two others, no one really wrote about sex in fiction. [The awards known as the Bad Sex in Fiction Awards were not launched until 1993, when it felt every author suddenly started to add one or two sexy paragraphs in order to spice up their titles]. Coverage for the book was everywhere. It went straight to the top of the bestseller list and left the publishing industry with three things: The birth of summer reading campaigns, the start of the sex and shopping novel and the beginning of marketing departments within all publishers.

[I deliberately used this example as it is so far back you can't claim it as your own. If you ever get asked this question, you'll need to find a book you can talk about that changed the publishing landscape. It is not an endorsement of Julie Burchill's political views.]

Interview Questions

A selection of genuine interview questions appear over the next few pages; all have been asked in previous book publishing interviews.

These have been divided into general questions, that everyone should be prepared for, to specific questions about publishing, the books and the marketplace around you. (Go back and read *Chapter One: Understanding Book Publishing*!) There may be some overlap; often the same question is asked in many different ways, and I want to ensure you are as prepared as possible. If you get invited to an interview, it is a good idea to practise answering as many relevant ones as you can.

In an interview where they are asking for a bilingual candidate or specific language skills, do not be surprised if part of an interview is conducted in the language requirements for the role.

If there are two jobs advertised, but you applied for only one, you might get asked, "I notice you've been quite specific in applying for the translation role, most people have applied for both, why haven't you applied for the other role as well?" If this is the case, have an answer ready.

All Assistant Level / Internship Level roles

- Do you like to just do your own tasks or are you willing to do other jobs?
- Do you prefer starting a task or finishing a task?
- How do you plan your day?
- What do you do to keep organised?
- How do you manage a busy email inbox?
- What is your current salary?
- What are your top three tips for staying organised?
- How do you like to communicate?
- How do you like to be managed?
- Give an example of a time you worked with difficult people.
- Have you ever been in a conflict situation at work and how did you manage it?
- Tell us about a time when you've worked with a difficult colleague and how you resolved it.
- Did you ever spot anything wrong in your last role and make suggestions as to how to fix it?
- Where do you see yourself in five years?
- Who is someone you admire?
- Tell me about your last role. What did you enjoy about it and what didn't you enjoy?

- Tell me what you did in a particular role.
- Tell us about something you would have done differently in hindsight.
- What organisation methods do you use?
- Who are our key competitors in the market?
- What upcoming books of ours are you excited by?
- Have you read our mission statement? What do you think?
- How do you stay up to date with publishing news?
- What do you know about the company?
- What do you think are the challenges facing publishing today?
- What experience do you have with the (latest digital trend)?
- What would you say/do if you were in the lift with the manager?
- Why do you want to be in publicity/marketing/editorial?
- Do you know any of our authors?
- Could you describe our list?
- What are you reading at the moment?
- What do you like to read?
- What was the last book you read?
- What are you most looking forward to in the role?
- What are your weaknesses?
- What did you learn from your internship?
- What is your favourite feature of InDesign?
- What part of the job do you think you will struggle with?
- What would you do if you don't know how to do something while we are away?
- What is your greatest achievement?

- Why is someone with a master's degree/PhD applying for this role?
- Why should we hire you?
- Without the relevant experience, why are you the right person for the job?
- Do you do any creative writing?
- What are you particularly proud of?
- What idea would you pitch to the Board?
- A lot of the job involves administrative tasks that are less creative. Would you find them boring? And if so, how would you cope with that?
- Can you talk about some of the books we are bringing out soon?
- Can you tell me about a time you found yourself with a task you don't normally deal with? How did you cope with that?
- Whilst you were at your publishing internship did they sign anyone new? Were they excited about anything happening at the time?
- Did you encounter anything during your internships that surprised you?
- Do you follow us on social media? What do you think we are doing well, or what we could improve on, in terms of our social media posts?
- How does your experience compare with lectures you attended as part of your MA?
- Who would you invite to a dinner party?

Academic Publishing

- Tell us what you know about our publications.
- How do you feel about open access?
- How do you keep up with science and publishing?
- Why do you want to work in academic publishing specifically?

- Why do you want to work in academic books and not trade?
- Are you going to stop your education at this point? Is there any reason you're not studying for a Master's or PhD?

Children's and Educational Publishing

- What do you know about the additional online resources that accompany the titles on this list?
- How will digital publishing affect children's publishing specifically?
- Who are your favourite illustrators?
- What books did you read as a child and how do you think they influenced your reading interest today
- How did you access books when you were growing up?
- What do you think the differences are in marketing for children as opposed to marketing adult books?
- What is the biggest problem teachers are facing right now?
- Which children's book published in the last year caught your attention and why?

Literary Agent's Assistant

- What are you most proud of in your life?
- What do you know about us?
- What do you know about our services?
- Do you know who our clients are?
- What made you pick publishing as a career path?
- What books do you like reading and give examples of authors in those genres?
- What do you know about how a literary agent works with an author?

> **TOP TIP**
> If you don't hear the question properly or are not sure what the interviewer means by the question, don't be afraid to ask them to repeat the question or explain further. Remember an interview is a conversation.

- Why do you want to work for an agent and not a publisher?
- Part of your role will be reading through all the initial submissions, have you any experience in writing reader reports?

Editorial Assistant

- What attracted you to the role?
- What do you know about the subject areas we publish in?
- Can you give an example of a book published in the last few years, from any publisher, that you think was published well, and explain what you liked about it?
- Do you write, and what do you write – fiction or non-fiction?
- Have you written blurbs before?
- How do you goal-set?
- How do you like to be managed?
- How do you manage balancing multiple different deadlines, and balancing work from several people who all want their work to be completed first?
- How do you organise your time?
- How do you work best? In a group or on your own?
- If you had your own list, what types of books would you want to be on it?
- One of the authors rings up very distressed and you cannot find one of the editors – what would you do?
- Part of your job would be reading the slush pile and other agented submissions. Have you read these types of manuscripts before?

- Tell me about a difficult situation and how you resolved it?
- We're a non-fiction imprint, but what sort of fiction have you read recently?
- What admin task do you struggle with?
- What are your strengths and weaknesses?
- What book are you currently reading?
- What book has impressed you recently?
- What do you think commercial fiction means?
- What current trend do you think could inspire a non-fiction book or series?
- Why do you want the job?
- Why do you want to work in publishing?
- Would you say you are social media savvy? Do you blog?

Marketing Assistant

- Give us examples of digital marketing?
- Tell us about a time something went wrong on a previous job and how you fixed it.
- Pick your favourite book/TV show/film/song and why?
- What has been a good example of an effective marketing campaign over the last 12 months?
- Give an example of a time when you were challenged in the workplace.
- How well do you know the publishing landscape (of the genres we publish in)?
- What was the Christmas bestseller?
- How proficient would you consider yourself in InDesign?
- Tell us a little about your experience in relation to the role?
- Which aspect of the role are you most excited about?
- Do you have experience with social media?

Rights Assistant

- What is a co-edition?
- What languages are you fluent in?
- Why do you want to work in Rights?
- Do you know anything about rights sales?
- Have you had any contracts experience?
- How do you go about negotiation?
- Have you been to any international book fairs?
- I see you helped with preparations for the London Book Fair, what did that involve?
- Tell me about a time when you had to manage multiple priorities.
- Have you managed any territories in your last role, if so which ones?
- What three things do you think are important for a business trip?

Production Assistant

- Why do you want to work in Production?
- Where do you think your career will lead?
- Tell me about a time when you worked with others as a team.
- I saw you worked in Editorial during an internship, why are you not pursuing a career in Editorial?
- What do you know about how production fits into the wider publishing process?
- How have you demonstrated your initiative in your current role?
- What do you know about the critical path?
- What experience do you have with the (latest digital trend)?

- If you had to choose between the quality of a book or meeting a deadline, what would you choose and why?
- Can you give me an example of when you've been tenacious?

Publicity Assistant

- How do you organise yourself with multiple priorities?
- Can you give us an example of where you improved the workflow of an organisation?
- If you had three tasks with the same deadline, how would you approach them?
- Can you give us two reasons you want to work for us?
- Can you tell us about one example of our marketing you like?
- Which do you prefer between marketing and publicity?
- Tell me about a time when you've used the skills you'd use in this role?
- You said you had an interest in publicity, why do you want to work in publicity?
- Have you had to convince/win anyone over in a situation? If so, how did you go about it?
- Have you ever had contact with the national press? What was it for and how did it go?

Sales Assistant

- Explain why you want to go suddenly into sales?
- What excites you about the role?
- How have you used Excel?
- How would you deal with people in the team being away all the time?
- What customer-facing experience do you have?
- What is 10% of 300?

- Do you have any experience with data analysis?
- How would you feel about presenting titles to customers?
- How would you deal with a difficult customer?
- Give us an example of a mistake you made, how you handled it and what you learnt from it?
- Do you see yourself staying in sales?
- This is an admin-heavy role, would you find this role boring?

ACTION POINTS

Go through the list of ten interview scenarios. How many scenarios can you find from your career history that you can talk about at interview?

Read through all the interview questions and practise, practise, practise your answers.

CHAPTER NINE

Interview Tests and How to Pass Them

"Sometimes it feels like the publisher is asking you to stand on your head and sing a Beatles song backwards in order to prove that you have the skills and competencies for the job advertised."

Suzanne Collier

For almost every interview within book publishing you should now expect some sort of practical test to confirm that you have the aptitude for the job.

Please do not be scared of these tests because if you have the skills for the role then you should pass. The aim of interview tests is to check you have the skills and competencies for the role, whatever the role is. Most of the tests are based around what you'll be expected to do in the job every day.

As there have been incidents of candidates cheating – using AI to write the test for them, come up with ideas or proofread the document, you might find the publisher will ask you to perform the test in plain sight, either on a Zoom call or when you are called to a face-to-face meeting. Please do not cheat.

Even with all the clients I help, I don't do the groundwork of the interview tests for them. I might give clients guidance and talk through the initial test before they start, so they have a better understanding of what the outcomes should be, or I'll run through a client's final version to check they haven't missed something. Alternatively, if they are required to give a presentation, I would comment on how the presentation comes across, but I would never complete an interview test for a client, because it would then be my work not theirs. At the end of the day, if you are successful getting the job based on someone else's work, remember it will be you turning up for work, not them, so don't be surprised, down the line, if you get fired.

Here are some of the popular tests conducted at a job interview for entry-level publishing roles.

I suggest you grab a notebook and pen to perform these tests. Please don't write in this book; you might want to repeat the tests or challenge a friend later.

1. Filing test

This is a test to check that you know your alphabet and can put things in order! Simple, yes, but it is amazing how many people cannot put a simple list of things in alphabetical order.

Without using the sort facility on your device, using a pen and paper, organise this list of countries into alphabetical order. Each is the file name of a country the publisher you are applying to work for sells to.

Myanmar
Morocco
Malaysia
Mozambique
Madagascar
Mali
Malawi
Mauritania
Mongolia
Moldova
Mauritius
Montenegro
Malta
Maldives
Micronesia
Monaco
Marshall Islands
Mexico

2. Microsoft Excel test

This is to test whether you can perform some basic functions in Excel. If you're given an Excel test it is likely you will be timed. I recommend you perform these tasks within 10 minutes.

On a computer, open any Microsoft Excel existing spreadsheet of numbers.

You need to perform the following seven actions within ten minutes.

Create four columns.

- Name
- Column 1
- Column 2
- Total

Now recreate the following sums as formulas, using a different row for each answer:

- A simple addition 59 + 75
- A simple subtraction 75 – 59
- A simple division and ensure that it is in the currency of GB Sterling with no more than two decimal places 295 ÷ 59
- A simple multiplication 75 x 59
- A simple percentage increase. What is 59% of 75, with no decimal places
- Add up the sum of each column using a formula, with the final column being a number to no more than two decimal places.
- Add up the number of rows in each column using a formula

(In addition to this, you might want to test yourself on creating a Pivot Table or a V Look Up, and sorting and filtering a spreadsheet containing a large amount of data, but these are not part of the test for this chapter.)

3. Microsoft PowerPoint test

This is a self-marking test. You need to be able to perform the following functions:

- Create a new presentation that contains three slides
- Choose a standard PowerPoint brand design
- Edit the Master Slide footer, so that your name appears in the bottom right corner of every slide
- On the first slide, animate the text so it swivels in
- Change the fill colour and text colour
- Ensure the transition between each slide is two seconds
- Create a text box on slide two and import in any text from a document
- Import a picture on slide three
- Save your presentation
- Convert your presentation into a video

Other computer software tests to expect include Adobe InDesign and Adobe Photoshop. Each test is likely to expect you to be able to create a document, add text or an image, resize text or an image, import a graphic and change the resolution.

4. Prioritisation test

This test is extremely popular for any entry level or assistant role. You should expect the complexity of the tasks to increase with the seniority of the role.

It is first thing in the morning, and these are the tasks allocated to you. Please put them in the order you will complete them and be prepared to discuss the reasoning in your job interview (some prioritisation tests may ask for your justification when submitting your answers).

1. Answer an email from the Managing Director who wants to know why Amazon is not showing the latest cover image for a major title.

2. Review and respond to 25 emails in the editorial submissions inbox that should have been answered two weeks ago.
3. Write a social media post for a book that needs to be promoted from tomorrow.
4. Instruct accounts to pay the advance due on publication for a book being published shortly.
5. Type up the minutes of the editorial and marketing meeting and circulate them.
6. Update the price information on the website for a title that is incorrectly showing £11.99 instead of £13.99.
7. Send out catalogue requests and a new account opening form to a prospective new customer who called yesterday wanting to open an account.
8. Check the ISBN on the back of a jacket proof that the editorial and production teams are waiting for.
9. Respond to an urgent request from the Sales Director, who is on a business trip in the USA, asking for the current stock level of a title.
10. Process an order for a major customer by passing it to the warehouse.
11. Chase the author of a new title who is late delivering their manuscript.
12. Cancel today's lunch booking at the Managing Director's favourite restaurant.

5. Editorial or proofreading test

Please mark up the following text. If you know BSI mark up, then you can use it, but the answers are purely based on your ability to spot the mistakes, not on using professional mark-up language.

> raffaëlli is the historian of the "banlieue" of Paris. His street scenes are tipical, life like, and modern, and they will be treasured in future year as veritable documents of the daily existence of the grt city. He wanders through the dreary "no man's land" outside the fortifications, and transfers to his block the most vivid portraits of the nondescript characters who swarm through that gaunt wilderness he is a man of

much mental refinement, who has had to struggled for every inch of the artistic success that now surrounds him. Richley endowed by nature he had no resources to fall back upon save his determination to conquer. In a few words M. Geffroy sums up the opening of this curiously career.

Raffaëlli has had many employments, has been engaged in many trades, has searched the town for work. He has been an office, has sung bass at the Théâtre Lyrique, has chanted salms in a church choir, and at the same time painted under the tuition of gerome at the ecole des beauxarts. He travelled through Europe, penetrating even so far as algeria, working in each town as he stopped returning to Paris he exhibited landscapes founded upon the studies he had accumulated in his portfolio, some pictures of the Louis the thirteenth style, some portraits, a view of the Opera. Suddenly he opened his eyes to a sight nobody had seen befour, disdained by the hole world, subjects that had never reached the dignaty of an entrance in art circles. He became the recorder of the suburbs of Paris and their wandering inhabitants.

Impressionist painting: its genesis and development
Author: Wynford Dewhurst
Published in the UK by George Newnes, Nineteen Hundred and four

6. Arithmetic test

This is usual for a role in sales, production, rights or anything where you are calculating numbers. Although calculators are on every device, how good are you without a calculator?

Calculate the answers to the following:

£6.99 + £13.99
10% of £14.90
250 x £4.57
672 ÷ 28
A 10% increase on £4,000

If a book is priced at £20, how much will a customer pay if their discount is set at:

    35%

    45%

    50%

If a sales agent receives 10% commission, how much commission would they receive on £146,500?

£3.50 + £5.99 + £12.99

7. Scenario test

A high-profile author has emailed the department email inbox complaining that the Commissioning Editor has not responded to their previous requests chasing an advance as well as the contract for their next book. The Commissioning Editor is out of the office that afternoon and uncontactable. Write a complete email in response, from beginning to end. What other actions would you take, if any?

8. Spelling test

Choose the correct spelling of each of the following words

Acceptable	Acceptible
Accomodate	Accommodate
Achievment	Achievement
Acknowlege	Acknowledge
Acquisition	Aquisition
Allright	Alright
Annualy	Annually
Apparent	Apparant
Archive	Arkhive
Believe	Beleive
Carribean	Caribbean
Colleague	Collegue
Confusian	Confusion

Curricullum	Curriculum
Definitely	Definately
Difficultey	Difficulty
Excede	Exceed
Experience	Experiance
Expendature	Expenditure
Gratefull	Grateful
Immediately	Immedietely
Incredibel	Incredible
Independant	Independent
Intelligence	Intelligance
Liaise	Liase
Memorandam	Memorandum
Neccessary	Necessary
Omission	Ommision
Organisation	Organisetion
Perceive	Percieve
Plagiarise	Plagerise
Productive	Producteve
Pronounciation	Pronunciation
Receive	Recieve
Reptition	Repetition
Restaurant	Restarant
Seperate	Separate
Shakespeare	Shakespere
Successful	Successfull
Underrated	Underated

The following tests are all self-marking and require you to choose books from your personal bookshelves to complete. Alternatively, if you are stuck, you can use this book as your example. If you're unfamiliar with talking or writing about books, these tests are a great opportunity to get some practice.

[If you do decide to use this book as your example, why not post your answer on social media and tag in @bookcareers? We're on most platforms.]

9. Copywriting test

This might be given in any role where you have to write summaries of books, so it could be for Editorial, Publicity, Sales, Marketing or Rights.

Take a book from your shelf and, without reading the cover copy, write:

   a. A 50-word summary about the book, as though it was going in an email to a journalist or customer saying why they should review or buy the book.
   b. A 150-word summary about the book, designed to go on the publisher's website, so it might have a headline or strapline and then information about the content.

10. Rights awareness test

This could be given in any Rights position, where they are assessing your enthusiasm and understanding for the role, and that you aren't just someone who has applied for a Rights job but really wants to work in Editorial.

Take any five books from your bookshelf. Which books do you think have the most potential for Rights sales and why?

11. Sales and Special Sales test

This is frequently given to see if you have potential for sales and a genuine interest in the part that sales plays in the publishing process, (again, probably checking you don't want to work in Editorial).

Take any book from your bookshelf. Which outlets, retail or online, do you think would be interested in purchasing the book, aside from traditional bookshops, Waterstones or Amazon?

12. Presentation Test

This could be given for any role where you may be required to talk about a book to colleagues, customers, the press or others, so could apply to every department, including Editorial.

Take any book from your shelf and stand up and talk about it for 45 seconds, in a way that explains its content (without giving away any spoilers), addresses the writing style, and why the person you are presenting to should either read or purchase a copy.

To test yourself properly, it is a good idea to film or record yourself and see how you sound, and what parts of your presentation you could improve on.

13. Social Media posts

This is a very common test for any role where part of the job requires you to post on social media.

Take a book from your shelf and write a social media post or create a reel or TikTok for the book. Your aim is to reach members of the public and, similar to the Presentation Test, encourage them to buy the book.

14. Psychometric and Aptitude Tests

It is not unheard of for Psychometric Tests to be used in publishing recruitment.

If you are to be given a psychometric test you should be advised in advance and have some time to prepare. Testing is likely to take place at first or second interview stage. There are so many varieties of psychometric tests, covering all sorts of areas such as numeracy, verbal reasoning, ability, work behaviours and personality.

The key is to answer the questions without being clever or giving them what you think they want. Good tests have a dishonesty score built in that makes it harder to cheat. There really are no right or wrong answers to many psychometric tests. It isn't like an examination; most of this is personality testing.

I've come across them when a major corporation was recruiting for their publishing division or where one person was required to slot into a complex team. At the time SHLTests (https://www.shl.com) were used.

One of the aptitude tests to assess the skills of the Sales and Marketing candidates involved being locked in a room for 45 minutes with a four-page document and told to prepare a presentation that you would deliver at the end of the time to a group of managers. Nerve-wracking, yes, but the thing to look for in these kinds of tests are the differences.

For example, if you are selling 100 books at £100 and 20,000 books at £10, when you are presenting to the panel, question what could happen if you reduced the price of the £100 book to £10, how many sales are possible? These kinds of tests challenge how much you think outside the box, so ensure you do think outside of the box.

For further information on Psychometric tests the best book for this is *Ultimate Psychometric Tests: Over 1000 Practical Questions for Verbal, Numerical, Diagrammatic and Personality Tests* by Mike Byron. (Kogan Page, ISBN 978-1398602380)

Interview test answers

1. Filing test

Madagascar
Malawi
Malaysia
Maldives
Mali
Malta
Marshall Islands
Mauritania
Mauritius
Mexico
Micronesia

Moldova
Monaco
Mongolia
Montenegro
Morocco
Mozambique
Myanmar

2. Microsoft Excel test

Did you manage to stick to time? The answers are as follows. The last column contains the formulas.

Name	Column 1	Column 2	Total	Formula
Addition	59	75	134	=(B1+C1)
Subtraction	75	59	16	=(B2-C2)
Division	295	59	£5.00	=(B3/C3)
Multiplication	75	59	4,425	=(B4*C4)
Percentage	59	75	79%	=(C5/B5)
SUM	343	327	4,577.06	=(B1:B5)
No of lines	5	5	5	=COUNT(D1:D5)

3. Microsoft PowerPoint test

This test is self-marking.

4. Prioritisation test

Prioritisation tests can, in some ways, be subjective, particularly in what action you choose first. I had six different industry professionals test this for the book, and each came up with a slightly different order. As long as you can justify why you put the answers in a particular order, you should be okay. My advice is always, go for the quick wins and 'chase the money'. The quick wins get a number of tasks off your desk and the money might not always be obvious; the money could be in having other teams sitting around waiting for you to action a task. Also paying money out could be another instance of 'chase the money'. Imagine what damage could be done if an author posted on social media, '"Is this publisher always so late in paying their authors?"'.

If I was undertaking the prioritisation task, this is how I would organise the answers, with the justification I used.

1. 1. Answer an email from the Managing Director who wants to know why Amazon is not showing the latest cover image for a major title.

    Whilst the Managing Director should take priority over everyone else, on this occasion I would acknowledge the email first. This should give the MD confidence that I am on top of tasks and understand their importance.

2. 6. Update the price information on the website for a title that is incorrectly showing £11.99 instead of £13.99.

    I would update the image on Amazon when I update the price of the book. I then would respond letting them know the jacket had been uploaded, the price of the book on the website had been amended.

3. 10. Process an order for a major customer by passing it to the warehouse.

    Orders are money into the company. Let's get the books invoiced and despatched as soon as possible.

4. 4. Instruct accounts to pay the advance due on publication for a book being published shortly.

    We want the author to feel valued and not risk them complaining the advance is late. If I was in touch with the author, I might also send them a courtesy email to let them know the payment instruction had been actioned.

5. 12. Cancel today's lunch booking at the Managing Director's favourite restaurant.

    Quick win, plus no one is likely to be there first thing. We know it needs to be done as soon as the staff are in to answer the phone because the restaurant is the Managing Director's favourite, so we don't want to upset them.

6. 1. Answer an email from the Managing Director who wants to know why Amazon is not showing the latest cover image for a major title.

    As well as confirming the restaurant cancellation to the Managing Director, I would add the issue with Amazon had been sorted out (the first action had been only to acknowledge the email; this confirms the action).

7. 8. Check the ISBN on the back of a jacket proof that the editorial and production teams are waiting for.

    Another quick win. It will take me less than 2 minutes plus other teams are waiting for this.

8. 9. Respond to an urgent request from the Sales Director who is on a business trip in the USA, asking for the current stock level of a title.

    Whilst this an urgent request, the Sales Director is in a time zone that is at least five hours behind the UK.

9. 11. Chase the author of a new title who is late delivering their manuscript.

    This is the first non-time sensitive task that is a quick win.

10. 5. Type up the minutes of the editorial and marketing meeting and circulate them.

    Departments are waiting for the minutes, but this will take some time, that is why it is the first item after all the urgent and important quick wins.

11. 7. Send out catalogue requests and a new account opening form to a prospective new customer who called yesterday wanting to open an account.

    Whilst this is a new customer, and a quick win, whether I complete this first thing in the morning or early afternoon, it won't make much difference so long as it goes out in today's post.

12. 3. Write a social media post for a book that needs to be promoted from tomorrow.

    I need to sit and think about this. I can ruminate over what I will write whilst completing all my earlier tasks.

13. 2. Review and respond to 25 emails in the editorial submissions inbox that should have been answered two weeks ago.

These are already two weeks late. Another day shouldn't make much difference so long as they are done soonish.

5. Editorial or proof-reading test

There were 21 deliberate mistakes.

Mistake	Correction
raffaëlli	Raffaëlli
Tipical	Typical
life like	life-like
year	Years
grt	great
Wilderness he	wilderness. He
Struggled	Struggle
Richley	Richly
curiously	curious
an office	in an office
Salms	Psalms
gerome at the ecole des beauxarts	Gérôme at the École des Beaux-Arts.
algeria	Algeria (Note: When this book was written, Algeria was part of France and could have been considered part of Europe, even though the country is on the African continent.)
stopped returning	stopped. Returning
Louis the thirteenth.	Louis XIII,
Befour	Before
Hole	Whole

dignity	Dignity
UK	United Kingdom
Nineteen Hundred and four	1904

6. Mathematics test

Although calculators are on every device, how good are you without a calculator?

£6.99 + £13.99 = £20.98

10% of £14.90 = £1.49

250 x £4.57 = £1,142.50

672 ÷ 28 = 24

A ten percent increase on £4,000 = £4,400

If a book is priced at £20 How much will each customer pay if their discount is set at:

35% = £13

45% = £11

50% = £10

If a sales agent receives 10% commission, how much commission would they receive on £146,500? = £14,650

£3.50 + £5.99 + £12.99 = £22.48

7. Scenario test

A high-profile author has emailed the department email inbox complaining that the Commissioning Editor has not responded to their previous requests chasing an advance as well as the contract for their next book. The Commissioning Editor is out of the office that afternoon and uncontactable. Write a complete email in response, from beginning to end. What other actions would you take, if any?

Answer – The actual words of the email are left to you, but you should acknowledge the email, say you are sure the Commissioning Editor has it all in hand and you will check and come back to them tomorrow.

(Remember in the interview question scenarios – do not blame another colleague). The other actions you could take are to check whether the contract has been raised, or with accounts to see if they have received the instruction to pay the advance.

8. Spelling test

Be honest with yourself. How many did you get right?

Acceptable
Accommodate
Achievement
Acknowledge
Acquisition
Alright
Annually
Apparent
Archive
Believe
Caribbean
Colleague
Confusion
Curriculum
Definitely
Difficulty
Exceed
Experience
Expenditure
Grateful
Immediately
Incredible
Independent
Intelligence
Liaise
Memorandum
Necessary

Omission
Organisation
Perceive
Plagiarise
Productive
Pronunciation
Receive
Repetition
Restaurant
Separate
Shakespeare
Successful
Underrated

The remaining tests in this chapter were all self-marking; it is for you, or a friend you discuss your answers with, to gauge how well you performed.

CHAPTER TEN

Going Freelance

"You need to be very determined, very patient and set on this career to succeed. You also (usually) need another source of income for a while."
>> Chartered Institute of Editing and Proofreading

Writing about how to run a successful freelance practice could be a book in itself. In this chapter, however, I intend to give you an overview of the key elements.

Book Publishing is an industry that appears to employ a vast array of freelances across a number of publishing functions, the most common being design, editorial, marketing and publicity. So going freelance and setting up on your own can seem like the perfect solution to common job-hunting and employment issues.

You might be under the impression that freelancing will allow you to bypass the whole recruitment issue, get yourself experience on the job, be based at a location of your choice, set hours that fit around your life, charge as much as you want and select your own clients and projects.

However, the reality of freelancing in book publishing can be tough. It is an industry that, in some areas, may already be overloaded with freelance staff. For many the pay is not great, the work erratic and you won't know where your next job or money is coming from. Often you will need a financial cushion to help you pay the bills. Also you will have to invest in your own training and advancement as well as market and publicise yourself in order to attain clients. Furthermore, it is unlikely a publisher will use you on projects where you have no prior experience.

The biggest hindrance to freelancers setting up in book publishing is that unless you have direct experience of working in a similar salaried role in-house, you are unlikely to have the experience and contacts to sustain a living. When the industry body for editorial freelancers, the Chartered Institute of Editing and Proofreading suggests that first-time freelancers will usually need another income in order to get started, then you may understand how real these issues are.

Of course, there are a wide variety of freelancers aside from editorial, but editorial freelancing is the most common route that novice publishing staff tend to take. In the past you might have seen adverts for training courses that pushed the mantra "become a proofreader, publishers need proofreaders: earn up to £500 per week". Although this advert is from more than 15 years ago, some freelancers struggle to make £500 a week in today's society, and if they do, there is no guarantee they will make that amount of money every week. This isn't because they are not good at their job, quite the contrary; this can apply to highly experienced and talented freelancers. It is because the market is saturated with editorial freelancers.

Also when costs are tight on book projects, as they invariably are, freelancers are often the first to feel the cuts, as they fall outside of the publisher's workforce. In the same way, whenever publishers are looking to reduce costs, the first overheads to go are usually the freelancers and contractors, and then the publishers will then either bring the work back in-house to their existing salaried staff or outsource overseas.

If you are considering freelancing in addition to being employed in a job, always check your current contract of employment before doing anything else. Many companies prohibit employees from taking on second jobs, freelancing or earning any income from additional employment without permission. To take on any freelance work can sometimes be a sackable offence, as well as cause a conflict of interest if you are working for a competing publisher or organisation.

Aside from this, when you are freelancing extra hours, alongside a full-time role, you may be too exhausted to fulfil your main job properly. People who work 24/7 do not make good employees.

Also remember, if you use any company property or resources without permission or try to complete your freelance work in office time, it is equivalent to theft. Theft is classed as gross misconduct, an offence that will result in instant dismissal. I am sorry if I sound a little harsh here but I have sadly had to deal with too many people who thought they could easily earn some extra money on the side of their day job, only to find they are without a day job and no freelance income either.

So, please read your current contract of employment before doing anything. Don't assume because someone else in the company is already freelancing in addition to their job you will be given permission too. Employers look at these requests on a case-by-case basis. When you ask permission be clear about the freelance work you intend to take on, who you plan to work for and how you will manage your workload. You may also need to re-enforce your commitment to your role with your main employer.

[If you're already freelancing outside of your main job and change employers, make it clear in writing that you wish to continue this work when you accept the role, and amend any clause in your new contract of employment accordingly before you sign anything. However, it is not unusual for a new employer to ask you to refrain from freelancing.]

Before you do anything or make the decision to freelance you need to investigate the viability of such a career move.

Do publishers use freelancers for such work?

Whilst you might see others freelancing or think that you are offering a valuable service, many publishers only use people who have worked for them previously in-house or who have come highly recommended.

It isn't automatic that because you are selling your services that a publisher will buy. The same goes if you've been working in-house, and then offering your freelancing services back to your former employer. When you first tell them you are going freelance, there are always lots of positive "oh yes, we will definitely come to you" comments. However, many people find as soon as they make the transition to freelancer, a lot of this potential work dries up. You need to look wider than your former employer for clients.

Please note, if you are a novice and for some reason an established publisher asks you do to some work for them, when you have no prior experience, ask yourself if it is because no one else will work for them?

TOP TIP

Always manage your client's expectations. Make it clear at the beginning how you work and when you are free to speak to them or answer emails. If they suddenly ask you to do something different, that was not agreed before you took the job and will take a lot of extra time, tell them there may be an extra charge. If it is a regular client, you might not charge, to keep them happy, but remember you are a business not a charity – you must be paid for the work that you do.

Is the freelance work viable?

Are you going to be paid a flat fee for the work you do or, if it is a sales or marketing role, is there some commission built into the fee? If it is a commission-only role, can you easily earn commission, or will you have to do a lot of work for no income?

How much might you be able to charge?

When you freelance you need to earn more than your take-home pay. You are now responsible for your taxes (income tax and, if you register for it, VAT), national insurance, pension, office light and heat, computer equipment, training, tea and coffee, subscriptions and holiday or sick pay; well, everything really. All of this costs money.

Is this enough to live on?

So, whilst you might think initially that, yes, you can make money freelancing, you might find that you are earning far less than in a salaried role, or that the fees you need to charge to make a living are far higher than other freelancers, so you will struggle to get any work.

What are you going to do if you get too little work?

Do you have any kind of financial cushion, and how will you pay the rent or the bills if you have a quiet few months? When you're freelancing you may find that you never have any work in July or August, or December or January. What are you going to live on if you have quiet periods? The reality is that even the most successful freelancers struggle from time to time.

How are you going to market yourself or advertise your services?

What is this going to cost? Will you have a website or use social media platforms to make people aware of what you offer?

Starting up as a freelancer

When you start up as a freelancer, you are effectively starting a new business and have to manage all the administration that goes with running a micro-business, in addition to the freelance work you intend to complete.

Business Training

As you are a start-up business, you may qualify for some free 'start your own business' training via the UK Government, your regional council or local business enterprise. Search on the internet to see what is available to you, but take care not to follow any spurious links that ask you for payment. Almost all start-up business help is offered free.

Whilst what is being offered is general business advice and not specific to the publishing industry, if you have limited commercial experience and have no idea how a business operates, this type of training can be very useful. The main organisations offering start-up business training for publishing freelancers are bookcareers.com and the Chartered Institute of Editors and Proofreaders (CIEP).

Business Plan

If you go on any start-your-business training course, you may be asked to prepare a business plan. Some parts of business planning are good, such as identifying your ideal customer, where you will find them and how you will market yourself. But often, the only time you need a formal business plan and cash-flow forecast is if you intend to borrow money or attain a grant to finance your business. Borrowing sizeable sums of money is something you are unlikely to do unless you envisage starting a large-scale business, so try not to spend too much time writing a full business plan you will never use.

Accounts and Taxation

In the UK, you will need to register with HMRC as self-employed whether you are working in another role that pays you via PAYE or not. From the moment you notify HMRC you'll be required to submit your own tax returns, so be sure to make a note of the business's start date. There is some helpful training and advice on starting up and what you can claim as a business expense on the gov.uk website, and when you first register as self-employed you are usually sent a welcome pack.

Sometimes it is best to employ a professional accountant to do your tax returns. Whilst you can complete them yourself, a good accountant can save you money long-term by making it clear what is a tax-deductible expense, and ensuring you take advantage of any tax relief that may be open to you. An accountant shouldn't cost you the earth, and it is often cost-effective to find one who works on one-off fees rather than on a retainer. A good accountant may also help you obtain some sort of tax rebate from your PAYE if your freelance expenses are more than your freelance income.

TOP TIP

Remember to plan your day and stick to it. You should control your email and workflow, not the other way around. If you find, regularly, that you wrongly estimate the time it takes to do a project, then learn from it! Don't keep making the same mistakes.

One tip is to have a simple way of raising an invoice and receiving payments, whether it is from a standard template or by using accounting software such as FreeAgent, that is designed for small businesses. It is surprising how many freelancers fail to address their invoicing and payment system properly when setting up. The easier it is for you to raise an invoice, the more invoices you will want to raise. You need to set your payment terms and be able to track when payments are made or become overdue and have a process in place for you to chase any late payments.

Insurance

Whatever services you intend to sell, it is imperative that you have appropriate Professional Indemnity Insurance. Even the smallest individual freelancer can make a mistake that results in a client suing you and claiming far more than a refund of fees. Don't put yourself at risk of losing everything for the cost of an insurance policy. Outside of the publishing industry, some large corporations require proof that you have adequate professional indemnity insurance before you are able to contract with them as a freelancer.

Equipment and Software

You may need to purchase equipment or software to start freelancing. As mentioned above, don't count on using equipment from any other employer where you may be working, either on contract or as a freelancer. Also ensure that any software or materials you use are from legitimate sources. If you're going freelance immediately after permanent employment, you will instantly realise – and probably miss – all the things you took for granted in your previous role. Here are just a few of them:

- A fast reliable internet connection
- Access to a full range of software
- Someone to fix all the IT issues
- Tea and coffee readily at hand (if you were office-based)

Online presence and branding

Once you have chosen your branding, I suggest you use exactly the same branding across all social media platforms, so that you instantly become recognisable everywhere, in the same way a major business can be easily identified. Use the same headshot, gravatar (global avatar) and colours.

You do not need to be on every single platform or spend ages curating posts for social media. Choose the one or two platforms where your potential clients will most probably be and aim to do those well. Whatever platforms you choose, always ensure you have a free LinkedIn profile and it is complete and up to date. A simple rule of thumb: if you are in the world of work, you need to be on LinkedIn.

It is absolutely essential that you check back and clean up any social media feeds or previous posts that may cause offence or be considered discriminatory to future clients. You are running a business now; you need to keep it professional. If you have set up a new account to promote your services, and are still running a personal account, too, any prospective client can look you up, see what you're discussing online, and they may decide that you're not the freelancer they want to work with.

It is likely to be a struggle to find paying clients as it is; don't make it any harder for yourself by ranting online. Your opinions may win and attract followers and possibly a few clients, but the odds are you will alienate and offend far more. It might not be a good stance to take even if you say you don't care about alienating and offending others, and you don't want to work with other people who don't share your opinions. However, publishing is a collaborative business; as a freelancer you are part of that collaboration. Some of your more lucrative potential clients may not want to be attached to you, especially when the market is flooded with others of a similar skillset who keep their opinions to themselves.

The purpose of social media is to act as a portal for people to get to know you, your work and the services you offer. Whilst you might attract client leads on social media, don't rely entirely on social media to keep in touch with clients.

Often it is best to use social media as a signpost to a website, such as Substack or another resource that allows clients to find out more and see your full portfolio. Within GDPR rules, you should be collecting email addresses at every opportunity, so if leads decide to leave the platform where you usually reach them, or it goes offline for a prolonged period of time, you are able to stay in touch. This is where a website for your freelance services may be helpful. If you decide to create your own website, unless there is an extraordinary reason why you need more pages, keep to anything between one and six webpages.

A one-page website could have your contact details and a list of your services all on the homepage.

A six-page website could be:

- Your home page
- Page(s) to cover your services
- An 'About Me' page
- A contact form with an option to sign up for a newsletter
- A portfolio of past work
- Testimonials

You don't need a blog or for anything on this website to be more than an extended business card. However, if you want to create extra content, post regularly, keep it up to date and use the guidance in *Chapter Three* about blogs.

Newsletter

It is not essential to have a newsletter or regular contact, but I do recommend you capture email addresses so you can email your subscribers as and when you need. For instance, when your assignments are sparse, a positive email that reminds subscribers of the services you offer, or that you have extra capacity, could bring in the work you need, as well as the opportunity to email at Christmas or holiday time informing them of your availability. Consider every email you send as a reminder that you exist.

Qualifications and Training

...ed professional qualifications or training in order to ...elancer in publishing, but if you plan to offer freelance ...rvices, then membership and accreditation from the Institute of Editing and Proofreading is essential. Other recommended editorial training is from The Publishing Training Centre and the Society of Indexers. Editorial training may be costly, but if you are trying to break into publishing, it is best to go to names instantly recognised by the UK book publishing industry. This way, those recruiting freelancers will know precisely that you have been trained to industry standards. A full list of training organisations appears in the online resources for this book.

TOP TIP
Always keep looking for freelance work, even when you are at your busiest. That way you should never be worried about where your next client is coming from. If you get too much work, you may be able to delay the project or subcontract to other freelancers you trust.

Where to find work

Firstly, please revisit *Chapter Three: Finding Jobs*. The chapter may be geared to those seeking permanent jobs within publishing, but go through it in your search for freelance work and pursue every avenue for freelance opportunities. Publishers are no longer averse to posting on job vacancy pages or advertising on social media for freelancers, in a similar way that they do for permanent employees.

They are also keen to improve equity, diversity and inclusion throughout their business, and this covers the freelancers they hire. A number now are also trying to improve the freelance pipeline and nurture new freelance talent. As part of this, you may see recruitment schemes aimed directly at freelancers at all stages of their career from Creative Access, Hachette, Penguin Random House and others.

The following resources may also give you access to freelance work:

1. **The Chartered Institute of Editing and Proofreading**

    As an Editorial Freelancer, becoming a member of the CIEP and having a full profile in their directory and being accredited by them can lead to more work, although it is never a guarantee. The CIEP directory of members is the first port of call for any experienced publisher who is looking for an editorial freelancer and has run out of initial contacts. The CIEP training, resources and networking is key for anyone who is working alone and wants to have a support network. It can also be a good resource if you have taken on too much freelance work and want to subcontract or recommend others. In the same spirit, others may do the same for you.

2. **Society of Indexers**

    If your editorial speciality is Indexing, then membership of the Society of Indexers can help you. In a similar way to CIEP, they also provide training, accreditation, networking opportunities and have a directory of members that anyone can search.

3. **Reedsy**

    Reedsy is an online marketplace that connects independent authors and publishers with freelancers in all areas of the publishing process, including editorial. They allow only experienced freelancers with at least five years of publishing experience to register with them, and once you have registered, your application will be vetted to ensure you meet their high standards. Therefore, if you are an experienced editor, typesetter, cover designer, indexer, book marketer, literary translator, publicist or ghost writer, Reedsy could become an effective resource to help you find clients or supplement your client base. You'll pay a commission of approximately 10% of every assignment you complete, so remember to adjust your fees accordingly.

CASE STUDY
Rachel Quin – Freelance Marketing Consultant

Before going freelance, I had four years of in-house publishing experience, plus several years of experience in my profession working outside of the industry. This was incredibly helpful when it came to pitching for initial projects, as I had the flexibility to work across publishing and other industries to diversify my project-base and build a steady stream of income.

I decided to take the leap into freelancing for a few reasons, the main ones being a desire for greater flexibility in my work environment post-pandemic (I was able to move out of London) and also because I felt like I'd learned everything I could in my current role. I wanted to be able to try new things, take on a variety of projects and do more copywriting.

While it may not have been my long-term plan to build a freelance career, it has been a hugely fulfilling decision. It has enabled me to upskill and grow as a professional much faster than I believe I ever could have in-house, while having the freedom to select my own projects and set a rate that I feel represents my ability and my hard work.

In terms of challenges, the first and most important is charging what you're worth. With so much competition on the market in recent years, it can easily become a race to the bottom; you need to advocate for yourself.

The second is nurturing your network. I've slowly and steadily built a base of reliable clients through hard work, mutual trust and respect, and great word-of-mouth. In such a small industry, maintaining good relationships with both publishers and other freelancers is critical if you want to make this a long-term endeavour.

4. **UpWork / Fiverr / PeoplePerHour**

    There are several other similar websites too, who all operate within the gig economy system. Entry-level freelancers often turn to these to find initial clients but, whilst you set your own fees, you may find you are competing for the lowest amount of pay and find you have difficult clients who then argue the final fee. However, if you are in need of income, they could help, but do use them with caution. All take commission fees on your work, so again, adjust your fees accordingly.

Unpaid work, Working for Free

I do not at any time in my, or your, career endorse unpaid work, unpaid work experience or working for free. All unpaid work ever gives you is more unpaid work. Any 'promise of exposure', leads or 'to get some experience' will not be helpful.

If you intend to take on work as a complete novice, then you might consider charging a lower fee, but do charge something that is more than the Living Wage. Once you have any experience, you should charge commercial fees. A reference or testimonial for work that you have done for free has little or no value compared to a reference for paid work.

Setting your fees

When it comes to setting your fees, there are a number of guides you can use, depending on the services you propose to offer.

For Editorial work, the CIEP has recommended rates depending on the work involved. The National Union of Journalists (NUJ) has a 'rate for the job' where you can see what someone else was paid for work undertaken.

If you are looking at other services, you should have an idea of how much you want to earn or what the service you are providing will cost.

Calculating your daily rate/rate per hour

One of the easiest ways to calculate your daily rate might be to set your desired annual salary and then divide it by a maximum of 225. Whilst there are approximately 253 working days in the UK, you will want to take some holiday, so allow 30 days. However, one of the joys of being freelance is that you can be more flexible with your working days and holidays and might decide to give yourself more time off than when you were employed.

When I was freelancing as a Sales Manager, I always calculated my daily rate on 180 days. This is because from 1 December to around 25 January, my services were not really required. No publisher really likes to have surplus staff in a short month such as December and sales don't really get going again until mid-January, as the industry is often still reeling from Christmas.

When setting your daily rate, or desired annual salary, you should take into account all the items you are now paying for – the equipment, software, holidays (imagine you are selling your time and, remember, you won't be paid for any days you are not working). This could come to as much as 20% above your previous full-time salary.

Also, when you are discussing the daily rate for a project, you could have a full rate for one day's work. However, if you were offered an extended contract or regular work – depending on how much would be forthcoming –you might reconsider your daily rate accordingly.

The key points to remember are that you need to be paid appropriately for your time and expertise, and the better you are paid, the more likely you will enjoy the work. There is nothing worse than being paid badly as a freelancer and begrudgingly working on a project as you know it is barely covering your costs.

Charging per project

If you decide to charge per project, estimate how many days the project will take, factor in slippage time, and charge your equivalent daily rate. Sometimes it is best to make the number of days clear to the client, so if the work is more complex and taking far longer, there could be the option of going back and asking for further payment.

Terms and Conditions

It is a good idea to set out some terms and conditions between you and a client when you are negotiating. Here are some situations to consider:

> **TOP TIP**
> Don't get too precious about only working for book publishers. Every company outside book publishing has some sort of publishing function and could use your skills and your experience. You might find they pay better than traditional publishers.

- Cancellation fees
- When they will pay you
- Late payment charges
- How often they can contact you
- What progress reports you will give them
- What if extra expenses occur
- Anything else that helps manage a client's expectations. For example, how many times you will allow them to change their mind or correct the work already submitted?

This doesn't need to be too complex and should be written in a way that isn't off-putting to anyone who wants to use your services. It does, however, need to be enough so that if there is any breakdown in a relationship or any dispute, you can refer to your terms and conditions. If you have these, it is best to send these out when you accept the work, so there is no misunderstanding.

ACTION POINTS

If you are considering going freelance do some research and ask yourself:

- Do publishers use freelancers for such work?
- Are there any specific qualifications, training or memberships that are essential for the role?
- How many freelancers are there currently offering such a service, and do they seem to be always busy?
- How do you intend to market your services and bring in new clients?
- How will you support yourself financially if there are gaps between clients or a client is late paying?

CHAPTER ELEVEN

How to Get the Career You Deserve

"May you all be doing a job you love and being paid the salary you so richly deserve."

Suzanne Collier

In the previous chapters you've learned how to job search in book publishing, and I hope you agree, this has been the ultimate insider's guide. This chapter is all about what happens when you've been offered a job and how to turn publishing into a career, no matter what the setbacks. You've put in so much work to get your dream job. Now is where the real work starts, that of keeping a job and building your career.

Accepting a Job

You've been offered your dream job and finally your career is moving in the right direction. Hooray! HUGE congratulations. How exciting!

Don't delay too long in accepting. You can do this by phone or email. Remember to tell them how delighted and excited you are to be joining them and are looking forward to working with them and, if not already mentioned, suggest a start date. Be as flexible as you can. If, for instance, they have a big event or conference and you can't formally start before the event, but you are free that day or evening, then try and make yourself available.

If you are still in the interview process for another job, don't instantly assume you will be offered the other job, even if all the signs are pointing in the right direction. If the alternative is a role you would choose over the job you have been offered, continue in the interview process and if you have the dilemma of choosing, there are ways around this. If you need to withdraw from an interview process because you've been offered a job elsewhere, then let them know, adding: "I hope to work for you at some point in the future" is best. Don't ignore them; always let them know you're withdrawing your application and why.

TOP TIP

Make sure you are making the most of your job:

- Read all the minutes of meetings
- Get involved
- Learn your market
- Put yourself forward for projects

The publisher should email you a contract of employment and confirm when they would like you to start. Go through the contract and read every clause. Check that the salary in the contract, the holiday allowance and working hours all conform to what you were advised.

Pay attention to the clauses about what you can and can't do as regards social media, working outside of your job, or any other activities that may affect your established social media feeds or alternate work. If necessary, in a friendly way, ask if it is possible to amend these clauses, ("Could I ask…", "Would it be at all possible to…") and make it clear what you are asking for and why.

They could refuse to amend them, but that is unlikely if your request is reasonable. Also query any other points that don't match what you understood to be true. These may include remote working, hybrid working and number of days in the office. Wherever you can, ensure these are clearly worded in the contract, or you have it in writing as a contract amendment.

You are probably in a rush to tell everyone about your new job and update your LinkedIn status to receive messages of congratulations, please don't be so hasty. I always advise delaying any announcement, especially on LinkedIn, until you've arrived at a new job, walked through the door and know it is the job for you. This applies to any new job in any industry; it is not exclusive to publishing. It is also why you should delay taking yourself off any Recruitment Consultants' books.

Of course, you are desperate to stop your job search but doing so before you've gone through your first day or week is a risky business. You need to be sure that the job you have accepted is what you expected and that you plan to stay there. The best way to be sure is by going through your first week. Then, if the job doesn't turn out to be what you wanted, or something else has happened (a company where I was working went into administration three days after a new employee began work), you can continue your job search without needing long explanations about what did or didn't go wrong.

When you've got more than one job offer at the same time

Like London buses, you wait ages for a job and two or three jobs come along all at once. You are looking for ages and suddenly you hit the jackpot and get offered more than one job at the same time. Congratulations! You probably already know which one you will take, and it might not be the one with the highest salary. If you haven't decided which job offer to accept, then write a list of the pros and cons for each one, such as location, tasks, promotion prospects, etc. The chances are you will know your decision before you reach the end of the list. But if you are stuck and don't know which job offer to accept, then talk through the situation with a qualified Careers Advisor. They won't make the decision for you, but they will be able to guide you through the process.

When you've just started a job and a second job offer comes through

This isn't as unusual as you think. It's your first day, week or month in a new role and, out of the blue, you are offered THE job, the perfect one you interviewed for ages ago. You really want to accept the job offer. You may be enjoying where you are, but the other role is almost exactly what you wanted. Alternatively, you may have discovered the role you accepted wasn't what you thought it would be.

If you intend to resign from your new job, the best thing to do is to come clean but do this in a friendly manner, even though the response is likely to be hostile. You want to part on good terms. The best way to approach this is by talking to your line manager face to face and saying something like: "I have a huge dilemma. I was interviewing for several roles at the same time and one of the others has come back to me. I am really enjoying working here, but the other role is perfect for me and... What do you think I should do?"

The odds are in your favour here, because no employer wants an employee who wants to be elsewhere. If your new boss is sensible, and the job you want to accept is as amazing as you believe it to be (remember, you cannot be certain of this), they will probably negotiate a day for you to leave. They might be a little angry, they possibly will suggest you are making the wrong decision, and the other company is terrible, but remain calm and deeply apologetic, saying, "I never intended this to happen." Ultimately, they should let you go.

A word of caution. Do not use this as a ploy to improve your salary, particularly when you are in an entry-level role. Often there is little manoeuvrability with set salary bands and, as you are still on probation, they might immediately end your probation period, even after you've turned down the alternative role.

Your first day

The first day in any new job can be daunting, and you should be told all that you need to know, and more. Be ready to write notes with your own notepad and pen, even though the company may supply you with them when you arrive.

Dress like it is your interview, usually smart casual, unless otherwise advised (no jeans on your first day). Once you've seen the dress code of others, then you can dress down if necessary. Remember, first impressions count.

Ask questions at every point where something is not clear or if you didn't catch the name of someone. Your first couple of weeks are the time to ask questions. In a few weeks' time, they might start to think "you should know this by now". Most importantly, make as many notes as you need in your pad so you can refer to them later. There is always a huge amount to take in at the beginning and you don't want to mis-remember things. Smile whenever you are introduced to new colleagues and, overall, look happy to be there.

The publisher may have a formal induction process and you may find others starting on the same day, even in a small company. You could be given a staff handbook about company procedures (read it, even if they say you don't need to). Don't get into a competition with other new starters, trying to curry favour with your new employers. At all times be interested, friendly and approachable.

If you are replacing a previous employee, there may be handover notes and instructions, maybe even a manual of how to complete certain tasks (though in some roles you may find you've been left no guidance whatsoever). If the previous employee who held the role is someone who is now working elsewhere within the company, you might be able to supplement any notes with a face-to-face chat during a tea-break or lunchtime. Read through these in full; the chances are they will be a great help and save you time and embarrassment. Overall, enjoy the experience, even though the first couple of weeks in any new job can be frustrating, as someone may be checking your work at every juncture.

TOP TIP

When aiming to put yourself forward for projects, ask questions such as:

- That looks interesting. Please can you show me how you put that together?
- That looks so much fun. How can I be involved?
- That looks time-consuming. Do you need any help with it?

Company Confidentiality

If you're active on social media, you might assume that you can broadcast everything that happens in a new role. The reality is that, aside from co-ordinated posts across the company, such as a timed cover reveal, it is advisable to ask permission about what you can and cannot post. There are probably already company guidelines, but always check, especially if there are any grey areas.

You can lose your job for discussing topics or incidents within or outside of your employment, even if you think what you are posting is harmless.

Having the words "all the views are my own" on your profile will not help you one bit if the content is a direct result of your employment with a publisher or your opinion ties back to your employer. Most companies do not want discussions or internal information broadcast. Anything that is tied to your job is, in theory, part of the publisher's online brand, even on your personal accounts.

As well as this, if you are asked to contribute to guest posts, appear on podcasts, or have any conversation with the media as a result of the job you do or who employs you, ask permission first. I have seen people lose their jobs for using the company name to forge their own online presence.

This has been in the form of publicly writing details of an editorial or sales meeting, talking to the press about workplace discussions, sharing office gossip or posting a simple "oh you'll never guess who came into the office today". Respect company confidentiality every step of the way, and you will go far.

Relationships with colleagues

At all times, even if a colleague feels like your best friend forever, and you may socialise with them outside of work, aim to keep the relationship on a professional footing. Whilst personal and deep relationships do occur, sometimes it can be difficult if the relationship breaks down whilst you are both working at the same employer; if this happens to you, one of you may find you will want to leave the company.

Overall, it is best to remember that new colleagues are acquaintances; they only become friends once they or you have left the company. Also keep communication professional at all times. "Dance like no one is watching and email like one day it will be read out in a deposition" is a popular meme, and it is something you should bear in mind in the workplace.

When things go wrong...

Not getting your perfect job

There are many reasons why you might not get what you think is your perfect job. It is easy and understandable to feel downhearted, particularly if your present employment situation is rather precarious, but you shouldn't be. Most clients I have worked with who didn't get their 'perfect' job have ended up with a better or more suitable role somewhere down the line. Here are a few of the many reasons why you might not have got the job, some of which are not down to you.

1. The publisher restructured the department and the job vacancy disappeared. It takes a lot of money to employ someone, and many employment decisions are not based on your salary, but on other factors. One might be headcount; that they are only allowed a certain number of employees to please the bank or shareholders. Another one might be profitability. In the old days of publishing, a publisher's profitability was gauged by the ratio of books they published to their number of employees. For example, a publisher with 40 employees and a turnover of £2 million, publishing 120 books a year, meant that the average turnover per each employee was £50,000 or three books. *The Bookseller* occasionally published this table but, since the 1990s – after so many publishing mergers – it has become difficult to calculate because of the way data is recorded at Companies House.

    It could also be that they advertised the vacancy automatically on an employee's departure but realised that they were functioning perfectly adequately without them.

    I know of one company that regularly restructures. Every time it restructures, a job vacancy appears and they advertise. Within six weeks they have restructured again and the role has disappeared. Another publisher always makes a raft of redundancies just before their financial year end, to help improve their financial outlook in their company accounts, even when they have had a good year. From time to time they issue annual contracts for a number of new staff, rather than recruit permanent employees, as it is more cost effective.

When you get rejected in this last situation, always take this as a sign that you had a lucky escape. A publisher usually quite fluid with job roles like this, might also be fluid with job redundancies.

2. There was an internal applicant. When you apply, especially for mid-level and senior roles, you might find yourself up against internal applicants. I know it is highly frustrating when a publisher advertises a role when there is already someone in-house, but, and I know it may be hard to believe, not all internal candidates get the promotion they want, whether they deserve it or not.

It can be really annoying, especially if the interview process was extensive – first and second interviews, tests or presentations – but be thankful that you got an interview, and got your face in front of the people recruiting. You never know, if something else comes up, or the internal candidate doesn't work out, they could knock on your door. I've regularly seen candidates who didn't get the job be offered consultancy or some contract work instead.

3. You've been told you have 'too much – or too little – experience' for the role. Sometimes this is an excuse or a way of letting you down gently. If you've been told you have too much experience, it could be a mismatch on salary expectations. One client told me recently that they had applied for a job below their level thinking they would be certain to get it, and didn't even get called back for an interview. Too little experience is the situation in reverse; you could be pitching for roles above your level.

Not all job titles are equal. For example, a marketing manager in a publishing house with a marketing budget of around £100,000 a year does not necessarily have the same job as a marketing manager in a publisher with a million-pound marketing spend, where they may be working with third-party agencies. In some cases, applying for marketing executive roles for a publisher with huge marketing budgets might be considered a step backwards in job title terms, but it is actually a step forward in real terms. If you do this, and prove you're more than competent at this level, you might be fast-tracked for promotion.

Please note, in most other industries an executive role is higher than a managerial one, someone quite senior. In book publishing, executive is usually used to label a position between Assistant and Manager.

4. "We loved you, but we've gone with someone else." Now this one hurts a lot. But when you get told this, please understand that there was probably something about the role that they were not telling you. You might not be a good cultural fit, and this wasn't an excuse to raise prejudices, but 'cultural fit' could be you coming from a company where everything was well-supported and you were going into a publisher where everything was run on a shoestring.

Sometimes the thing they haven't disclosed could be a nightmare scenario. Whilst on the outside they look like they are a great place to work, internally it could be a combat zone, and they don't want to be responsible for you handing in your notice if they aren't 100% sure you will cope. Fortunately, these situations are now few and far between in publishing houses of today, but it can still occur.

Certain signposts for this would be at the interview stage when they ask worrying questions:

- "Have you ever had a conflict with people you work with? If so, how did you deal with it?"
- "How do you deal with a demanding colleague?"

Yes, these questions can be asked commonly of first or second jobbers, but as you go up the food chain, be wary and be thankful; you've had a very lucky escape.

There have been several incidents where I've told clients they've had a lucky escape, and they really didn't want to work at a particular publisher. Some people might thrive in a combative environment, but when you're leaving one difficult situation, the last thing you want to do is head into another. You may want a demanding and busy job, but one without the anxiety.

On other occasions, you might be told: "We loved you, but we've gone with someone else." They may know the job might be short term, the company could be up for sale and, again, they don't want to shift you from a permanent situation into something unstable.

Another reason for this could be because they advertised the role, and someone with a completely different set of experiences applied and they modified the role to fit them.

I'm going to use another marketing example: a publisher advertises for a marketing administration role. You match all the skills and competencies perfectly; you've even worked with the sister company and know everyone there.

However, someone with lots of TikTok experience also applies. The publisher hadn't really thought of doing TikTok properly; it was in their mind, but it wasn't a priority. They interview the TikTok candidate and, whoosh, they suddenly see a whole new world. They build what was the marketing administration role around the TikTok person and make it a marketing executive role. This happens more often than you think. So, if you almost match a job, or if it's a similar but not quite the job you want that has been advertised, don't be afraid to put in an application.

But whatever the reason you didn't get the role, there is nothing much you can do, other than move on. If the publisher didn't believe you were the right candidate, then it clearly wasn't the perfect job after all. That said, it is not unusual for the publisher to make a mistake with their appointment. It happened to me once, as discussed in *Chapter Eight: Interview Questions and How to Answer Them*.

Not making your probation

It is not uncommon for those new to the industry to struggle to adapt to an entry-level or assistant role. Most of the time this is down to a lack of prioritisation (it is why prioritisation tests are a key part of the interview process) and poor productivity, where you are taking too long to complete tasks (you are too slow), or unprofessional behaviour. This might initially be raised with you as: "This seems to be taking you a long time to process", or: "Why hasn't this been done yet?" or: "Why did you do it like that?"

If you don't rectify the problems immediately, you could be called into a meeting where you are given performance objectives and targets to adhere to. When this first happens, don't be afraid initially to ask for help from your line manager. Ask them clearly: "Please can you show me how you would like this to be done?" or: "How would you like me to prioritise this, as I've been taught differently?"

Also, if they give you a task that is not clear, before you go off and work on it, say to them, "So, I am clear, you want me to do this, and this, and I do it by checking this document and writing an email. The deadline is…" This now gives them the opportunity to correct you – or put you on the right path – before you do the work.

You may be sent for some time-management training, or it is suggested you work shadow a colleague. It is a good idea, at this time – when these problems first arise – to seek some external help or support from a career coach or mentor. Do it now, and not at the point when you are on a full and final warning. If the worst happens, and they ask you to leave, remember you can only truly say you work in book publishing when you've been fired at least once.

Career Planning

There are several actions you can take to ensure you are progressing your career:

Keeping up with developments

I wrote a lot about keeping up with industry developments in *Chapter One: Understanding Book Publishing* and *Chapter Two: Getting Started* and that shouldn't stop now you are working in the industry. Ensure you keep up your knowledge, and some of this should now be easier, as your employer is likely to have paid subscriptions to a wide variety of industry journals, including *The Bookseller*, *BookBrunch* and *Publishers Weekly*. Even if you are working in a narrow field, keep an eye on what is happening in all areas of the publishing business and the wider world. In particular, keep up with current affairs, so if you are in a meeting or conversation and a manager mentions a topic, you will feel confident about contributing to the discussion.

> **TOP TIP**
>
> If your employer won't automatically pay for training, ask them and see if you can come to some arrangement. An arrangement might be:
>
> - If they pay for all the course you commit to stay with them for at least another 12 months.
> - They pay one half of the course fee and you pay the other half.
> - They pay for the course, but you pay them back on a monthly basis. If it is a course that relates to a skill that isn't part of your job, say commissioning, they give you commissioning tasks as part of this.

Training

Investing in your own self-development is key to successful career progression.

Many years ago, Greg Evaristo, currently a non-executive director of Bonnier, asked me: "How much of your salary have you spent training yourself in the past year?" He was surprised when I answered, "at least £1,500", and told me that he asks that question of everyone, but I was the only person who had actually said that I had invested in my own self-development.

Please do not wait for an employer to initiate training for you; if you don't value yourself, why should anyone else value you? Even though your employer may pay for you to access a raft of online training such as the IPG Skills Hub, BookMachine Campus and LinkedIn Learning, work out what skills you need for your next role (and beyond) and aim to get trained in them now. Overall, if you are ever offered any in-house or formal training, paid by your employer, take it.

Also, commit to training yourself for a least one hour a week outside of normal working hours. This might be by spending time learning how to do that tricky calculation in Excel, perfecting your use of InDesign or training in soft skills, such as communication, assertiveness or leadership, or reading a book to increase your knowledge.

If there is an expensive formal training course that you wish to attend, and it is outside the remit of your current role, you might ask your employer if they will contribute to some of the cost (maybe 50% or more) and you will pay the rest. Alternatively, as part of the negotiation, if they pay 100%, you might agree to commit to staying with the company for at least another 6 or 12 months after you complete the course.

Another option, especially if paying the lump sum for the course is difficult, ask your employer if they could pay for the course in full, and you would reimburse them monthly from your salary. If it is publishing industry-led training, such as through the Publishing Training Centre, check to see if there are any industry-led grants that might assist you with some of the cost. Organisations that sometimes help with training bursaries include The Printing Charity.

TOP TIP

If you want to be promoted within the company, carefully read its latest business plan. If you know what your employer's plans are, you'll be able to plan your own journey.

Pushing for Career Progression

You've landed your new job and already you are thinking of what your next role will be and you are trying to find ways to push for promotion. Please don't be in such a hurry. There appears to be a lot of pressure in today's society to be instantly promoted or to move up the career ladder every few months, but companies don't work like that. Promotions don't automatically come from career longevity or because you are good at your job. Promotions are mostly because the person in the role above you has left and there is a job to fill. Or the company is expanding and a new role is being created.

Rather than focusing on promotions, job titles and the status symbols of a successful career, focus instead on the tasks you are doing now, the responsibility you are being given and how these can expand within your current role. You don't necessarily need to be the best at what you are doing at the time, but you need to have the vision to see beyond your job, and beyond the immediate situation. However, you should remember that the other people within the company may not share your views.

These are some of the many ways you can do this:

If you are working in a department but would much prefer to be in another one, then where you can, take an interest in what the other department is doing. Sometimes an invitation to be involved in a project (of course, with your line manager's permission) may be forthcoming. For example, I was working in Accounts and the Sales Director mentioned something about the cost of the Sales Conference. I asked what happened at a Sales Conference and what it was for, and I got invited along.

My next role was working in Sales for the Sales Director; they knew I was keen to progress and had shown an interest so they approached me when they had a vacancy. Many of my coaching clients have managed to attain cross-company moves in similar ways, just by talking to cross-department colleagues about their work. They've been given books to read and write reports on, invited to attend events, and included in projects where possible.

When you are working in a department you are happy with and want to progress, express interest in others and their projects, whilst still maintaining your own role. "That looks interesting, what does that involve?", "That looks interesting, is there anything I can help with?", "That looks very complex, how do you go about doing it?" or "I'd love to know how to do that, would you have any time to show me?"

If you see a particular colleague who is overloaded or stressed, offer to help or assist, maybe by taking something that might be routine for them but challenging for you. You need to be wary of taking any administrative work from them, if you are not learning or doing something differently, or where it isn't part of a senior role. You want to be stretched in quality of work, not in quantity.

When you're in a team meeting and a new project is being allocated, this could be your time to speak up and ask for more or different responsibilities.

There are, hopefully, plenty of opportunities to use your initiative in your current role. Some can be by simplifying systems, automating processes or looking at the bigger picture. When you see a solution to a problem, something that could benefit the whole team or company, and that doesn't involve spending any money, have the confidence to raise your idea. Maybe first verbally with your line manager and following this up in writing.

You also can use your initiative when making decisions that usually fall under your remit. This could be as simple as how you prioritise your work or having to make a decision when your line manager is unavailable and it is an urgent situation.

> **TOP TIP**
> It is imperative that as soon as you receive it, read your job description. If something goes wrong, it will be brought up and you may be asked why you either had not read it or not adhered to it. Time and effort were spent putting it together and it is there for a reason. Also, when you have an appraisal, you might ask why you spend more times on some tasks, but don't get the chance to do others in the job description.

Whatever your role, or planned career path, be interested, helpful, curious, adaptable, and use initiative where you can, without overloading your current, and probably already overfull, workload. In career guidance we have a phrase 'planned happenstance'. Planned happenstance is the act of fate or luck creating the situations that you are in. It is about you finding ways to create the situations that will help progress your career.

Most of the time people will say they were in the right place at the right time, but the truth is you created the situation, either by offering to help, being supportive, showing an interest, or using your initiative. Go out in the world and create your own situations for career success.

CHAPTER TWELVE

Questions, Answers and Jargon Busters

"To solve any problem, here are three questions to ask yourself: First, what could I do? Second, what could I read? And third, who could I ask?"

Jim Rohn

The following questions have all been asked and answered at bookcareers.com Job Club meetings, and I usually answer more than 40 questions in a session. I have tried to answer most of the questions elsewhere in this book, but here are the most popular that need direct answers.

How can you make your application stand out when hundreds of people are applying for the same role? (There are many variations of this question!)

The key is to read and understand the job advertisement and tailor your application accordingly. You don't need gimmicks or even 100% of the job requirements if you can show a genuine interest and the potential to do the job well. By doing this, you should automatically be in the top 20% of applicants of any job you apply for, as 80% of applicants won't bother to do this.

How can I become a book editor?

It is highly unusual for someone to instantly become a book editor. The usual career path is Editorial Assistant to Assistant Editor or Junior Editor to Editor. If, however, you have unique and specialist subject expertise, it is possible to attain an editor role as your first publishing job, but it is likely you will have other career experience too.

Is publishing an ageist industry?

I have found book publishing to be one of the least ageist industries. It recruits people of all ages and values the experience that comes with senior members of staff as much as it appreciates junior members of staff.

Is it possible to get an entry-level Editorial Assistant role if you are over 40? Is this a realistic goal?

There is no reason why someone who is not at the entry-level stage of their career shouldn't apply for entry-level roles, but what you are likely to find is the entry-level salary won't meet your expectations (or, maybe, your financial needs). In addition, the work is likely to be highly administrative and your capabilities may far exceed the tasks given, and you will become bored very quickly.

What is the best way to get work experience?

You don't need publishing work experience to get a publishing job. You need office experience, which you can get in any industry anywhere, or even gain while you are still in education. If you want to learn how to gain some publishing skills, visit *Chapter Two: Getting Started*, that lists many of the ways to get publishing experience.

I'm stuck in a cycle of applying for roles but not getting interviews, other than those for almost exactly same role as I'm currently in, and the feedback is always – "better suited candidates". What can I do?

If this is happening to you, and especially if you are applying for roles that are a step up, look back and review how you are expressing your current experience. It could be that your application reads like you don't have the experience or haven't learned anything new in your current role.

Have you included all your achievements, and all the things you did in the role that made a difference to the wider company? When you started, were you liaising with suppliers, but as you gained experience, were you co-ordinating or managing the relationship with suppliers?

Do you see how subtle changes of vocabulary can make all the difference to your application, providing of course, you have done the things you have said at the appropriate level? Otherwise, you will end up like the next question.

I'm always getting first interviews but never getting invited back or offered a role. What am I doing wrong?

This is probably a case of overstating your experience rather than pitching yourself at the right level. You might have said you managed tasks but when questioned further about how you performed them, the interviewer realises that your competence level is below what is needed for the position.

By all means, add your achievements and responsibilities, but ensure they are accurate representations of what you did and not trying to win a bragging competition. For example, if you said you had managed all the marketing collateral with an outside agency, it would give the impression that you had a certain level of responsibility; however, you were only co-ordinating or supplying all the marketing collateral with an outside agency. In your covering letter, you could add that you have experience working with an outside agency, as you've been supplying them with all the marketing collateral, and you're now ready to take the next step up. Honesty is always best.

I'd like to know how to build a relevant portfolio to attach to the CV when applying for publishing jobs (literary or academic writing or editing, and the administration chores associated with it).

A portfolio is only necessary when you have something visual you want to show, such as marketing graphics, cover designs or book layouts. Otherwise, it will be sufficient to add a third page to your CV, with a list of published articles and their linking URLs.

For a visual portfolio, it is best to arrange them in a separate PDF and send it across with your application. While you may have an online portfolio, too, you might want to link it, but I would advise sending both the PDF and URL, not the URL alone because it may not get clicked. Also, any administrative duties you want to record should be described on your CV and not in a portfolio.

What are good jobs to gain relevant experience to talk about in a CV? For example, would an office job or a receptionist role help?

Any role that gives you any kind of experience or transferable skills should be mentioned on your CV. There is a tendency for entry-level applicants to not include some summer jobs or voluntary work because they feel it is not relevant. However, for example, if you are applying for a role within a children's publisher and you worked during the summer holidays at a children's summer camp, your ability to relate to children and understand their likes and dislikes could demonstrate your commitment to working with children's books.

Is it difficult to find an entry-level job in publishing without having done any internships before?

No, it is not difficult to find an entry-level job in publishing without having done any internships, so long as you have some basic office or work experience in any industry. Focus on the office skills required, not the publishing experience. If you have absolutely no experience at all, other than your education, you might want to consider a publishing apprenticeship or continuing your education by studying for a Master's in Publishing. See *Chapter Two: Getting Started*, to help you decide on your best options.

Which do you think is better: freelancing or working in a publishing house?

The best and most successful freelancers are those who already have in-house experience. The usual career path is to start off as a salaried employee and then, if you wish, switch to freelancing, bearing in mind all the points discussed in *Chapter Nine: Going Freelance*. Also take into account that once you have been freelancing, you may find it difficult (but not impossible) to get another salaried job, mainly because you are used to having so much flexibility in your life.

Does not having a social media presence reduce your chances of getting a job in publishing or writing? If so, how can a person mitigate against this other than by creating an online portfolio or blog?

You do not need to have a personal social media presence or any kind of online presence to secure a publishing role. Focus on your skills and competencies for the role, and if you need social media experience, it is far easier to contribute to someone else's social media, one that has an established following, than to create your own.

I have been trying to find a job for months, and my biggest problem may be that I have not had a job in the field before. To get experience in the industry, where can I look for volunteer work in the business?

I recommend you do not volunteer or work for free for a publisher. If you are looking for industry-related volunteer opportunities, then *The Publishing Post* and the Society of Young Publishers are highly recommended. Aside from this, please remember that all working for free ever gets you is more free work. It is unlikely to lead to a job (and in the UK free work falls under the Minimum Wage and National Living Wage guidelines).

How do I demonstrate that I am passionate about books and literature?

In your application, talk about the books you have read or come across that relate to the publisher you are applying to join. You don't have to have knowledge of every book they have published, but if the advertisement asks for someone who reads voraciously, be prepared to discuss all the books you have read recently, what makes you select a book to read, and how long it usually takes you to read a book.

What matters more: a CV with loads of experiences or a very good Covering Letter?

Both a CV and (if requested) a Covering Letter have equal importance in a job application. Think of your CV as a Statement of Fact, that shows where you have been and the experience gained, and your Covering Letter detailing what you can do, the experience you can bring and how you match the role advertised.

The new (three-question system) seems impenetrable to me. I look pretty good on paper (see my CV), but I haven't been able to get through to the second round in my applications where there was a three-question system, each requiring 200-word answers. Do you have any tips on how to stand out in those?

The recruitment processes that require answers to questions can look impenetrable to some and easy to others. *Chapter Four: Recruitment Processes* and *Chapter Eight: Interview Questions and How to Answer Them* should both help. The key is to remember you are answering these questions like how you might answer an interview question, and ensure you stick to the theme of the question and the key components of the role.

For example, if the question asked you to describe a time when you had to stick to a deadline, and the role for which you were applying was all about sticking to deadlines, you should describe the processes you took to ensure that you didn't miss a deadline, whether it was something you did in a job, or how you planned your work and timetable so you didn't miss a deadline for submitting an essay or dissertation.

How do recruiters make a decision for an assistant position where they state publishing experience is not needed?

This would very much depend on the role, but what they are probably looking for is a sign that you have the potential for the role, or an experience that might match some of the skills for the role. You can show your potential for the role by reading and understanding the job advertisement, as well as the books and output for that particular publisher.

For example, if you were applying for a Marketing Assistant role where prior publishing experience was not required, you could look at their website and social media, sign up for their newsletter, and perhaps discuss some of this in your application. You might write something along the lines of: "I liked the marketing you did for such and such book, and the way you engaged the audience..." and then give specifics about what you thought worked and why. This would demonstrate to the publisher that you have both a keen interest in and understanding of what marketing is and how it is used, even though you may not have marketing experience.

Are there any departments that aren't so competitive to get into?

Editorial, purely by the nature of the work, will always be the most competitive department to get into. Other departments seem to go through fashions. For example, in the past few years, Publicity and PR has become the new Editorial, in that it is the latest popular career choice, maybe driven by an awareness of celebrity culture.

The competitiveness of the department will reflect the number of people employed in specific roles. For example, Editorial will usually have a reasonable number of employees, as it is integral to the publication of books. Publicity and PR will always be highly competitive as there might only be one publicist dealing with many, many books. The number of people working in Sales has dropped as the number of customers and the way that sales to customers takes place has changed. Until quite recently, publishers had huge forces of sales representatives travelling around the UK; now they may have a skeleton staff on the road and a number of Key Account Managers based in-house, with a few days of travelling.

Marketing, once only staffed by one or two people, has been the biggest expanding department in recent years, due to the way that social media marketing, and selling direct to the consumer, has come to the forefront. Production has always been seen as unfashionable, and is probably one of the most overlooked departments as regards career opportunities. However, with the advent of technology and the expansion of the conglomerates, many senior management roles for Production are no more, and you might find your career halting at Senior Production Controller level.

If I had to prioritise departments in order of their popularity, it would be: Editorial > Publicity > Marketing > Rights > Production > Sales > Administration.

So, in theory, if you searched for positions in the least popular departments, the order would be: Administration > Sales > Production > Rights > Marketing > Publicity > Editorial.

Is it easy for someone who has bookselling experience to get a job in book publishing?

If you'd asked me this question a few years ago, I would have said with confidence: "Yes, it is easy to move from bookselling to publishing. This is because you know: a little about how the publishing industry works; have been on the receiving end of publishers' marketing; understand book buying; have good customer service skills and know what helps a book to sell through."

However, in today's climate, publishers are looking for so much more in skills and commercial acumen. So, if you want to move from bookselling to publishing you need to have some added value – you need to have been organising events, specific promotions, be active on social media (e.g. X, Facebook, TikTok, Blogging).

But above all, you need to show you are proactive and can think for yourself. As well as this, you need to have up-to-date computer skills – a basic level of Word and Excel is not enough. This advice might be reviewed again in the future, but for the time being, get involved. Knowing about publishing is not enough; commercial skills are the start.

How do you become a Literary Agent?

Literary Agents start their career in different ways, some by working as an Assistant to a Literary Agent, though those roles can be harder to find than Editorial Assistants. A lot of people come up through the Editorial route of working for a publisher and then transferring across to a Literary Agency. Working in Rights is also seen as a direct route into a Literary Agency role as the main point of acting as an agent for an author is to sell the rights in the author's books. But like working in book publishing, there is no set career path; everyone finds their own way.

If you are unable to network in person, how can you best keep in touch and network in other ways?

The joy of social media means that you can network online with others. You do not have to attend events in person to make meaningful connections with others. If an event has live streaming, you might be able to follow it, or connect with people by using the event's hashtag and engaging with those who are live posting. You can then connect with them on other platforms such as LinkedIn.

I'm never sure what tone to take in my Covering Letter. I want to make sure my enthusiasm and character is evident, but is taking a formal tone more important?

The best thing to do is to try and match the tone of the job advertisement. If you follow the guidance in *Chapter Six: Covering Letters That Work*, and dissect the advertisement phrase by phrase, tying your experience to the skills and competencies they have requested, it should be easier to meet the tone of the advertisement.

How far in advance can you apply for jobs? I'm currently wrapping up an MPhil, so I see openings, but I still have several months before I graduate.

I've monitored the recruitment process and often it takes between 8 and 12 weeks, if not longer, from the placing of the advertisement to someone starting their first day. It is recommended you start applying for jobs approximately 12 weeks before you're available, because as you can see, recruitment is a slow process. The jobs you should avoid in this period are advertisements that stress "immediate start", because in those cases they really do want somebody instantly.

I'm in a role with a long notice period. Should I resign and start looking for another job whilst working my notice?

Do not resign from your role thinking you will walk into another role, even if you have all the perfect skills. Sadly, life isn't like that. What I suggest is you look for a new job, and when you've been offered another job, at the point of resigning from your current role, see if you can negotiate your notice period. Very often, employers will be flexible about leaving dates, especially if your notice period is longer than one month. (A month's notice is the standard notice period once you have passed probation.)

I am based outside of London and Oxford, which I understand are the main cities where most publishers have their main offices. How can I find a publishing role that doesn't rely on me relocating?

Thankfully there are now far more publishing jobs available outside of London and Oxford than at any other time. There are lots of different opportunities, but you might have to hunt them down. Several publishers have set up regional offices in different locations. There are also one or two publishers that say that they'll negotiate remote working, but the current favoured working pattern tends to be hybrid – three days in the office, two working from home.

What you'll probably struggle to find, particularly at entry level, is a fully remote working opportunity because you'll need to be taught how to do the role, and this will probably be done face to face in the office. You'll also need to meet the team and have occasional face-to-face meetings. Many people who say they are remote working still have to go into a London office at least once a month.

I want to get into editorial. Will paying for a training course in proofreading or copyediting give me an advantage?

Don't get training for the sake of training thinking it will get you a job. It won't necessarily give you an advantage; in some cases, it could hold you back as they will think you will get bored quickly in an entry-level Editorial role. Remember what publishers are looking for at entry level is office skills. Office skills are not exclusive to book publishing, but 80% of publishing entry-level jobs require office skills. Focus on that and not on the publishing or editorial experience.

How do I keep going in the face of endless rejections?

Firstly, I would review the parts of your job application process where you are failing. Remember, if you're getting interviews but not the job, then it is a mixture of your CV, Covering Letter (or application questions), as well as your interview performance.

But if you're not getting called to interview, review your initial application. Sometimes we get complacent or so formulaic in our applications, we forget to spend time writing a well-tailored Covering Letter. Remember, it is better to write quality applications for jobs you really want rather than applying poorly for every single opportunity you see advertised. It then becomes a question of how do you keep going?

Sometimes it might be a good idea for you to take a deep breath, go off for the afternoon and do something that gives you pleasure. One of the tools I use, whenever I'm having a really difficult time, is to open a box I have put aside. It is full of happy memories, photographs, press cuttings, things that remind me I'm good at what I do (even someone like me has moments of self-doubt) and it will completely take my mind off what's happened. Or I'll go and watch an episode of my favourite television programme.

Whatever you do it is important to give yourself a break before starting over again. Picking yourself up after rejections is one of the hardest things to do, but if you're sending hundreds and hundreds of applications, there must be a reason within your application that indicates why you're not going further, and it doesn't always relate to not having the right experience.

Is publishing really competitive?

Judging by the volume of numbers applying for each entry-level job, publishing is a competitive industry to enter. There are always far more applicants than there are jobs advertised. One major publisher informed me that on average they have only four Editorial Assistant vacancies a year but they receive more than 300 applicants for each. Some publishers report 600 applicants for a single editorial job.

As you progress up the ladder, there are fewer applicants, so for a senior role, there could be 20–60 applicants with the relevant experience. If, however, your question referred to publishing being really competitive in that people are out for your job all the time and back-stabbing you, then the answer is no. Publishing is a very collaborative environment; we all believe in teamwork and we all socialise and fraternise with people from other publishers who in a different industry might be seen as direct competitors.

Do publishers run graduate or entry-level training schemes?

Yes, from time to time, a number of book publishers may run graduate or entry-level training schemes; however, there are many entry-level positions within book publishing that may lead to a similar career path. You can find current entry-level training schemes at https://www.bookcareers.com.

Am I allowed to freelance outside of my job?

This question arose when a client got in touch as she'd been freelancing outside of her job and her employer had fired her "for cheating by using their skills outside of the company"! The truth is, you need to consult your contract of employment as it will give you guidance as to where you are allowed to freelance or whether you need to seek permission first.

If you already freelance, and you are about to sign a contract of employment with a new publisher, make this clear and ask for the no freelancing clause to be amended accordingly. For example, when I started bookcareers.com, I sought permission from my employer to do this. Every employer I have worked for since has been aware, and there has been a clause in my contract covering the work I do for bookcareers.com.

JARGON BUSTER!

These are terms or acronyms that you may find in publishing job advertisements.

Adobe A software company that produces many popular programmes such as Acrobat, InDesign, Illustrator and Photoshop.

Agenda A list of items to be discussed at a meeting, usually sent in advance of the meeting.

Acquisition This usually refers to a title where the publisher has bought the rights from another publisher, rather than commissioned or originated themselves. It can also be a term for a corporate takeover.

Aggregator A company that licenses material from a variety of publishers.

AI/AIS/ATIS Publishers have their own terms for this, but this is an Advance Information Sheet or Advance Title Information Sheet or a New Title Information Sheet. It is usually a one-page comprehensive summary of everything about a book that tells everyone the book is coming. It contains the Title, Subtitle, Author(s), ISBN, full bibliographic details and a summary of what the book is about, along with promotional plans and a mini biography of the author, as well as a thumbnail of the cover image.

AOB Any other business. This is usually added at the end of the agenda of a meeting after all the previous items on the Agenda have been discussed and allows attendees to raise items not previously discussed.

Agile A certified system of project management that is responsive to change in its approach. Agile originates from technical/IT teams but some publishers use it across all other functions.

APAC The Asia-Pacific region.

Backlist A publisher's already-published titles (as opposed to frontlist/forthcoming) usually still in print.

Biblio A publishing management software system designed for book publishers and produced by https://www.virtusales.com. Its capabilities cover all parts of the publishing process from acquisitions, production, marketing, sales, distribution, inventory control and royalties. It can send automatic Onix feeds and updates to suppliers.

BIC Originally called Book Industry Communication. BIC is a membership organisation that works across publishing, bookselling and libraries in order to improve the supply chain. They are the overseers of matters such as Metadata, book classifications, and improving distribution across the industry.

BISAC The US method of subject classification of books. This is controlled by the Book Industry Study Group.

Blad A sample section of a book, often used to help promote and sell full-colour illustrated books.

Book job transparency #bookjobtransparency An industry initiative to encourage employers to add salaries or salary bands to every job advertisement.

BookScan *see* Nielsen BookScan's Total Consumer Market.

Bradbury Phillips A rights and royalty management software system that is designed to handle all the functions of publishers' rights departments and literary agencies.

B2B Business to Business; one business selling to another business.

B2C Business to Consumer; one business selling to consumers.

Canva Online graphic design software that has overtaken the use of Adobe Photoshop in a number of publishers.

Cast off An estimate of the number of printed pages of a book, based on the number of words in the original typescript.

CMS A content management system, similar to a publishing management system.

CMYK A print colour process that uses the acronym for Cyan (a shade of blue), Magenta (a shade of red), Yellow and Key (Black). Blue, red and yellow are the three primary colours from which all colours can be manufactured. Technically, neither black nor white are colours – black is cyan, magenta and yellow together, and white is the absence of all three.

Co-edition An edition of a book that the publisher has licensed to other publishers (usually international). They come off the same printing, with a few changes such as text or colophon. This type of publishing makes books that are usually expensive to produce, such as full colour illustrated books, more cost effective.

Colophon The design, symbol or trademark that represents an individual publishing house or an imprint of a publisher. This is usually displayed on the spine of a book.

Commission To initiate or create a new book or to acquire the rights of a book from an author. This is similar to an acquisition, except it is original material. You may also commission a freelancer.

Copy-editing Editing a work for consistency and style, ensuring the text flows and limiting errors. There might be slight changes to sentence construction and a few suggestions, but mostly you are not changing the author's original words.

Copyright The legal protection given to any work produced by authors or illustrators (and others). It is enshrined in both UK and international laws.

Copywriting The act of writing persuasive text, usually for marketing purposes.

Critical path The schedule or workflow that takes a book through an editorial, production and sales process. This workflow is usually rigidly kept to in a publishing house and arranged so that the timing of each stage meets with the demands and deadlines of internal and external stakeholders (e.g. the manuscript being delivered, the copy-edits completed, the major retailers notified). Adhering to a critical path allows the publisher to manage and anticipate the workload of each department.

CRM (Customer Relationship Management) system A database where all customer records and interactions are kept and updated. There are lots of different systems available, but the principles are the same. Salesforce is one of the major CRM systems.

DACH region Germany (D), Austria (A), Switzerland (CH) region.

Data-driven Driven by the ability to interpret and make decisions based on data.

Demonstrable experience That you have proven experience in the tasks or functions required.

Desk-editing This is similar to a developmental editing but often includes additional editorial responsibilities, that support the Commissioning Editor, such as writing the cover copy or liaising with the Copy-Editor or freelancers.

Developmental editing Editing a work and making structural and substantial changes as well as suggestions to the author regarding context, style, facts, additions or deletions of text. A developmental edit can significantly improve the quality of the work.

Diary management Booking appointments, meetings and often arranging travel and preparing all the back-up materials (agenda, documents, previous minutes) for these meetings.

Digital savvy Someone who is interested in the tech and digital world and ahead of others in advancements, new trends and how they are being used.

Diplomatic Being able to keep the peace and control a difficult situation without upsetting anyone, especially when situations may get heated.

Distribution The process of despatching books or other goods to the end user.

Distributors The part of the business that is responsible for the despatch of books or other goods to the end user. In the case of publishers and printed books, one distributor may distribute for many different publishers.

D2C (Direct to the Consumer) One business selling direct to the consumer.

Dummies Mock-ups of finished books and products.

EMEA Europe, the Middle East and Africa.

Emotionally intelligent The ability to understand and control your emotions as well as understand and influence the emotions of the people around you.

Endmatter The pages at the end of a book. These might be the bibliography, index, publisher's or author's credits, and picture credits.

Entry-level A starter-level job that is designed for someone with limited expertise or knowledge; a novice.

Executive In other industries an Executive can be a senior or Director level role. In book publishing it mostly refers to a job level that is between Assistant and Manager.

Fixed-term contract A short-term contract (of employment) that has a definite ending date.

FMCG (Fast moving consumer goods) Products that are sold quickly, at low cost and high volume, such as food and household items.

Freelance reps The Sales Representatives of a publisher who are self-employed and, whilst they are not salaried employees of the publisher, usually behave like employees.

Frontlist The new, forthcoming and recently published books from a publisher.

House style A set style devised by the publisher for all the works they publish, so there is consistency across all issues for items such as capitalisation, anglicisation and other spelling and grammar. A set House Style allows new employees to quickly integrate with a publisher's editorial preferences.

Imprint The brand name that a collection of books are published under. A publishing house may have many different imprints, with different colophons, that they use to reflect the different style or categories of books they publish.

In-house Something that is done directly by the publisher (in the publishing house) as opposed to outsourcing.

Interpersonal skills The skills and behaviours that represent effective and collaborative communication between people in a workplace environment.

ISBN (International Standard Book Number) This is a unique 13-digit number that is given to each individual book or book product.

ISSN (International Standard Serial Number) This is a unique 8-digit number that is given to each newspaper, magazine or journal.

Key title A major title from any publisher that is important to them in either sales, income or importance.

KPI Key performance indicator.

Mac-literate The familiarity with and ability to use Apple Mac computers.

Mailchimp A popular email marketing platform that allows you to email large mailing lists as well as automate and measure responses.

Marketing plan A strategic plan of advertising, marketing and promotion to engage an audience and sell product.

Mass-market paperback An inexpensive paperback, without illustrations, with a wide distribution. It is usually an A format (110 mm × 178 mm).

Metadata The bibliographic information that is a key aspect of making a book discoverable.

Mono books Books that have no colour and are printed in black only (mono is an abbreviation of monochrome – remember black is technically not a colour).

NBI sheet (New Book Information Sheet) Also known as an AI.

NetGalley An online platform that allows publishers and authors to promote digital review copies to book advocates and industry professionals.

Nielsen BookScan Total Consumer Market A subscription service used by publishers to assist with competitor analysis, pricing, category analysis, market size, and other sales and marketing data. It collates electronic sales data directly from tills and despatch systems worldwide. Nielsen BookScan provides weekly bestseller charts to *The Sunday Times* and other media.

Non-trade This usually refers to retail customers, organisations and sales outlets that are not traditional bookshops but have the capacity to sell books.

Numerate To be good at working with numbers and calculations.

Open access Where a publication is free for all to read without any subscription, financial or other barriers to accessing it.

Pedagogic methodologies The processes and methods of how tutors approach teaching and learning to a fixed curriculum.

Peer review system The process of journal articles being reviewed by peers (people with similar backgrounds to the author) to evaluate and verify their accuracy.

People manager A person who can manage a team of people, even though they may or may not be at management level.

Pivot Table A function in Microsoft Excel that allows you to extract, calculate, summarise and analyse data in a spreadsheet.

PMP certified A person who holds a Project Management Professional certificate.

POS (Point of Sale) material Promotional items that are used to display or promote a book at the point of sale (usually in a bookshop). For example, a display stand for books, a dumpbin or a cardboard cutout.

Prelims The preliminary pages at the front of a book. For example, the title, copyright and contents pages.

Prince 2 A project management qualification that focusses on moving projects through predefined stages.

Print on demand (POD) A method of printing books, where the printing only takes place once an order is received. This allows a publisher to not hold stock of the book and only print to order, often supplying a single copy at a time.

Print ready files The final files of a printed book that are ready to be sent to the printer.

Problem-solving skills The ability to identify problems and suggest workable solutions or to adapt to unexpected challenges.

Proofreading Reading a work and correcting errors. You may also check for consistency, but you are not rewriting the text.

Quark Xpress A brand of desktop publishing software for page layouts, print and digital publishing creative tasks.

Reader report A critique or analysis of a title often undertaken before a publisher commits to publishing. A Reader is someone who has experience in the subject area or genre of the publication.

Reissue A book that has been previously published that is now being republished again, sometimes with an update, in a new format or with a different cover image.

Remainders Books that are sold off in bulk for a heavily reduced price (approx. 95% discount) after their sales have dropped to a nominal figure and substantial stock remains.

Review copies Books that are sent out to press and other media in order to solicit a published review.

RGB A digital colour process that uses the acronym for Red, Green and Black.

Roadmap The workflow of a process.

ROI (Return on Investment) How much money has been spent in order to attain the required result.

Royalty The income from a book or other product paid to an author by the publisher on each copy sold.

Sales pitch A short speech or sentence aimed at persuading someone to make a purchase.

ScholarOne A brand of software used in the workflow and management of scholarly journals.

Self-starter A person who can undertake or initiate a project or task without being given instruction as to what to do; a person who uses their initiative.

SEM (Search Engine Marketing) The process of increasing the visibility of a title or publisher by using paid advertisements that help increase the rankings on search engine results pages.

SEO (Search Engine Optimisation) The process used to optimise metadata and other information on a book, website or product, so it can become easily findable on search engines.

Serial rights The right to publish extracts from a publication in a newspaper or magazine. These rights can go for thousands of pounds, essentially paying the publisher and giving them free publicity – more than something for nothing!

Showcard A large display card, usually white mounted board, decorated with the book cover or other promotional material, to display in a bookshop or at an event.

SLA (Service Level Agreement) The minimum level of service that is expected from a supplier.

Slush pile The phrase used to describe the unsolicited manuscripts that have been submitted to a publisher by anyone who is hoping to get published.

Social media visuals Any graphics or photographs that accompany a social media post.

Stakeholder Any person who has an interest or concern in a particular process, function or publication.

STM An acronym for Scientific, Technical and Medical.

Stison A publishing management software system produced by https://www.stison.com. Its capabilities cover all parts of the publishing process from acquisitions, production, marketing, sales, distribution, inventory control and royalties. It can send automatic Onix feeds and updates to suppliers.

Strong administrative skills Skills that show you are well organised in general office administrative tasks, such as booking meetings, answering the telephone, arranging travel, entering into databases, communicating with others and filing.

Subsidiary rights Additional rights to publish that may come with the right to publish a book. For example, translation rights.

Supply chain In book publishing this is the name for the process and stakeholders involved in the technology, manufacture, distribution, despatch, sales, and return of products.

Target-driven A person or team who is focussed on achieving pre-set goals or targets.

TCM (Total Consumer Market) *See* Nielsen BookScan Total Consumer Market.

Third-party An external supplier or service that acts as though it is part of the publisher, as it is integral to the publisher's success. For example, third-party sales representation or third-party distribution.

Title Management System This is another way of saying CMS, Content Management System. Popular Title Management Systems include Biblio and Stison.

Trello Collaboration and project management software that helps organise workflows and responsibilities.

UAT (User accessibility testing) The process of testing a service or format to ensure it is accessible to all required users.

Unsolicited submissions Manuscripts that are submitted to a publisher by anyone who is hoping to get published, without the publisher directly requesting to see the work in question.

VLOOKUP A function in Microsoft Excel that enables you to find things in a table or a range by row.

WordPress A free open-source website software on which a number of websites and blogs are built.

Working knowledge Sufficient understanding of how a process, system or component works without having demonstrable knowledge or a deeper understanding of it.

May you all be doing a job you love and being paid the salary that you so richly deserve

And if you're not, we need to talk!

Sign up for the How to Job Search in Book Publishing training course on https://www.bookcareers.com/htjs or book a one-to-one appointment.

APPENDIX 1

Additional resources

A full selection of additional resources for this book can be found at https://www.bookcareers.com/

Online resources include:

Entry Level and Diversity schemes
Job Search Spreadsheet
Networking Groups
Publishing Courses and Master's Degrees
Recommending Reading
Recruitment Consultants
STAR worksheet

Useful hashtags for social media:

#bookcareers
#bookjobtransparency
#workinpublishing
#discovercreativecareers
#jobsinbooks
#publishingjobs
#publishingcareers
#publishinghopefuls

Apprenticeships

Find an Apprenticeship https://www.gov.uk/apply-apprenticeship

Institute for Apprenticeships (IFA) https://www.instituteforapprenticeships.org

LDN apprenticeships https://www.ldnapprenticeships.com

Degrees and Higher Education Search

UCAS, the Universities and Colleges Admissions Service https://www.ucas.com

Discover Uni https://discoveruni.gov.uk/

Times Education Supplement (TES) https://www.timeshighereducation.com

Job Boards, Networking Groups and Training Organisations
Note – Some of these have membership or other fees

bookcareers.com https://www.bookcareers.com

BookMachine https://bookmachine.org/

Book Marketing Society https://www.bookmarketingsociety.co.uk

Byte the Book https://bytethebook.com

Chartered Institute for Editors and Proofreaders https://www.ciep.uk

Creative Access https://creativeaccess.org.uk

The Galley Club https://www.galleyclub.co.uk

Editors and Proofreaders Alliance of Northern Ireland https://www.epani.org.uk

FLIP (Female Leadership in Publishing) https://www.the-flip.co.uk

Get Into Book Publishing https://getintobookpublishing.co.uk

The Publishing Post https://www.thepublishingpost.com

Publisher's Publicity Circle https://www.publisherspublicitycircle.co.uk

The Publishing Training Centre https://www.publishingtrainingcentre.co.uk/

The Society of Indexers https://www.indexers.org.uk

The Society of Young Publishers https://www.thesyp.org.uk

Spare Room Project https://thespareroomproject.co.uk

Membership Trade Associations aimed at Employers, but they often have job boards, training and mentoring opportunities

Association of Authors Agents https://agentsassoc.co.uk

Association of Freelance Editors, Proofreaders and Indexers of Ireland

https://afepi-ireland.com

ALPSP (Association of Learned Professional and Scholarly Publishers) https://www.alpsp.org

BIC https://bic.org.uk

Book Aid International https://bookaid.org

Booksellers Association https://www.booksellers.org.uk

British Printing Industry Federation https://www.britishprint.com

The Creative Industries Council https://www.thecreativeindustries.co.uk/partners/creative-and-cultural-skills

Discover! Creative Careers https://discovercreative.careers

Independent Publishers Guild https://www.ipg.uk.com/

International Association of Scientific, Technical and Medical Publishers https://www.stm-assoc.org

International Publishers Association https://internationalpublishers.org/

The Publishers Association https://www.publishers.org/

Publishing Ireland https://afepi-ireland.com

Publishing Scotland https://www.publishingscotland.org

Cyhoeddi Cymru (Publishing Wales) https://cyhoeddi.cymru

Society Publishers Coalition https://www.socpc.org

Industry Charities

The Book Trade Charity BTBS https://www.btbs.org

Printing Charity https://www.theprintingcharity.org.uk

Trade Press (these usually carry job advertisements as well as news; some are behind a paywall, but often have free elements)

Book Brunch https://www.bookbrunch.co.uk
The Bookseller https://www.thebookseller.com
Publishers Lunch https://lunch.publishersmarketplace.com
Publishers Weekly (USA) https://www.publishersweekly.com
Publishing Perspectives https://publishingperspectives.com
Quill and Quire (Canada) https://quillandquire.com
Scholarly Kitchen https://scholarlykitchen.sspnet.org

Other Useful Links

Arts Council https://www.artscouncil.org.uk
Association for Publishing Education https://www.publishingeducation.org
Bologna Book Fair https://www.bolognachildrensbookfair.com/
Book Trust https://www.booktrust.org.uk
Bradbury Phillips Rights Software https://bradburyphillips.co.uk/
Career Development Institute https://thecdi.net
Directory of Open Access Journals https://doaj.org
Editeur https://www.editeur.org
Frankfurt Book Fair https://www.buchmesse.de
Freeagent http://fre.ag/42hofr7l (affiliate link)
Inspired Selection https://www.inspiredselection.com
London Book Fair https://www.londonbookfair.co.uk
National Centre for Writing https://nationalcentreforwriting.org.uk
National Union of Journalists https://www.nuj.org.uk
Nielsen Book Data https://nielsenbook.co.uk
Reading Agency https://readingagency.org.uk/
Redwood Publishing Recruitment https://www.redwoodrecruitment.com
Royal Literature Fund https://www.rlf.org.uk

APPENDIX 1

ShimmrAI https://shimmr.ai
The Society of Authors https://societyofauthors.org
Speakers for Schools https://www.speakersforschools.org
Stison Publishing Solutions https://www.stison.com
Unite the Union https://www.unitetheunion.org
Virtusales (creators of Biblio) https://www.virtusales.com/features
Writers Guild https://writersguild.org.uk

APPENDIX 2

Recommended Reading

Ahead of Her Time: How a One-Woman Startup Became a Global Publishing Brand by Judy Piatkus, Watkins Publishing

Book Commissioning and Acquisition by Gill Davies, Routledge

Book Makers: British Publishing in the Twentieth Century by Iain Stevenson, British Library

A Book of One's Own by Lucy McCarraher, Rethink Press

The Business of Digital Publishing: An Introduction to the Digital Book and Journal Industries by Frania Hall, Routledge

Butcher's Copy-Editing: The Cambridge Handbook for Editors, Copy-editors and Proofreaders by Judith Butcher, Caroline Drake and Maureen Leach, Cambridge University Press

Children's Writers' and Artists' Yearbook, Bloomsbury

Clark's Publishing Agreements: A Book of Precedents by Lynette Owen, Bloomsbury

The Content Machine: Towards a Theory of Publishing from the Printing Press to the Digital Network by Michael Bhaskar, Anthem Press

Curation: The Power of Selection in a World of Excess by Michael Bhaskar, Piatkus

How to Get a Job in Publishing: A Guide to Careers in the Booktrade, Magazines and Communications by Alison Baverstock and Susannah Bowen and Steve Carey, Routledge

Faber & Faber: The Untold Story by Toby Faber, Faber & Faber

From Pitch to Publication by Carole Blake

How to Market Books by Alison Baverstock, Routledge

How to Pitch a Book by James Spackman

How to Succeed as a Freelancer in Publishing by Emma Murray & Charlie Wilson, How to Books

Inside Book Publishing by Angus Phillips and Giles Clark, Routledge

The Insiders' Guide to Independent Publishing, Independent Publishers Guild

Loose Connections: From Narva Mantee to Great Russell Street by Esther Menell, Westhill Books

My Back Pages: An undeniably personal history of Publishing by Richard Charkin with Tom Campbell, Marble Hill Publishers

New Hart's Rules: The Handbook of Style for Writers and Editors, Oxford University Press

The Oxford Handbook of Publishing by Angus Phillips and Michael Bhaskar, Oxford University Press

The Professionals Guide to Publishing by Gill Davies and Richard Balkwill, Kogan Page

The Publishing Business by Kelvin Smith and Melanie Ramdarshan Bold, Bloomsbury

Selling Rights by Lynette Owen, Routledge

Shelf Life: A History of the British Book Trade by Michael Robb, History Press

Shimmer, Don't Shake: How Publishing Can Embrace AI by Nadim Sadek, Forbes Books

Single Journey Only: A Memoir by Ursula Owen, Salt Publishing

Stet: An Editor's Life by Diana Athill, Granta Books

This Book Means Business by Alison Jones, Practical Inspiration Publishing

The Truth About Publishing by Stanley Unwin with Philip Unwin, George Allen & Unwin

Weidenfeld & Nicolson: Fifty Years of Publishing by John Curtis, Weidenfeld & Nicolson

Writers' and Artists' Yearbook (Online at https://www.writersandartists.co.uk), Bloomsbury

www.ingramcontent.com/pod-product-compliance
Ingram Content Group UK Ltd.
Pitfield, Milton Keynes, MK11 3LW, UK
UKHW041825190225
455323UK00004B/12